APPLIED INFORMATION SECURITY:

A HANDS-ON GUIDE TO INFORMATION SECURITY SOFTWARE

First Edition

RANDALL BOYLE Ph.D.

University of Utah

Editor-in-Chief: Eric Svendsen
Acquisitions Editor: Bob Horan
Editorial Project Manager: Kelly Loftus
Production Project Manager: Debbie Ryan
Operations Specialist: Arnold Vila

Prentice Hall
is an imprint of

www.pearsonhighered.com

ISBN-13: 978-0-13-612203-6
ISBN-10: 0-13-612203-5

ABOUT THE AUTHOR

 Dr. Randall Boyle received his Ph.D. in Management Information Systems from Florida State University. His research areas include deception detection in computer-mediated environments, the effects of IT on cognitive biases, the effects of IT on knowledge workers, and e-commerce. He has published in journals such as *Journal of Management Information Systems*, *International Journal of E-Collaboration*, and *Journal of International Technology and Information Management*.

Dr. Boyle has received the college teaching award at the University of Alabama in Huntsville, the Marvin J. Ashton Excellence in Teaching Award, and the Excellence in Education Award at the University of Utah. He has taught a variety of classes including Information Security, Network Defense and Countermeasures, Telecommunications, Systems Analysis and Design, Decision Support Systems, Web Servers, and Introductory MIS courses.

Dr. Boyle is currently Director of the Master of Science in Information Systems (MSIS) program, David Eccles School of Business, at the University of Utah.

DEDICATION

This book is dedicated to my wife, Courtney. Thank you for supporting and encouraging me during the writing of this book. I love you.

Thanks to Jason Koop for the great reviews.

Contents

INTRODUCTION

DESCRIPTION

Applied Information Security guides students through the installation and basic operation of software that is used in the IT security industry today. The primary audience is upper-division BS majors in Information Systems, Computer Science, and Computer Information Systems. This book is also intended for graduate students in MSIS, MBA, MACC, or other MS programs that are seeking a broader knowledge about IT security. The added practical knowledge about IT security greatly enhances MS programs in other areas. This book can also be used in executive training programs or by anyone interested in learning the practical side of IT security.

IT security is a rapidly growing area within the information systems landscape. Students hear about security incidents on the news and watch movies (or TV programs) that popularize the use of IT security in the real world. Students are often motivated to take an IT security course to learn more about what they have been exposed to in the media. This book gives them hands-on experience with some of the tools they may have heard about.

A book covering the breadth of IT security software presented in this book has not been produced before. Several thousand pieces of software were reviewed for possible inclusion in this edition. In each category the best free Windows-based software was chosen.

INTENDED AUDIENCE

This book was written for students with limited computer experience. Typically students have already taken an introductory course about information systems or computer science. College-aged juniors enrolled in an IT security class will use this book along with an IT security textbook like Panko's *Corporate Computer and Network Security*, or Whitman and Mattord's *Principles of Information Security*.

This book gives students real-world experience using actual software that may not be presented in a traditional textbook. Both practical and theoretical books are necessary to adequately train a student to be able to add value to an organization. This book focuses on the practical side of IT security.

WARNING

This book is NOT a "hacking" book. This book is designed to provide students interested in IT security with the tools necessary to secure their computers and information systems. It is not designed to give them the tools necessary to break into other systems. Anyone familiar with IT security software will attest to the fact that the software demonstrated in this book is relatively benign. Malicious software does exist and was intentionally left out.

Students are discouraged from using software illegally, inappropriately, or immorally. Do NOT scan any machine that is not your own. Using these programs to gain unauthorized access to other computer systems or harm them in any way is illegal.

There are programs set up to monitor illegal computer activity and you will eventually get caught if you engage in illegal behavior. If you are uncertain about what you are doing, please STOP. Ask your instructor for more direction. Curiosity is admirable but you may find that going to jail is no fun at all.

The author, publisher, and instructor have given, and will continue to give, strong warnings against all illegal use of software. Any illegal or inappropriate use of the software listed in this book is the sole responsibility of the reader.

FOR THE INSTRUCTOR

Applied Information Security reduces the amount of preparation an instructor has to do because it provides him/her with approximately 100 homework assignments ready to give to their students. These projects have been tested in both undergraduate and graduate classes across several semesters. Many students say that doing hands-on projects is the best part of the class.

Students learn how to use the tools they will need when they start working in the real world, and they get more excited about the class. Throughout this book students learn to use software in a building-block fashion that introduces them to progressively more complicated software. Later chapters refer to skills learned in earlier chapters. Step-wise learning method increases memory retention and integration across software categories.

One of the main criticisms of IT security classes is that they are "too theoretical." Students hear "security" and they think it's going to be a really fun class. Sometimes, however, they are disappointed when they are presented with a class that deals exclusively with theoretical concepts and lists of suggested guidelines. A healthy dose of real-world software projects that support in-class lectures can change student attitudes right away.

Each project contains instructions to take a screenshot by pressing Alt-PrtScn or Ctrl-PrtScn at specific points in the project to show that students have completed the project. These screenshots are then pasted into a document and emailed to the instructor. Grading an entire semester of projects can be done in a couple of minutes. Screenshots will be unique due to when the screenshot is taken. For example, a student will likely have a unique IP address or unique file name when they complete each project. Any sharing or cheating will be obvious.

Using this book in addition to a regular theoretical IT security book will greatly reduce the time and effort required to prepare an IT security course. It will also get students excited about the course and give them hands-on experience using real world IT security tools.

GETTING STARTED

Sometimes in life, the more knowledgeable you are about a given topic area the harder it is to teach it to someone who knows little about that area. This is especially true of IT security. It takes a lot of time and effort to really understand the fundamentals of information security. It requires an in-depth understanding of networking, databases, a variety of operating systems, programming, and IT hardware. You also need plenty of curiosity, a strong desire to learn, and the ability to learn on your own.

There isn't a single person on the planet that knows everything about information security. You don't need to know everything. You just need to know one thing. You can decide what that is and then become an expert in that particular part of the IT security field. It just takes time and hard work.

Hands-on Experience

This book was designed to give you experience using a broad array of IT security tools. It will help give you an idea of the type of tools IT security experts might use on a daily basis. It will also equip you with a repertoire of useful tools that you could use on your first IT security job. Too many students graduate with a degree in IS from well-know colleges and only know what they were taught—hand waving pie-in-the-sky. This book will introduce you to a broad array of practical IT security tools and how to use them.

There is a lot more to learn about each tool presented in this book. Entire books could be written about any given tool you will use. Please feel free to take time to become more familiar with each tool. We will only introduce each tool and show you the basic functionality. You won't become an expert by completing these projects.

TAKING SCREENSHOTS

To show that students have completed their projects they will be required to take screenshots of their work. They will take a screenshot at the end of each project to show they successfully completed the project. They will then paste these screenshots into a document. If students need a word-processing program, they can download a free copy of the OpenOffice® suite (http://www.openoffice.org/). They will then turn in their project screenshots to their instructor. Instructors can choose the quantity and variety of projects to assign to their students.

To get a screenshot of the current window you press Alt-PrtScn.

To get a screenshot of the whole computer screen you press Ctrl-PrtScn.

FREE WINDOWS-BASED SOFTWARE

The software in this book is freeware and will run on any computer with Windows XP® SP2/SP3. If you have the Windows Vista® operating system, some of these programs may not work. Hopefully the next version of Windows will not have this problem. This is not intended to be a comprehensive manual for all IT security software. There are a lot of other great pieces of software that were not included due to space limitations. Each piece of software is worth exploring more thoroughly. Online help manuals for each piece of software in this book are available at the links listed throughout the book.

This manual focuses on helping beginners have a good first experience with a wide breadth of security software. A few of the best pieces of software in each category were selected to represent the whole category. More experienced users may find the introductory projects presented in this book simplistic. The projects are intended to give the beginning user a survey of the field, not advanced training.

COMPUTER SCANNING INSTRUCTIONS

For projects that require scanning, your instructor will provide you with an IP address of a test machine. If you aren't familiar with what an IP address is, please ask your instructor or read about IP addresses on the Internet. If you are working on this book without attending a formal course, you are welcome to scan your own computer by using the IP address 127.0.0.1 or your real IP address that you will learn about later.

Some of the examples below use the IP address 155.97.243.201. This was the author's University of Utah IP address at the time this book was written. Please do not use this IP address for any of the exercises in this book. This IP address range runs several honeypots and intrusion detection systems (some of which you will learn about) to monitor various activities. All scans on this IP address range will be logged. Please get a valid IP address from your instructor or use your own IP address.

You will need to know your own IP address for some of the projects. Your IP address may change over time. You can find out what your own IP address is by going to http://whatismyipaddress.com/ or you can use the loopback adapter address 127.0.0.1 mentioned earlier. If your instructor gives you a different IP address to use, please use that address. Do NOT scan the Department of Defense, FBI, CIA, or any other site that hasn't given you permission to do so.

SOFTWARE, SUPPLEMENTS, AND UPDATES

The software you are going to use in this book will be available for download on the Internet, or will be available on WebCT®/Blackboard® if your teacher chooses to upload them. If one of the links listed doesn't appear to be working, then please check Google or WebCT/Blackboard for a current link. Almost all of the programs listed below can be found by searching Google®. They are all well-known and virus/worm free. All of the programs in this manual were tested on a Windows XP SP2/SP3 desktop machine. If you have the Windows Vista® operating system, some of these programs may not work. Hopefully the next version of Windows will not have the same compatibility problems.

The Web site for this book will contain a current listing of links to each of the pieces of software and a few files necessary to complete a couple of the projects. The Web site can be found at http://www.pearsonhighered.com/boyle. We recommend you make a folder labeled "**security**" on your C: drive to store all the software that you will download. Creating this folder will make software organization and operation easier. This book is written with the understanding that you did create a security folder on your C: drive. All the programs in this manual will match the directions in the book if you create the C:\security folder on your C: drive.

Updates to the projects and errata can be found at http://www.pearsonhighered.com/boyle. Links and software will change. We will try to keep any changes updated on the Web site.

The list of good, free software will change every year as new software becomes freeware. If you know of a piece of *free* Windows-based software that is more *useful* and *easier to use* than the ones listed below, please feel free to email a link to Randy.Boyle@utah.edu and it may get included in the next edition. Please do not send emails about shareware, trial versions, or anything you are trying to make money on.

REMOTE TEST MACHINES

If you do not want to load the software listed in this book on your own computer, your instructor can set up a standard Windows XP SP2/SP3 box for you to use remotely as a test machine. You can use Remote Desktop® (part of Windows XP) to remote into the test machine and run the projects.

If your instructor doesn't know how to enable multiple, concurrent Remote Desktop connections, you can Google the instructions and give them to him/her. Hopefully your network administrator already has several remote machines set up for your class to use. Instructions on how to use Remote Desktop are shown in a later project.

Having a safe environment where you, as a student, can test software is nice because you don't have to worry about causing problems on your own machine. You will also have fewer installation issues, downloading problems, and compatibility conflicts. Overall, it will save your instructor countless hours answering emails if he/she sets up a remote test machine.

DOS PROMPT

Some of the projects use DOS-based programs and will require you to run them in a DOS window from a specific directory. When you download the programs in this book, you can put them in the C:\security\ directory (mentioned earlier) and run them from there. When you are asked to run a program, you will go to **C:\security** and then type in the command. For example, C:\security\john hackme.txt.

SOFTWARE INSTALLATION AND UN-INSTALLATION

Some of the programs you will install/run will require administrator privileges. Most users are administrators on their own computers. If you are not, you'll have to ask the owner of the computer to make you an administrator account. It's probably easier for you to use a remote machine set up by your instructor. None of the programs listed in this book are viruses/worms/malware.

Once you have completed a project please feel free to uninstall or delete the software. Most of the software listed below can be automatically uninstalled. You can also go to Control Panel, Add/Remove Software, and then select the software you want to uninstall.

IMPORTANT: If you are a beginning computer user, it's highly recommended that you uninstall every piece of software that you use in this book after you are done. Newbies tend to blame the IT security software in these projects for unrelated external problems such as a city-wide power outage, their spouse spilling Coke® on their router, or their ISP failing to offer service that day. Uninstalling the software in this book helps reduce the overall anxiety level for IT security neophytes.

CREATE A VIRUS-SCAN EXCEPTION FOLDER

If your anti-virus software gives you a warning that any of the programs are viruses, you'll need to create an exception folder. The anti-virus program will not scan the files/programs in the exception folder you will create. Instructions on how to get McAfee® and Norton® anti-virus scanners to create exception folders are listed in Appendix A.

Most common anti-virus scanners will have the ability to create an exception folder. If they don't have this option, you may want to get a better anti-virus scanner. It may take a small amount of cognitive effort to figure out how to make an exception folder if you are using an anti-virus scanner that is not listed in the Appendix.

COMPRESSED (ZIP) FILES

Many of the files you will open, and subsequently install, will be compressed (Zipped). Windows XP comes with a standard zip/unzip program. There are a variety of compression programs including WinZip (http://www.winzip.com/index.htm), 7-Zip® (http://www.7-zip.org/), WinRAR® (http://www.rarlab.com/), etc. We recommend you use 7Zip or the built in Windows zip program. We will use both in this book.

CHAPTER 1: DOS COMMANDS

Below are a few widely used DOS commands that are used by IT security professionals on a daily basis. Although DOS commands may seem archaic to those that grew up on Windows, many of the best security programs still use a command-line interface. Learning command-line will become easier with practice. Knowing how to use a command prompt will make the transition to the Linux operating system much easier. Many IT security tools are currently written exclusively for Linux and use only a command-line interface.

These are just a few of the most basic commands available to all users with a command prompt. A larger list is available by typing "help" at the DOS prompt. All versions of Windows have a command prompt for you to use. To pull up a command prompt you can go through the start menu. You can also click Start, Run, and then type **command.** (See Figure 1-1.)

Figure 1-1: How to open a command prompt.

IPCONFIG

The ipconfig command will give you a listing of the basic IP information for the computer you are using. You will get information about your IP address, subnet mask, and default gateway (the computer that connects you to the Internet). Write this information down because you will use it in later projects involving port scanning, remote administration, penetration testing, etc. You will enter items 1 and 2 at the command prompt.

1. Type **ipconfig**
2. Type **ipconfig /all**
3. Take a screenshot. (See Figure 1-2.)

Figure 1-2: Output from the ipconfig command.

```
C:\>ipconfig /?

USAGE:
    ipconfig [/? | /all | /renew [adapter] | /release [adapter] |
             /flushdns | /displaydns | /registerdns |
             /showclassid adapter |
             /setclassid adapter [classid] ]

where
    adapter         Connection name
                    (wildcard characters * and ? allowed, see examples)

    Options:
       /?           Display this help message
       /all         Display full configuration information.
       /release     Release the IP address for the specified adapter.
       /renew       Renew the IP address for the specified adapter.
       /flushdns    Purges the DNS Resolver cache.
       /registerdns Refreshes all DHCP leases and re-registers DNS names
       /displaydns  Display the contents of the DNS Resolver Cache.
       /showclassid Displays all the dhcp class IDs allowed for adapter.
       /setclassid  Modifies the dhcp class id.

The default is to display only the IP address, subnet mask and
default gateway for each adapter bound to TCP/IP.

For Release and Renew, if no adapter name is specified, then the IP address
leases for all adapters bound to TCP/IP will be released or renewed.

For Setclassid, if no ClassId is specified, then the ClassId is removed.

Examples:
    > ipconfig                ... Show information.
    > ipconfig /all           ... Show detailed information
    > ipconfig /renew         ... renew all adapters
    > ipconfig /renew EL*     ... renew any connection that has its
                                  name starting with EL
    > ipconfig /release *Con* ... release all matching connections,
                                  eg. "Local Area Connection 1" or
                                  "Local Area Connection 2"

C:\>_
```

Figure 1-3: List of possible switches available for a given DOS command.

In the second command we wanted more information so we used the **/all** switch to give us more information. Now you know how to get the following information for any computer:

✓   The IP address (in this case: **155.97.243.201)**

✓   The MAC address (in this case: **00-13-D3-52-74-35)**

✓   The computer that connects to the Internet (Default Gateway) (in this case: **155.97.243.193)**

This information will come in handy when you do the rest of the projects. If you want a listing of all the possible switches available for a given DOS command you can just type the name of the command followed by a question mark. (See Figure 1-3.) For example, if you wanted to see all the switches for ipconfig you would enter the following command.

```
C:\>ipconfig /?
```

THOUGHT QUESTIONS

1. What is the practical difference between an IP address and a physical (MAC) address?
2. What is the "Default Gateway?"
3. What do DNS servers do?
4. What is a subnet mask?

PING

Ping is a command that will tell you if a host is reachable and alive. (Think back to the movie: The Hunt for Red October.) It sends out a packet that asks the target computer to send back a message saying it's actually there. It also tells you how long it took to get back and if any of the packets were lost. This is useful should you need to determine whether a server/computer is running.

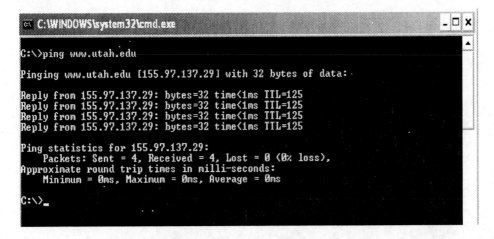

Figure 1-4: Information from PING command.

1. Type **ping www.utah.edu**
2. Take a screenshot. (See Figure 1-4.)

THOUGHT QUESTIONS

1. Why does it send 4 packets?
2. What is a TTL?
3. How do packets get lost?
4. Does each hostname have an IP address assigned to it?

Trace route is a command that allows you to see every computer (including routers) between you and a target of your choosing. You can type in the name of the computer/Web site (e.g., www.utah.edu) or the IP address of the computer (155.97.137.29).

1. Type **tracert www.utah.edu**
2. Take a screenshot. (See Figure 1-5.)

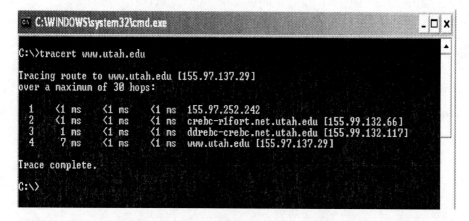

Figure 1-5: The trace route command shows every computer between you and a target of your choosing.

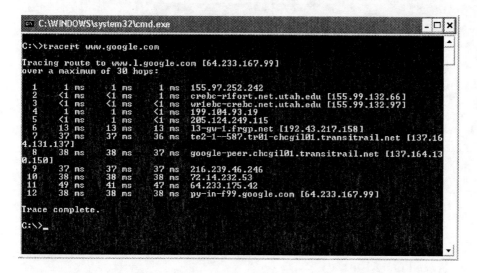

Figure 1-6: Trace root command using Google as target.

If you try the same command on www.Google.com, you might get a much longer list because it has to go through more computers to get to one of Google's servers. (See Figure 1-6.) You can see that there are 11 computers between this computer and www.google.com. You can also see that the packets moved quickly (38 ms).

THOUGHT QUESTIONS

1. How many computers do you go through each time you click on a Web site?
2. Why are some links slower than others?

3. Who owns all those computers/routers that route the packets?
4. How does the tracert program actually work (Hint: TTL)?

NETSTAT

Netstat is the command that lists all current network connections, connection statistics, and routing tables on your computer. The default netstat command will give you a listing of all the ports open on your computer as well as the foreign address of the computer to which you are connected.

Ports are like doors on your house. Information packets are addressed to a specific IP address (location) and port number (point of entry). Your house works the same way. It has an address (location) and door (point of entry) where packages are delivered. Netstat can tell you which programs are sending or receiving information to/from your computer.

1. Type **netstat**
2. Take a screenshot. (See Figure 1-7.)

Figure 1-7: NETSTAT lists all current connections, connection statistics, and routing tables.

Note: As you can see, this computer has multiple ports open with the www.umail.utah.edu:https server. (Microsoft Outlook is open.) The only problem is we don't know which program is opening all those ports. You can use the –b switch to get information about which program is opening each port.

3. Type **netstat –b**
4. Take a screenshot. (See Figure 1-8.)

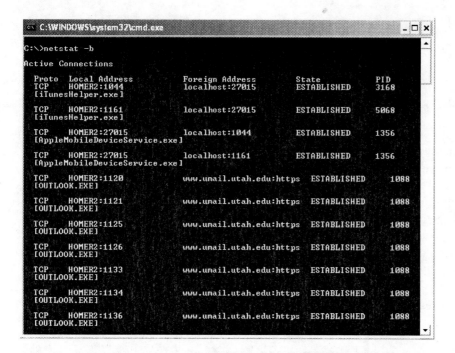

Figure 1-8: Information obtained using –b switch.

Note: Now we know that Outlook.exe is opening a lot of ports to send/receive email. Using the –b switch we can find out if any rogue program is opening a port. This is useful when you want to identify programs that are sending/receiving information. You don't want rogue programs sending/receiving information without your knowledge. You can get a listing of all the switches for any DOS command by typing "?" after the command. To find out all the possible switches associated with the netstat command type the following:

5. Type **netstat ?**
6. Take a screenshot. (See Figure 1-9.)

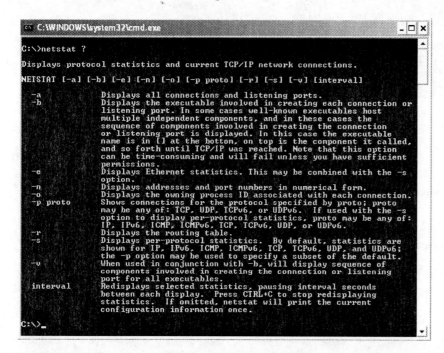

Figure 1-9: A "?" after a command provides a listing of all switches.

1. How can netstat help you track the information coming in and out of your computer?
2. How can netstat help you diagnose network problems?
3. How would the routing table (**netstat -r**) be useful?
4. Why would someone need different statistics for IP, IPv6, ICMP, TCP, UDP, etc.?

NSLOOKUP

Nslookup is a command that will give you all the IP addresses that are associated with a given domain name from the local DNS server. (It's like an Internet phone book.) For example, if you wanted to find the IP addresses of www.cnn.com you could use Nslookup to identify them.

1. Type **nslookup www.cnn.com**
2. Take a screenshot. (See Figure 1-10.)

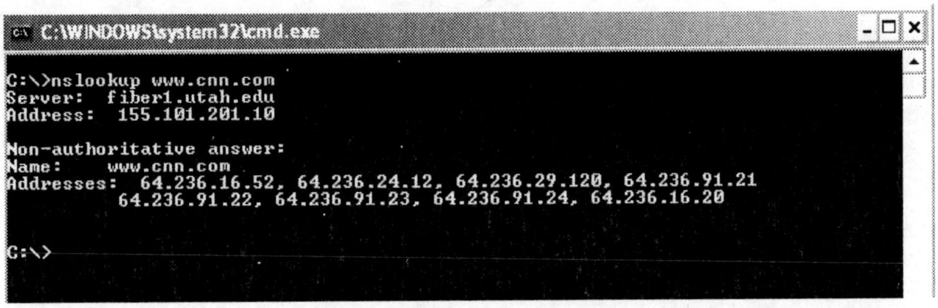

Figure 1-10: Nslookup command gives IP addresses associated with a given domain name from the local DNS server.

1. Why are there multiple IP addresses associated with a single domain name?
2. Why did Nslookup query fiber1.utah.edu instead of querying www.cnn.com directly?
3. How could someone use Nslookup in an unethical manner?
4. How do domain names and IP addresses get registered?

DIR & CD

For some of the projects you will need to move between directories (folders) on your computer using DOS commands. The dir command gives you a listing of the files, programs, and subdirectories in the current directory.

Directories (called folders in Windows) are shown with a <DIR> before the name of the directory. Files and programs (executables) are shown with their file size. Notice in the screenshot below that Adobe is a directory and Fport.exe is a program. Below are identical listings of directories, programs, and files shown in a command prompt and Windows Explorer®.

1. Type **dir**
2. Take a screenshot. (See Figures 1-11 and 1-12.)

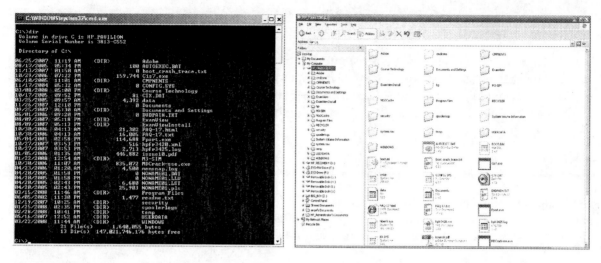

Figure 1-11: Listing of directories, programs, and files using the command prompt.

Figure 1-12: Listing of directories, programs, and files using Windows Explorer.

Note: You will also need to be able to move between directories. In Windows you just double-click on the folder and it opens up. To move back you click on the tree structure to the left. However, in DOS you use the **cd** (change directory) command to change directories.

First, you will need to learn how to move back to the C: prompt. Using the **cd . .** command you can move back one folder in the tree structure. When most Windows XP users open a DOS prompt, this will open up in their directory. To get back to the C: drive you will enter **cd ..** multiple times.

3. Type **cd . .**
4. Type **cd . .**
5. Take a screenshot. (See Figure 1-13.)

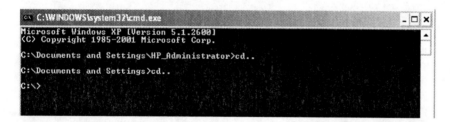

Figure 1-13: Changing directories using the cd command.

Note: Then get a directory listing of all the directories, files, and programs on the C: drive.

6. Type **dir**
7. Take a screenshot. (See Figure 1-14.)

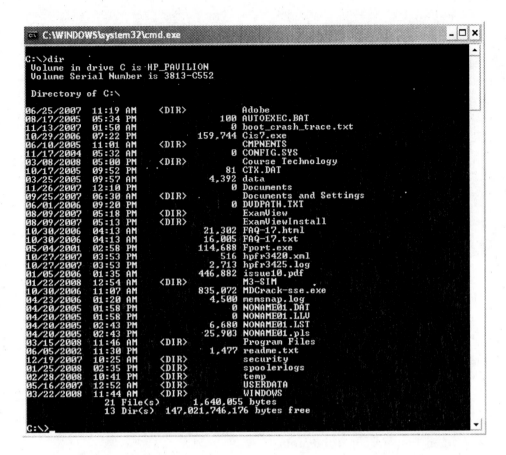

Figure 1-14: Directory listing on the C: drive.

Note: If you look at the directory listing, you can see that WINDOWS is listed as a directory (folder). Changing the command prompt into the WINDOWS directory is easy.

8. Type **cd windows**
9. Take a screenshot. (See Figure 1-15.)

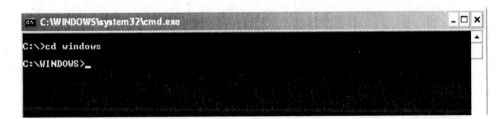

Figure 1-15: Changing command prompt into WINDOWS directory.

Note: Now get a listing of the files in the WINDOWS directory you are in.

10. Type **dir**
11. Take a screenshot. (See Figure 1-16.)

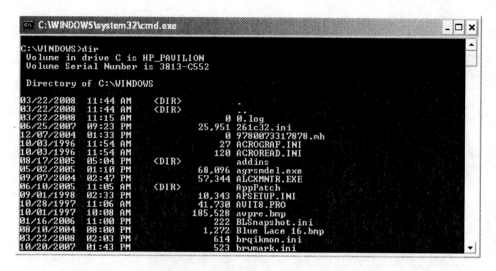

Figure 1-16: Listing of files in WINDOWS directory.

Notice that the files and directories are different. You can now move back and forward between directories (folders) through the DOS prompt.

THOUGHT QUESTIONS

1. Can you use the DIR command to show only directories? Executables? How?
2. Can you edit text files from the DOS prompt? How?
3. Can you start programs from the command prompt?
4. Can you change the color of the text and background in the command prompt? How?

CHAPTER 2: PASSWORD AUDITORS

All major corporations run password audits to assure that users have strong passwords. If just one user has a weak password, the entire company is at risk. Criminals only need one weak password to access an entire computer system. A password audit will identify those weak passwords. Network administrators will notify users that they need to change their weak passwords. Password audits are a critical part of an overall corporate security policy.

Below are some of the most well known password auditors (crackers) available and in use today. You will run them on your own passwords to see how secure they are. You will also see how to make secure passwords that will be difficult to crack. Using a secure password will go a long way to ensuring the confidentiality and integrity of your data.

JOHN THE RIPPER & FSCRACK

One of the most well known password auditing programs is John the Ripper® (JtR). You can read all about it and get a copy from http://www.openwall.com/john/. It has been used for many years and has proven to be both robust and easy to use.

Once you have downloaded JtR you will have a folder called john1701 in the security directory. JtR is a command-line program. Foundstone® created a graphical user interface (GUI) called FS Crack® to make using JtR easier. Without the GUI front end you would have to run JtR in a command prompt (DOS). You can also download a handy user's guide to FS Crack if you have other questions.

1. Download JtR from http://www.openwall.com/john/.
2. Scroll down and click on the link labeled John the Ripper 1.7.0.1 (Windows—binaries, ZIP, 1360 KB).
3. Click Save.
4. Select the C:\security folder.
5. If the program doesn't automatically open, browse to C:\security.
6. Right-click john171w.zip.
7. Select Extract All, Next, Next, Finish.
8. Download FS Crack from http://www.foundstone.com/us/index.asp.
9. Click Resources, Free Tools, FS Crack.
10. Click on the link labeled Download This Tool Now.
11. Click Download Now.
12. Click Save.
13. Select the C:\security folder.
14. If the program doesn't automatically open, browse to C:\security.
15. Right-click fscrack.zip.
16. Select Extract All, Next, Next, Finish.
17. Browse to C:\security\fscrack\.
18. Double-click the file labeled Foundstone FSCrack v1.0.msi to run the installation program.
19. Click Next, Next, Next, Close.
20. Download the sample password database from http://www.pearsonhighered.com/boyle.
21. Click Download hackme.txt.
22. Click Save.
23. Select the C:\security folder.

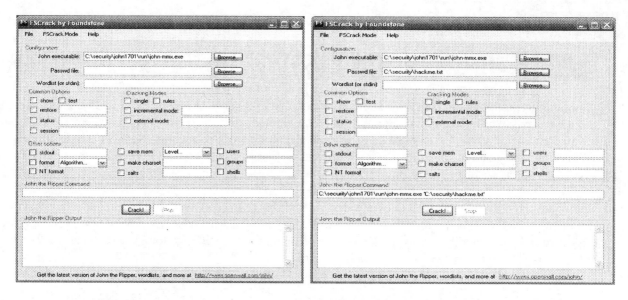

Figure 2-1: Designate the cracking program.   Figure 2-2: Designate the password file.

24. Double-click the FS Crack icon on your desktop.
25. Click browse to select the john-mmx.exe program. (See Figure 2-1.)
26. Click browse to select the password file called hackme.txt located in the C:\security directory. (See Figure 2-2.)
27. Click Crack and see how many passwords you get in 2 minutes.

Note: You also need to make sure you have a copy of the hackme.txt file in the current directory. You need to give john.exe something to crack. The cracked passwords are stored in a file called john.pot in the C:\security\john1701\run directory. (You can delete john.pot and run it again to show a friend what you've learned.)

28. Take a screenshot showing passwords you have cracked. (See Figure 2-3.)

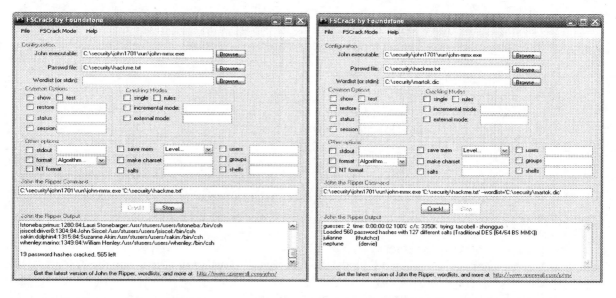

Figure 2-3: Cracking passwords.   Figure 2-4: Using an alternate dictionary file to crack passwords.

You just did your first password audit! You can also run dictionary attacks on the sample password file. (See Figure 2-4.) You will find sample dictionary files (martok.dic and puffs.dic) at http://www.pearsonhighered.com/boyle. Additional dictionary files are available on the Internet. These are sample password dictionaries that you can run against the password file. See the FSCrack Users' Guide you downloaded for more details. If you are really adventurous, you can run john-mmx.exe in the command prompt without the GUI interface.

THOUGHT QUESTIONS

1. How does the cracking program actually "crack" the password?
2. Can a cracking program like JtR crack any password?
3. If you used a larger wordlist, would it crack the passwords faster?
4. Can you use foreign language wordlists?

LCP

LCP® is a nice graphical password auditing tool with built-in functionality used to test the passwords on your own system. In the prior project you audited a standard password database. In this example, you will audit the passwords on your own computer to see how strong they really are. Many systems administrators test their own user passwords on a regular basis.

1. Download LCP from http://www.lcpsoft.com/english/download.htm.
2. Click Download English version with installer.
3. Click Save.
4. Select C:\security.
5. If the program doesn't automatically open, browse to C:\security.
6. Run the lcp504en.exe installation program.
7. Keep clicking Next until it completes the installation process.
8. Click Start, Programs, LCP, LCP.
9. Download the PWDump01.txt file from http://www.pearsonhighered.com/boyle.
10. Click Save.
11. Select C:\security.

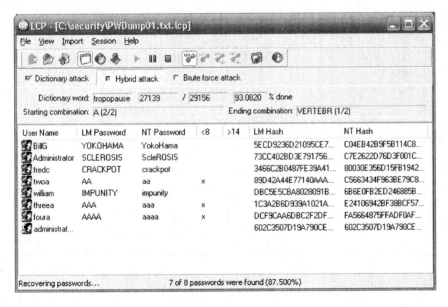

Figure 2-5: Passwords that have been cracked.

12. In LC4 click Import, Import From PWDump File.
13. Select the PWDump01.txt file in the C:\security directory.
14. Click Session, Begin Audit (or click the little blue "play" button).
15. Take a screenshot showing how many passwords were cracked. (See Figure 2-5.)
16. Click Import From Local Machine.
17. Click Session, Begin Audit (or click the little blue "play" button).
18. Type a short note about the results. (Did it crack your passwords?)
19. Do not take a screenshot of your cracked passwords.

THOUGHT QUESTIONS

1. Where are these passwords stored on your computer?
2. Can MAC or Linux passwords be cracked?
3. Can someone access your computer by guessing your password?
4. Are there additional options that would make guessing passwords faster?

OPHCRACK

Ophcrack® is another password auditing tool that functions differently from the prior two auditing tools and can yield better results in certain situations. The writers of Ophcrack explain it this way: "Ophcrack is a Windows password cracker based on a time-memory trade-off using rainbow tables. This is a new variant of Hellman's original trade-off, with better performance. It recovers 99.9% of alphanumeric passwords in seconds."

You must have a high-speed connection to complete this project. You will download a large file from the Web. Downloading it at your university will be much faster because LAN speeds are typically many times those of regular home connections. A typical Internet connection from home will take about an hour to download the entire file. It's worth the download time. Start the download before dinner and you won't have to wait for it.

1. Download Ophcrack from http://sourceforge.net/project/showfiles.php?group_id=133599&package_id=148704.
2. Click on the link labeled ophcrack-win32-installer-3.2.0.exe.
3. Click Save.
4. Select the C:\security folder.
5. If the program doesn't automatically open, browse to C:\security.
6. Double-click ophcrack-win32-installer-2.4.1.exe.
7. Click Next, Next.
8. Select Download Alphanumeric Tables from Internet. (Choose the smallest download.) (See Figure 2-6.)

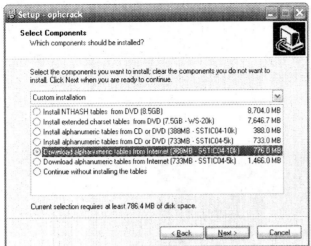

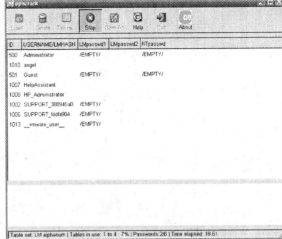

Figure 2-6: Downloading Ophcrack tables.   Figure 2-7: Cracking passwords with Ophcrack.

9. Click Next, Next, Install. (You must have a high-speed Internet connection to complete.)
10. Once the download is complete click Start, Programs, Ophcrack, Ophcrack.
11. Click Load, From Local SAM. (This is your local password database.)
12. Click Launch.
13. Take a screenshot. (See Figure 2-7.)
14. Let it run for a couple minutes and see if it cracks your password. (It will even crack fairly strong passwords!)
15. Don't take a screenshot of your cracked password. Just make a note that it did, in fact, crack your password.

THOUGHT QUESTIONS

1. What are rainbow tables and what do they look like?
2. How do rainbow tables differ from dictionary or brute-force attacks?
3. If you had a faster computer, would it crack the passwords faster?
4. Would a larger encryption key make it harder to crack a given password?

FGDUMP

Fgdump is a utility for dumping passwords on Windows machines. Once you have dumped your password, you can crack it with JtR or LC4. Pwdump® was the original program but started having problems with anti-virus programs preventing it from running correctly. Fgdump® will take care of those problems. Many of the more expensive password auditing tools will have pwdump/fgdump functionality built in. You must have administrator access on your computer to do this exercise.

1. Download fgdump from http://swamp.foofus.net/fizzgig/fgdump/downloads.htm.
2. Select fgdump_1.7.0 no source in Zip format.
3. Click Save.
4. Select the C:\security folder.
5. If the program doesn't automatically open, browse to C:\security.
6. Right-click fgdump-2.1.0-exeonly.zip.
7. Select Extract All, Next, Next, Finish.
8. Browse to C:\security\fgdump-2.1.0-exeonly\.

9. Confirm that fgdump.exe is in this folder.
10. Open a command prompt (DOS prompt).
11. Get to C:\. (Review the DOS tutorial in Chapter 1, if necessary.)
12. Change directory to C:\security\fgdump-2.1.0-exeonly\. (You can get their directly by typing: **cd security\fgdump-2.1.0-exe**)
13. Type **dir** to get a listing of all the files in the current directory. (See Figure 2-8.)

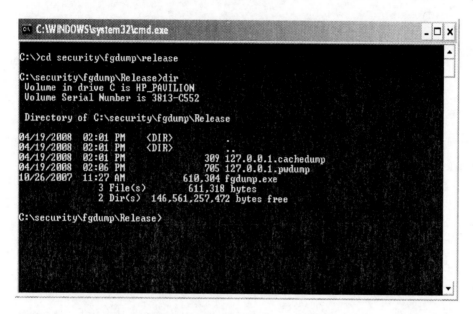

Figure 2-8: Verify that fgdump.exe is in the directory.

14. Type **fgdump**
15. Take a screenshot. (See Figure 2-9.)

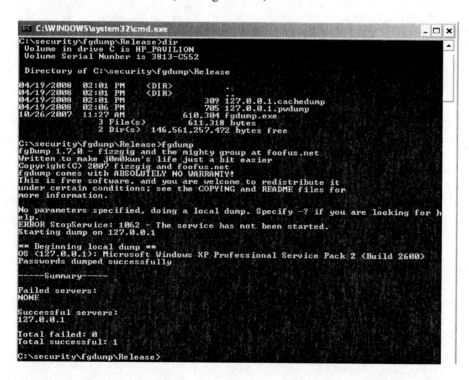

Figure 2-9: Dumping passwords with fgdump.

Note: You now have dumped all the encrypted passwords from your local machine into a file called 127.0.0.1.pwdump and it is saved in the current directory.

16. Repeat the John the Ripper project and use this new password file (127.0.0.1.pwdump) instead of using the hackme.txt password file. (You can also use LC4 and import your pwdump file.)
17. If it cracked your password, then *don't* take a screenshot of the JtR results. (Make a note saying that it cracked your password.)
18. If it *did not* crack your password, then take a screenshot.

THOUGHT QUESTIONS

1. Could someone get the password database from your computer?
2. Could someone remotely access your password database?
3. Are the passwords stored in plain-text or encrypted?
4. How could you keep these passwords from being stolen?

FREE WORD AND EXCEL PASSWORD RECOVERY

Security professionals get requests from individuals on a regular basis asking them for help unlocking Word®, Excel®, Access®, files. Individuals are worried about security so they try to secure their documents with the built-in features in Microsoft products. However, they sometimes forget the passwords they use.

There are a large number of products on the market that can help you recover your passwords if you used a Microsoft product. Below is a free version that can help you. It will walk you through dictionary and brute-force attacks.

1. Download Free Word and Excel Password Recovery® Wizard from http://www.freewordexcelpassword.com/index.php?id=download.
2. Click "Download Free Word / Excel password recovery wizard now."
3. Click Save.
4. Select the C:\security folder.
5. If the program doesn't automatically open, browse to C:\security.
6. Right-click FreeWordExcelPasswordrecoverywizard.zip.
7. Select Extract All, Next, Next, Finish.
8. Browse to C:\security\FreeWordExcelPasswordrecoverywizard\.
9. Double-click FreeWordExcelPasswordrecoveryWizard.msi.
10. Click Next, Next, Next, Close.
11. Download the sample password protected Excel file from http://www.pearsonhighered.com/boyle.
12. Click on both CrackMe_1234.xls and Martoc.dic.
13. Click Save.
14. Select the C:\security folder.
15. Double-click the Free Word / Excel Password Wizard on your desktop.
16. Click Next.
17. Click Select File.
18. Select the file CrackMe_1234.xls. (You can also create a blank Excel spreadsheet and protect it with the password "1234".)
19. Take a screenshot. (See Figure 2-10.)
20. Click Next.

21. Select all recovery options.
22. Click Select dictionary.
23. Select the file Martoc.dic. (You can find additional wordlists at ftp://ftp.openwall.com/pub/wordlists/.)
24. Take a screenshot. (See Figure 2-11.)
25. Click Go.
26. Take a screenshot.

Figure 2-10: Select a file to recover.

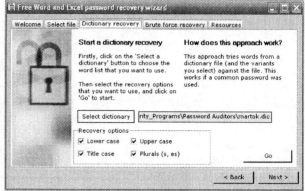

Figure 2-11: Select a dictionary.

27. Click Next.
28. Change the ending length till it reads 7.
29. Change the Characters to include all numbers and special characters.
30. Take a screenshot. (See Figure 2-12.)
31. Click Go and watch the progress bar on the bottom.
32. Take a screenshot. (See Figure 2-13.)

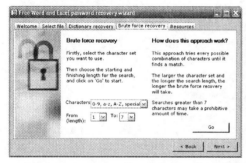

Figure 2-12: Select brute-force options.

Figure 2-13: Recovered password.

There are other programs that can crack passwords much more quickly but the goal of this project was not to show the most effective way to crack Word/Excel passwords. The goal of this project was to show that they can be cracked.

Although the built-in encryption systems may be more convenient, it's more prudent to use third-party encryption software to secure your files. They will be much harder to crack and do not have inherently weak encryption algorithms.

THOUGHT QUESTIONS

1. Are there additional programs that can "recover" your passwords more quickly?

2. Is the password system used in this Microsoft application inherently and intentionally weak?
3. Would third-party encryption software keep your documents safer?
4. Are there options that could speed up the cracking process?

REVELATION

Sometimes people forget the password they entered but can't see it because it's hidden by asterisks. There are several little programs on the Web that can remove the asterisks used by programs to hide your password. Revelation® is an easy-to-use program that shows the password in another window without removing the asterisks in the original window. Revelation works on a variety of programs that hide their passwords in this manner.

1. Download Revelation from http://www.snadboy.com/.
2. Click on the download for Revelation v2.0.
3. Click Save.
4. Select the C:\security folder.
5. Browse to C:\security.
6. Right-click RevelationV2.zip.
7. Select Extract All, Next, Next, Finish.
8. Browse to C:\security\RevelationV2\.
9. Double-click SetupRevelationV2.exe.
10. Click Run, Next, Next, Next, Next, Finish.
11. Click Start, All Programs, Snadboy's Revelation V2, Revelation.
12. Take a screenshot.
13. Open the file CrackMe_1234.xls in C:\security. (The password is 1234, if you didn't get it in the last exercise.)
14. Click the Office button, Prepare, Encrypt Document. (This will get you to the screen where you change the password in Office 2007.)
15. Take a screenshot of the window with the hidden password. (See Figure 2-14.)
16. Click and HOLD the crosshairs in the Revelation program. (If you don't keep your mouse button held down, it won't work.)
17. While holding down your left mouse button, drag your cursor over to the window with the hidden password and release.
18. Take a screenshot of the revealed password in Revelation.

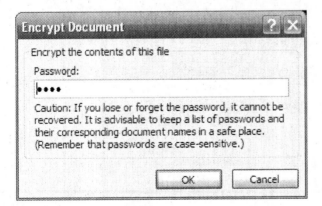

Figure 2-14: Password hidden by asterisks.

1. Why allow asterisks to show in the password box? Are they necessary?
2. Could someone gain advantage by knowing the number of characters in your password?
3. Could this tool be integrated into other security software to automate this task?
4. How does it change the asterisks to characters?

CAIN & ABLE

When people see Cain & Able® for the first time they start clicking buttons wildly. This is an EXTREMELY bad idea. Cain & Able comes with a lot of functionality that most beginning students are not ready to use. Yes, you can cause problems on your network and get in trouble. Do not run Cain & Able at your workplace or on school labs. Only run it on your personal computer or on a computer set up by your instructor.

Please feel free to click on any of the tabs and look at the functionality available. However, it would be best for you to go through the rest of the projects in this book before you do anything else. Cain & Able integrates a wide array of functionality into a single piece of software. It's also pretty easy to use.

A longer project using Cain & Able is shown at the end of this book. It's introduced at this point because it has a handy cracking feature for Microsoft Access databases. It also has an integrated password cracker. We will go through a project showing how to use the Microsoft Access cracker and leave the other features for later projects.

1. Download Cain & Able from http://www.oxid.it/cain.html.
2. Select "Download Cain & Abel v4.9.17 for Windows NT/2000/XP."
3. Click Save.
4. Select the C:\security folder.
5. Browse to C:\security.
6. Double-click ca_setup.exe.
7. Click Next, Next, Next, Next, Finish.
8. Install WinPCap, if you haven't already installed it.
9. Download the sample Access Database file from http://www.pearsonhighered.com/boyle.
10. Click on HackMe_tiger1234.mdb.
11. Click Save.
12. Select the C:\security folder.
13. Run Cain from Start, All Programs, Cain, Cain.
14. Take a screenshot. (See Figure 2-15.)
15. Click Tools, Access Database Password Decoder. (See Figure 2-16.)
16. Click on the "…" button to the right.
17. Select the file HackMe_tiger1234.mdb that you downloaded earlier. (You can also create your own Microsoft Database and set the password to "tiger1234" without quotes.)

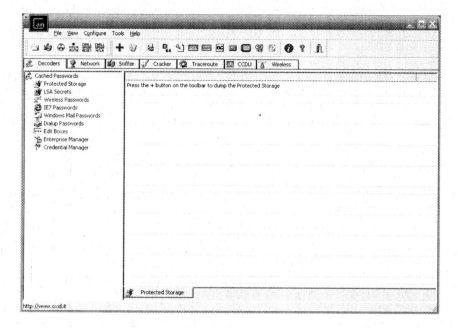

Figure 2-15: Cain start page.

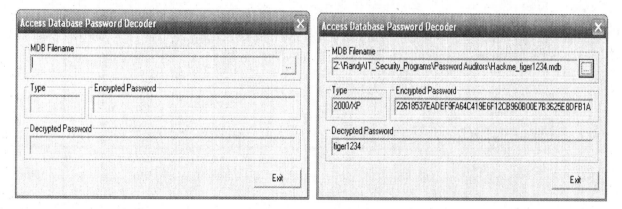

Figure 2-16: Database decoder.

Figure 2-17: Decoded password.

18. Click Open.
19. Take a screenshot of the decoded password. (See Figure 2-17.)
20. Open the database and change the password to your last name followed by any number sequence.
21. Repeat the decoding process starting at step 9 and see if it cracks your new password.
22. Take a screenshot.

Again, don't click on any of the additional features in Cain & Able until you know what they do. Randomly clicking on buttons can be harmful. You will learn more about Cain & Able later.

THOUGHT QUESTIONS

1. Did the length or strength of the password slow down the cracking of the password?
2. Why did Cain & Able crack the password so quickly?
3. Would a stronger password even help?
4. Does Cain & Able integrate a password cracker with other security tools?

DEFAULT PASSWORDS

Many people are surprised to know that their computers, routers, and printers may come with a default password. Sometimes people do not change the default password for their computers, routers, and printers. This may open them up to an attack from an outsider. There are also lists of "backdoor" passwords (on some devices) that will always work regardless of what you make the new password.

This project is not intended to give access to all default/backdoor password lists. Rather, its intent is to show the reader that these lists do exist and it is absolutely necessary to change the default password on any new devices (i.e., a new wireless router). Failing to do so will unnecessarily open your system up to a potential attack.

1. Go to http://www.phenoelit-us.org/dpl/dpl.html for a limited list of default passwords.
2. Search the left-most column for the manufacturer of your computer, router, printer, etc.
3. Take a screenshot.
4. If there is more than one device that you own shown, take additional screenshots.

THOUGHT QUESTIONS

1. Why have default passwords?
2. Do all devices have default passwords (e.g., routers, switches, firewalls, desktops, cars, vending machines, alarm systems, etc.)?
3. Is there any way to disable default passwords?
4. Does "flashing" the device remove new passwords?

PASSWORD EVALUATOR

Let's evaluate your current password to see how good it really is. Having a strong password can save you a lot of headaches because the chances of a criminal being able to break into your computer (home or work) are pretty good. Just because a cracker steals your password database does not mean he knows your password. He still has to crack it.

A strong password can keep your data safe despite it being stolen. George Shaffer has written several interesting online tools that help users learn more about strong passwords. These are great tools to help users understand the difference between strong and weak passwords.

1. Go to http://geodsoft.com/cgi-bin/pwcheck.pl.
2. Enter one of the passwords you use on a regular basis. (Include a minor change if you feel it necessary.)
3. Click Submit.
4. Take a screenshot. (See Figure 2-18.)
5. Take note of the problems with your password (in my case, a number sequence and a dictionary word).
6. Try entering a password you might actually use and you think is strong.
7. Take a screenshot of the results.

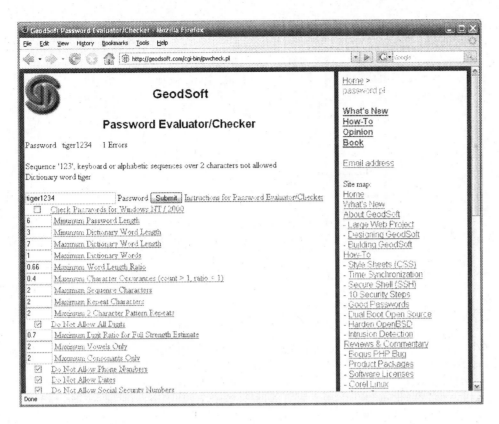

Figure 2-18: Password Evaluator.

THOUGHT QUESTIONS

1. Why did you choose the password you currently have?
2. Could others follow the same logic and choose a similar password?
3. Do hackers/crackers know that users follow these same patterns when they choose their passwords?
4. Do you use the same password for multiple accounts?

PASSWORD GENERATOR

You have just seen how difficult it is to create a good password. Weak passwords are typically easier to remember. However, it is possible to create a strong password that is fairly easy to remember. The following Web site will show you what a strong password might look like. George Shaffer has written another good tool that will automatically generate strong passwords.

If you have done the prior password auditing projects and want to make sure you have a strong password you might want to consider using one of the passwords generated by this Web site. They will be fairly difficult to crack. If you don't see a password that you can easily remember, just keep clicking submit until you see one you like.

1. Go to http://geodsoft.com/cgi-bin/password.pl.
2. Click Submit several times and watch the passwords at the top change.
3. Take a screenshot. (See Figure 2-19.)
4. Click Submit again.
5. Take a screenshot. (See Figure 2-20.)

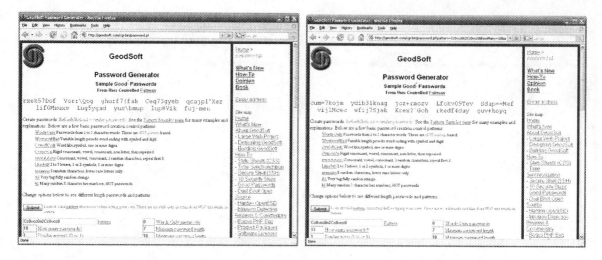

Figure 2-19: Passwords generated automatically.   Figure 2-20: Additional passwords generated.

THOUGHT QUESTIONS

1. Do you think one of these passwords would be easy for you to remember?
2. Why are these good passwords?
3. Why do special characters (e.g., @#$%^&*) make passwords difficult to crack?
4. Why does a change of case help make a stronger password?

CHAPTER 3: DATA RECOVERY & SECURE DELETION

After taking an introductory course on IT security most people say that one of the most useful skills they learned was how to recover a lost file. When a user deletes a file, the file is usually not permanently deleted. Deleting the file marks the space on the hard drive as "free space" where additional files can be written. That means the file is still there, but it might be overwritten by another newer file. The programs below try to recover files, or parts of files, that have been deleted and marked as free space.

Whenever you are using a computer it's a good idea to remember that pretty much everything you are doing can be recorded. It's highly likely that more is being recorded about you than you would like. All your actions, data, secrets, and private information can be stored on a computer for a long time. The same goes for all electronic devices including cell phones, digital cameras, Ipods©, etc. All electronic devices need to be completely destroyed when you are getting rid of them. Never throw away a computer (or cell phone) without pounding the hard drive with a hammer for a minimum of 2 minutes on each side.

The following are programs that can be used to recover data, automatically delete tracking data, and permanently wipe data from your computer. Many of these programs can also be used on various types of media connected to your computer including USB drives, cameras, external drives, etc.

RECUVA

Recuva® is a useful program by Piriform®. In the past, file recovery software was somewhat expensive and not user-friendly. It was a great source of revenue for those individuals that had the software and knew how to run it. Their customers were extremely grateful to have their "lost" data recovered. Recuva scans the entire empty memory space for possible files to recover.

As mentioned above, most users errantly believe that data is gone forever when they empty it from the Recycle Bin. This is incorrect. It merely marks the space as open to be written over if another file needs to be stored. Your operating system writes over these open spaces and subsequently "damages" the previously deleted file. With some simple knowledge of how a given file (e.g. document, image, database, etc.) is formatted you can easily recover part of the file.

Below is a picture of Angel's Landing at Zion National Park in Utah. (See Figure 3-1.) If it were partially written over by another program it might look like the second image. (See Figure 3-2.) Using a simple hex editor you can recover partial files that may be damaged and not open automatically with the default application. (See Figure 3-3.) There is software available that will automatically recover partial images without using a hex editor but they are not free to use. Learning to use a hex editor to recover partial files is beyond the scope of this introductory book but is a great skill to have. Let's look at a simple file recovery example using Recuva.

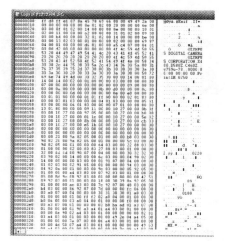

Figure 3-1: Original image.   Figure 3-2: Partial image.   Figure 3-3: Hex editor.

1. Download Recuva from http://www.recuva.com/download.
2. Click Download from FileHippo.com.
3. Click Download Latest Version.
4. Click Save.
5. Select C:\security.
6. If the program doesn't automatically open, browse to C:\security.
7. Run the rcsetup121.exe installation program. (Due to different versions, the filename may be slightly different than the one listed here.)
8. Run the rcsetup121.exe installation program.
9. Select Run, Ok, Next, I Agree, Next.
10. Uncheck Install optional Yahoo! Toolbar.
11. Click Install, Finish.
12. Click Start, Programs, Recuva, Recuva (or you can double-click the Recuva desktop icon).
13. Select the drive from which you want to recover files. (C: is always a good bet, but you can use your USB if you have it handy.) (See Figure 3-4.)
14. Click Scan. (See Figure 3-5.)

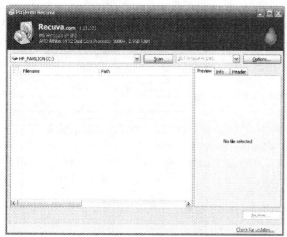
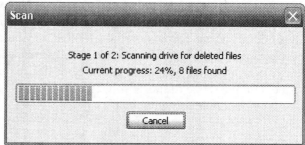

Figure 3-4: Select drive to scan.   Figure 3-5: Recuva scanning a drive.

15. After the scan completes, click on any of the recovered files listed with a graphic extension (e.g., .jpg or .bmp) until you see a picture on the right-hand side of the screen.
16. Take a screenshot. (See Figure 3-6.)

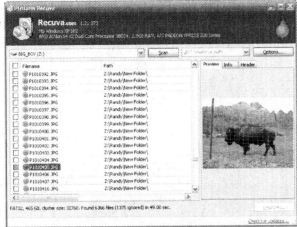

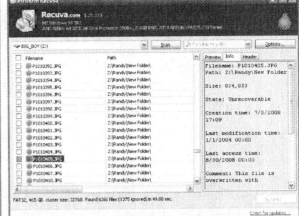

Figure 3-6: Recovered image that was previously deleted.   Figure 3-7: Details for a recovered image.

17. Click on the Info tab to see the details for the file.
18. Take a screenshot. (See Figure 3-7.)
19. Check one of the recoverable graphic files. (Even some of the "unrecoverable" files are actually recoverable.)
20. Click Recover.
21. Save it to your desktop.
22. Open the picture you recovered.
23. Take a screenshot.
24. Repeat this process on your USB to confirm that it can recover files on a removable drive.
25. Take a screenshot.

THOUGHT QUESTIONS

1. Would this work on your cell phone if it were connected to your computer?
2. What effect does the "condition" of the file have on its ability to be recovered?
3. What other recovery options does Recuva come with?
4. Does Recuva have the ability to find a deleted file by its specific file name?

ERASER

Immediately after people learn that all files they deleted in the past could be recovered they want to know how to permanently delete their files. It's not that they are trying to hide anything, they may just want to protect their privacy. Honestly, most of the people reading this book have looked at a Web site or done something on a computer they regret doing. They didn't know so much information was being stored about them on their computers. You can think of file shredders as "fresh start" programs. Everyone wants a fresh start. This is how you get one.

Individuals and companies also need to make sure all confidential data are deleted from hard drives before they dispose of them. Recovering files from discarded hard drives is extremely easy and fairly entertaining. Going through someone's garbage is becoming increasingly profitable for criminals. Eraser® will delete any previously deleted files on your hard drive. It will not delete any files that have not been previously deleted. In other words, your existing data will not get erased. It only wipes the free space.

1. Download Eraser from http://www.heidi.ie/node/6.
2. Click Download.
3. Click Download for Windows XP.
4. Click EraserSetup32.exe.
5. Click Save.
6. Select C:\security.
7. If the program doesn't automatically open, browse to C:\security.
8. Double-click Eraser.exe.
9. Click Next, Accept, Next, Next, Next, Next, Next, Finish.
10. Take a screenshot. (See Figure 3-8.)
11. Click New Task.

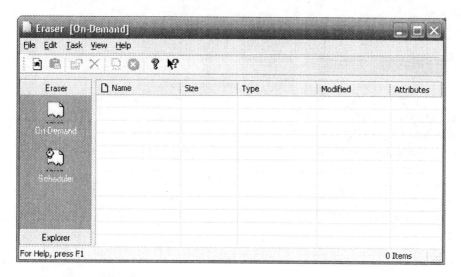

Figure 3-8: Eraser file shredder.

12. Select the drive you want to clean. (A small USB works faster than your hard drive.)
13. Click OK. (See Figure 3-9.)

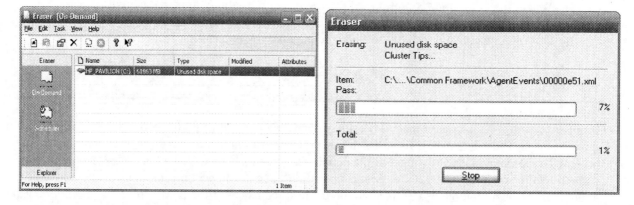

Figure 3-9: Select a drive to clean.   Figure 3-10: Wiping free disk space.

14. Take a screenshot when it finishes. (If it takes too long, you can click Stop and take a screenshot.) (See Figure 3-10.)
15. Click New Task. (You're now going to delete a file or a folder.)
16. Select Files in a Folder.
17. Click the browse button.

18. Select a file you want to permanently delete. (Create a document if you don't have anything to delete.) (See Figure 3-11.)
19. Click OK, OK. (That file is now permanently deleted and cannot be recovered.)
20. Take a screenshot.

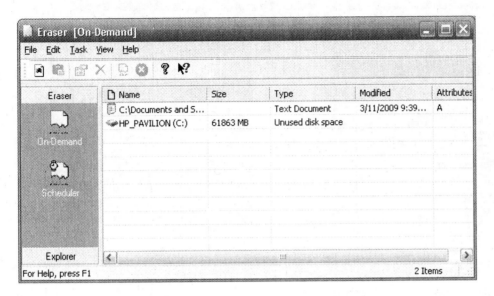

Figure 3-11: Permanently deleting a file.

Note: There have been examples of files being recovered even after permanent deletion using expensive equipment like electron microscopes. This would be expensive and difficult to do. If you smash your hard drive with a hammer and/or drill several holes in it, you won't have too much to worry about. Never throw away a hard drive without thoroughly destroying it.

THOUGHT QUESTIONS

1. What methods does Eraser use to "shred" the files?
2. Can you right-click any file and shred it directly (or securely move it to another directory)?
3. Why does it take so long? Could it go faster?
4. Why isn't this functionality included with Windows?

WEB BROWSER HISTORY

One of the more common questions that newbies (non-computer people) ask is how they can see which Web sites their spouse, son, daughter, significant other, roommates, etc. have been looking at. They are unaware that most Web browsers have built in logging functions to keep track of all Web sites visited. It's surprising how many people just don't know this exists.

In the following exercises you'll see that there is a tremendous amount of information logged about your computer activities. It's turned on by default. If you are using Internet Explorer® and want to try Firefox® you can download it from here (http://www.mozilla.com/en-US/firefox/). This exercise will use both Internet Explorer and Firefox.

1. Open your Web browser.
2. Press Ctrl-H to see your browser's history (Internet Explorer & Firefox). (See Figure 3-12.)
3. Take a screenshot.

4. Open up a folder from a prior day.
5. Take a screenshot.
6. Right-click any one of the prior days (or today) and click Delete. (See Figure 3-13.)

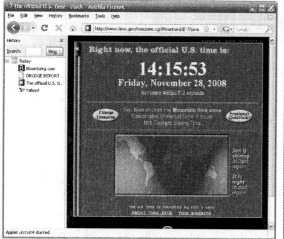

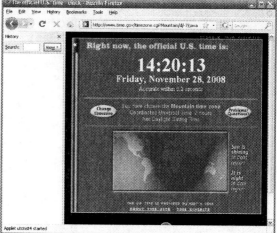

Figure 3-12: Internet Explorer browser history.

Figure 3-13: Deleted browser history.

7. In Firefox Click Tools, Options, Privacy.
8. Adjust your browser history from 90 days to 10 days. (See Figure 3-14.)
9. Take a screenshot.
10. In Internet Explorer click Tools, Internet Options.
11. Click Settings under the Browser history subsection.
12. Adjust your browser history to keep only 10 days. (See Figure 3-15.)
13. Take a screenshot.

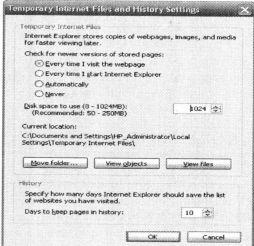

Figure 3-14: Adjusting Web browser history.

Figure 3-15: Adjusting temporary Internet files.

THOUGHT QUESTIONS

1. Why do you want to keep your browser history?
2. Do the benefits of having a browser history outweigh the potential costs of it being used inappropriately?

3. How could someone use your browser history for malicious purposes?
4. Could you edit the history file manually to show any browsing history you'd want to?

COOKIE MANAGEMENT

Some people are aware of the fact that your browser saves a history of all Web sites visited. However, they may not be aware that hundreds of cookies are being stored on your computer. Cookies are placed on your computer by your Internet browser when you visit Web sites. They store information about you and the Web sites you've visited. Cookies are also a way of tracking which Web sites have been visited. Most people are shocked when they see how many cookies are being kept on their computer.

Invariably people also ask why cookies are necessary. It turns out that cookies can be beneficial in certain cases. For example, cookies can be helpful for beginning computer users that don't want to keep re-entering their passwords every time they visit a site. However, in the end, the risks of allowing cookies may outweigh the benefits. Deleting cookies on a regular basis is a good idea. We will do this in later projects. Let's see how many cookies are on your computer.

Most new computers hide your system files and your cookies by default. For some people this is a great idea because it keeps them from damaging important system files. It's the equivalent of locking the hood of your car so you can't get to the engine. However, for this exercise you'll have to unhide all the hidden files on your computer. It's time to pull back the curtain and take a look at the wizard.

1. Open Windows Explorer by clicking Start, All Programs, Accessories, Windows Explorer.
2. Click Tools, Folder Options.
3. Click the View tab.
4. Check the "Display the contents of system folders" box. (See Figure 3-16.)
5. Check the "Show hidden files and folders" option. (See Figure 3-17.)
6. Uncheck the "Hide protected operating system files" box. (See Figure 3-18.)
7. Uncheck the "Hide extensions for known file types" box. (See Figure 3-19.)

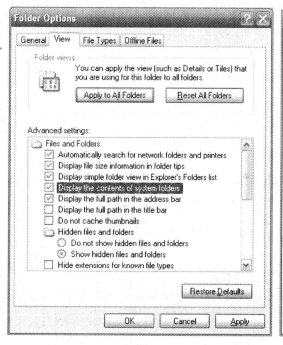

Figure 3-16: Enable the display of system folders.

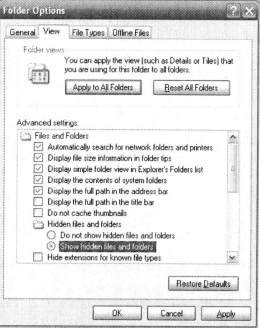

Figure 3-17: Show hidden files and folders.

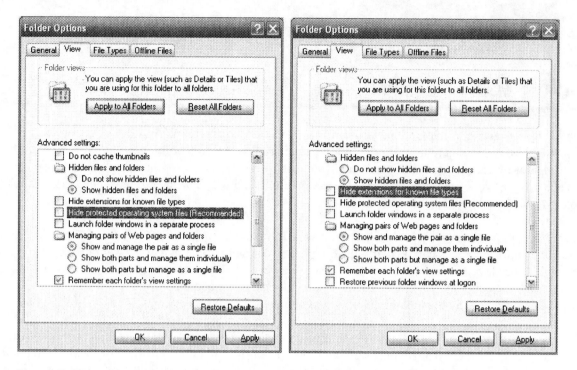

Figure 3-18: Show protected operating system files.   Figure 3-19: Show extensions for known file types.

8. Go to C:\Documents and Settings\[your user name]\Cookies (without brackets).
9. Take a screenshot. (See Figure 3-20.)

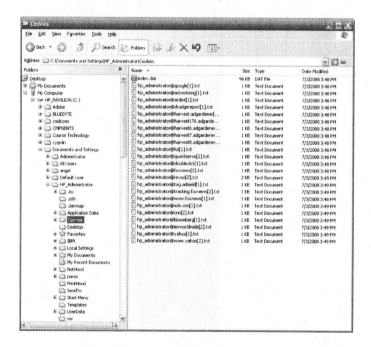

Figure 3-20: View cookies on your hard drive.

Note: You can also look at some of the cookies stored on your computer through your Internet browser. The following will show you how to view cookies stored by each browser (Internet Explorer and Firefox) and each of the values they store.

10. In Firefox click Tools, Options, Privacy.

11. Click on Show Cookies. (See Figure 3-21.)
12. Open one of the folders to see the contents of the cookie.
13. Take a screenshot showing the values associated with any one of the cookies. (See Figure 3-22.)

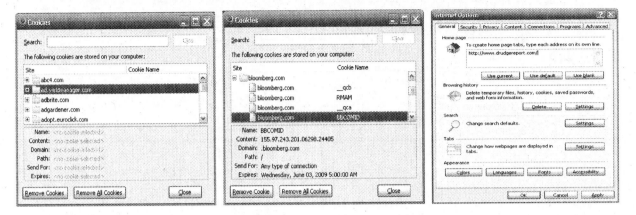

Figure 3-21: View cookies.   Figure 3-22: View contents of a cookie.   Figure 3-23: Internet Explorer options.

14. In Internet Explorer click Tools, Internet Options. (See Figure 3-23.)
15. Under the sub-section marked "Browsing history" click Settings.
16. Click View Files. (See Figure 3-24.)
17. Click the column "Type" to sort the temporary files by file type.
18. Scroll to the bottom to see your cookies listed as Text Documents. (See Figure 3-25.)

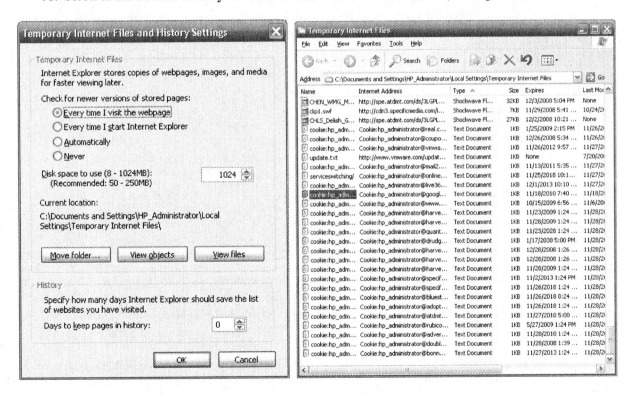

Figure 3-24: Temporary Internet files settings.   Figure 3-25: Listing of cookies.

PREF▯
ID=925f57c1edfdc0b7:FF=4:TB=2:LD=en:
NR=10:TM=1215121731:LM=1215635279:S=
up0Oosr5_oSL8PI7▯google.com/▯1536▯
9497440000▯30089125▯1190558896▯
29942274▯*▯NID▯
17=bhgAhLyOLoGwo3TiYOV1SAWT2sapLxC0O
ib6F1V5aAK05DMxhnENiwjOLVXgvQePvEsR7
oO1z3sKADLgv1Fr0MGgJbgncPRo8-Utk1m5v
6koTdGym0wf60T5uRQLPUrM▯
google.com/▯1536▯649866624▯
3011573101▯7716215201▯29968880▯*▯

Figure 3-26: Contents of a cookie.

19. Double-click one of the cookies to open it.
20. If a pop-up asks you if you want to open it, click "yes."
21. Take a screenshot of your cookie. (See Figure 3-26.)

It's a good idea to delete all your cookies and temporary files on a regular basis. Subsequent projects will show you how to delete all the cookies, temporary files, browsing history, and other logs. Wiping your machine once a week is not only prudent but will also show you how much information is recorded in a short period of time.

THOUGHT QUESTIONS

1. Can unintended Web sites or hackers see all the cookies on your computer?
2. Could a cookie collect information from your computer and send it to a Web site?
3. Do certain Web sites require cookies? Why would they require cookies?
4. Why are so many of the cookies from online advertisers? Why do they want information put on your computer?

CCLEANER

You have just seen that most people have a large number of cookies, temp files, and various logs that are used to capture information about them. Deleting these files can free up system resources and protect your privacy. In addition to deleting your browser history, CCleaner will also empty your Recycle Bin, Clipboard, memory dumps, etc.

CCleaner® is a great free tool that will delete all those annoying files that need to be cleaned up. If you change the configuration settings CCleaner will delete those files permanently using secure deletion (more than just regular deleting). None of these files will be recoverable after you run CCleaner with secure deletion. The DOD 5220.22-M standard is a sufficient secure deletion standard.

1. Download CCleaner from http://www.filehippo.com/download_ccleaner/.
2. Click Download Latest Version.
3. Click Save.

4. Select C:\security.
5. If the program doesn't automatically open, browse to C:\security.
6. Double-click ccsetup206.exe. (The number "206" will change with each version.)
7. Click OK, Next, I Agree, Next.
8. Uncheck all boxes except the one named Add Desktop Shortcut.
9. Click Install, Finish.
10. Double-click the CCleaner icon on your desktop.
11. Click Analyze.
12. Take a screenshot.

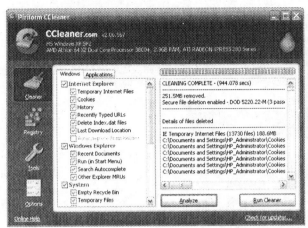 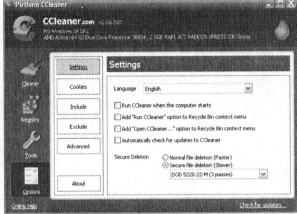

Figure 3-27: Cleaning files with CCleaner.   Figure 3-28: CCleaner settings.

STOP here if you do not wish to delete your temp files, cookies, etc. Temp files remember your passwords when you visit Web sites and help some pages load faster. If you don't mind entering your username and password when you visit Web sites, then proceed. The more you find out about the extent of tracking done on your own computer the less you want to put up with it. Running CCleaner once a week is a good idea. (This weekly cleaning deleted about 250 MB.) Most people delete about 2 GB of information the first time they run CCleaner.

13. If you choose to delete these files, you can click Run Cleaner. (If it's your first time, it can take up to 30 minutes if you have a lot of junk on your computer.)
14. Take a screenshot and look at how much it deleted. (See Figure 3-27.)
15. Click on Options, Settings.
16. Select secure file deletion (slower) using the DOD standard. (See Figure 3-28.)
17. Open your Web browser and click on five of your most commonly visited Web sites.
18. Click on www.google.com.
19. Go back to CCleaner and click Analyze.
20. Click Options, Cookies.
21. In the "Cookies to Delete" pane select google.com and press the right arrow to keep the google.com cookie. (You just created an exception for the Google cookie.)
22. Take a screenshot. (See Figure 3-29.)
23. Click on the Cleaner icon and run CCleaner again.
24. Note the large number of cookies and temp files deleted from just six Web sites.
25. Take a screenshot.

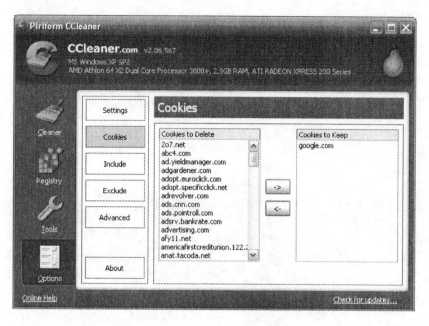

Figure 3-29: Making exceptions for cookies.

THOUGHT QUESTIONS

1. Why isn't secure deletion an option included with Windows XP?
2. Why are there different levels of secure deletion?
3. Can you set CCleaner to run automatically?
4. Will CCleaner delete other logs in different programs other than Web browsers?

CHAPTER 4: PACKET SNIFFER

Packet sniffers are used to analyze intercepted network traffic as it is travels across a network. You can pick up packets of information that may or may not be intended for your computer. Packet sniffers are an extremely valuable tool for network administrators. Network administrators use them to diagnose a wide array of everyday problems on both wired and wireless networks.

You will do a couple of basic exercises to learn how packet sniffers work on a fundamental level. Most people are shocked when they first see a packet sniffer because they didn't realize (1) that there were that many packets going across a network; (2) that a single packet had that much information in it; and (3) that someone else could look at their packets. Seeing a packet sniffer work for the first time can be overwhelming. The trick is to go slow and try to understand each part one at a time.

Packet sniffers are used by IT security personnel to gather information about potential targets or hackers, watch hackers send traffic over a network, manipulate man-in-the-middle attacks, perform penetration testing, etc. It would be well worth your time to learn all the functionality that is built into Wireshark®.

There are several other packet sniffers available on the market today that you could learn how to use. Wireshark was chosen because it has excellent functionality and beginning students find it easy to use. Learning how to actually use a packet sniffer is a critical skill for anyone interested in a career in IT security.

WIRESHARK (INSTALL AND CAPTURE)

One of the most well-known packet sniffers is Wireshark (formerly named Ethereal®). This is a flexible and powerful tool. Any IT security professional worth his/her salt will know Wireshark. Most professionals know it well. Wireshark has been getting better and better with every release. It will likely be around for a long time as the industry standard packet sniffer.

You will install Wireshark and do a few examples to give you a small taste of what Wireshark can do. In addition to loading Wireshark you will also have to load WinPCap® in order to actually capture the packets being sent over your network.

1. Download Wireshark from http://www.wireshark.org/download.html.
2. Click Download Windows2000/XP/2003/Vista Installer.
3. Click Save.
4. Select C:\security.
5. If the program doesn't automatically open, browse to C:\security.
6. Double-click Wireshark-setup-1.0.0.exe.
7. Click Next, I Agree, Next.
8. Select Desktop Icon.
9. Click Next, Next, Install.
10. Click Next to install WinPCap.
11. Click Next, I Agree, Finish.
12. Click Next, Finish.
13. Double-click the Wireshark icon on your desktop.
14. Click Capture, Options.
15. Take a screenshot. (See Figure 4-1.)

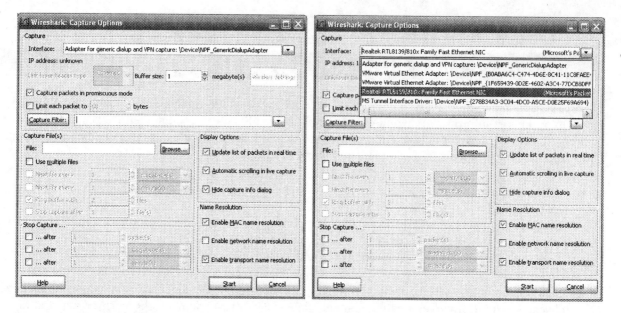

Figure 4-1: Wireshark configuration screen.   Figure 4-2: Select your network card.

16. Select your Network Interface Card (NIC) in the Interface drop-down menu at the top of the screen. (See Figure 4-2.)

Note: Your NIC will undoubtedly have a different name. If you don't know which NIC is your active network card, you should keep trying them all until one of them works. Then memorize the model name and number of your NIC. If you are still looking for a Realtek® NIC like the one shown in the screenshots above, please stop and ask your instructor for help.

17. Close ALL other programs you currently have open except your word processing program (MS Word, OpenOffice Writer®).
18. Click Start.
19. Let it run for 30 seconds.
20. While you are waiting open a Web browser and go to www.google.com.
21. Click Capture, Stop.
22. Scroll up until you see a green and blue area. (These are the packets you captured when you requested Google's main page.)
23. Take a screenshot. (See Figure 4-3.)

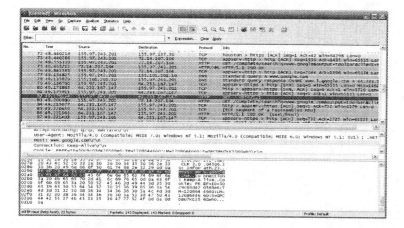

Figure 4-3: Captured packets.

24. Scroll down until you see a line that has GET / HTTP/1.1. (You may have to try more than one until you get to the packet that shows "www.google.com" in the bottom pane.)
25. Select click that row.
26. In the bottom pane you will see a bunch of numbers to the left. (It's the packets contents in hexadecimal.) Just to the right you will see the content of the packet in a column.
27. Select the text: www.google.com.
28. Take a screenshot.

You just picked packets off your network and looked at their contents. There may have been a lot of traffic that you couldn't interpret. Don't worry about the information on your screen that is difficult to understand. As you learn more about IT security and TCP/IP it will begin to make more sense. In the next project you will use a filter to capture only Web traffic going over port 80.

THOUGHT QUESTIONS

1. What do the different colors mean?
2. Why does your computer get packets that are addressed to another machine?
3. How many packets does your computer send/receive in a single mouse click when you visit a Web site?
4. Could you organize or filter the traffic to make it easier to understand?

WIRESHARK II (CAPTURE WEB TRAFFIC)

Now you are going to filter out all the "extra" packets you captured and just look at Web traffic. Too often you will capture much more information than you will ever want or need. Being able to filter out the traffic you don't want is an important skill. Before you can filter packets you need to understand a little bit about "ports."

Ports are like doors and windows on your house. Your house has several points of entry (including doors, windows, chimneys, etc.) through which people could enter your house. Computers work the same way. Each point of entry on a computer is called a port. Information comes into a computer through a port. Each port is given a specific number so it's easier to remember. Below are some of the more common port numbers that you'll need to know:

Port 80—Web   Port 23—Telnet   Port 143—IMAP (email)

Port 20—FTP (data)   Port 25—Email   Port 443—SSL (encrypted)

Port 21—FTP (supervisory) Port 110—POP (email)

Your house has an address to locate it and a front door for people to enter. Your computer works the same way. It has an IP address to locate it and a port to enter. You can filter packets by IP address or by port number. A thorough understanding of TCP/IP will greatly aid your understanding of how packet filtering works. There are many great tutorials available on the Web that will teach you the basics.

Below are instructions on how to filter out all packets EXCEPT Web traffic by creating a filter for just port 80. This will capture all the Web traffic going to all the computers on your local network. Reread the last sentence. Yes, you read that correctly, it will even capture Web traffic intended for other computers on your network. This is one of the reasons why packet sniffers are important to learn.

1. With Wireshark open click Capture, Options.
2. If you haven't already done so, select your Network Interface Card (NIC) in the Interface drop-down menu at the top of the screen. (Your NIC will undoubtedly have a different name.)
3. Type tcp port 80 in the box next to Capture Filter. (See Figure 4-4.)

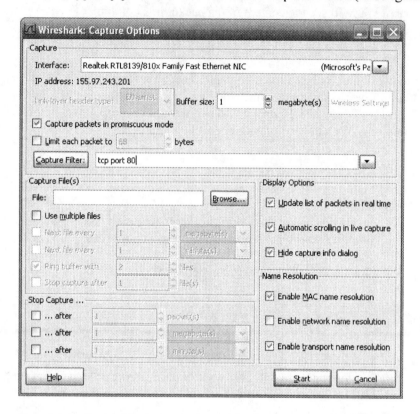

Figure 4-4: Configuring Wireshark to capture port 80 traffic.

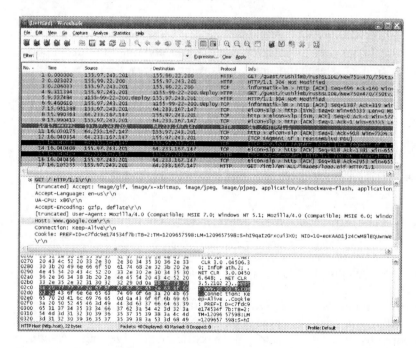

Figure 4-5: Viewing the contents of a packet.

4. Close ALL other programs you currently have open except your word processing program (Microsoft Word®, OpenOffice Writer®, etc.).
5. Click Start.
6. Open a Web browser and go to www.google.com.
7. Click Capture, Stop.
8. Scroll down until you see a line that has GET / HTTP/1.1. (You may have to try more than one until you get to the www.google.com packet.)
9. Select click that row.
10. In the bottom pane you will see a bunch of numbers to the left. (It's the contents of the packet in hexadecimal.) Just to the right you will see the content of the packet in a column.
11. Select the text www.google.com.
12. Take a screenshot. (See Figure 4-5.)

By filtering only Web traffic (port 80) there was much less information to capture. You'll also notice that one simple visit to www.google.com generates a large number of packets. Some of these packets are used to guarantee that you received the Web page and that it wasn't damaged. Others are used to transfer text and pictures used in the Web page. You may have also captured packets going to other computers on your network.

If you can see what other people are looking at on the Web, they can see what you are looking at. Doing this project helps individuals understand that Web surfing is not anonymous. There will always be someone that can see what you are looking at. Looking at inappropriate materials while you are at work is the acme of foolishness. Chances are good that your systems administrator is able to see exactly what you are looking at.

Many systems administrators watch their employees' Web surfing activities during work hours. It's completely legal. They have also fired employees for viewing inappropriate material at work. It's well within their rights to do so. There are commercial software products that track all employee Web surfing activities. When you are at work… do your work.

THOUGHT QUESTIONS

1. Why does your computer send so many packets? Why not send just one BIG packet?
2. What do SYN, ACK, FIN, GET mean?
3. Why do some packets have sequence numbers?
4. Why does your computer send packets to the Web server that you requested data from?

WIRESHARK III (CAPTURE AN EMAIL)

Let's do another filtering example using Wireshark to capture an email. We will send an email to a generic hotmail.com® account and capture it as it's going over the network. We will look at the contents of the email without opening an email program. We will be able to capture any email going over our local network and read its contents (as long as it's not encrypted). Most email traffic is not encrypted. However, many providers are starting to set up encrypted email for their users.

1. With Wireshark open click Capture, Options.
2. If you haven't already done so, select your Network Interface Card (NIC) in the Interface drop-down menu at the top of the screen. (Your NIC will undoubtedly have a different name.)
3. Type tcp port 80 in the box next to Capture Filter. (Use port 80 for Webmail or port 25 for email if you are using a local client like Outlook.) (See Figure 4-6.)

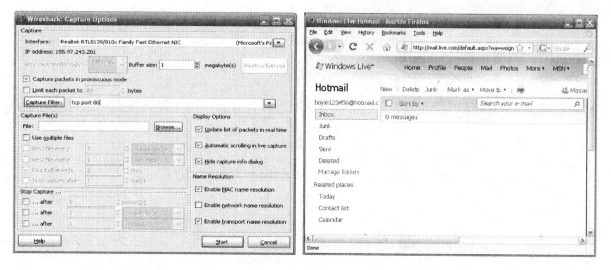

Figure 4-6: Configuring Wireshark to capture port 80 packets.　　Figure 4-7: Hotmail.com inbox.

4. Close ALL other programs you currently have open except your word processing program (MS Word, OpenOffice Writer) and your Web browser.
5. Direct your Web browser to www.hotmail.com. (If you already have a hotmail account, skip to step 12.)
6. Click Sign Up (to get a free hotmail account).
7. Click Get It (free).
8. Under the Create a Windows Live® ID enter a fake Windows Live ID and a hotmail.com extension. (Write down the information you enter and make sure it's not real; mine was boyle123456@hotmail.com.)
9. Enter fake information for all the required fields marked with an asterisk. (My name is always john doe, and I'm from Utah; born in 1980.)
10. Click "give me the classic version." (See Figure 4-7.)
11. Click New (to get a new email).
12. In the "To:" field put your real email address (or the same email address you just created).
13. In the Subject line put TEST.
14. In the body of the email put the words "EMAIL TEST" and copy/paste it until it fills up the body of the email message. (This will help us identify the packet when we see it.) (See Figure 4-8.)

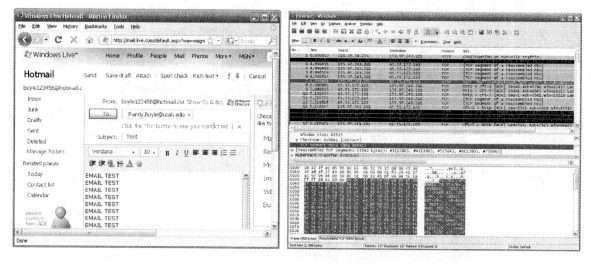

Figure 4-8: Sending a test email.　　Figure 4-9: Viewing the contents of the captured email.

15. Go back to Wireshark and click Start.
16. Got to Back to your hotmail account and click Send.
17. Go back to Wireshark and click Stop.
18. Click on the line that has Post /mail/sendmessage in the Info field. (Mine was the seventh packet.)
19. Click on the bottom window pane where you see a column of words saying EMAIL TEST (the body of the message we just sent).
20. Take a screenshot. (See Figure 4-9.)
21. The To, From, and Subject fields are in the earlier packets captured.

You just picked up your email off the network that was on its way to www.hotmail.com. Unless specified your emails are NOT encrypted. Most people are unaware of this and send confidential information on a regular basis over unencrypted email systems. It's a good idea **NOT** to send sensitive information over email.

You can learn how to encrypt the emails you are sending. Ask your network administrator about how to automate the process of sending encrypted emails. If your network administrator doesn't know how to set up encryption for emails, it's time to get a new admin.

It's important to understand that Wireshark picked up the email you just sent off the network. It can just as easily pick up ALL email traffic going over your network. One of the main concepts you will learn by doing these projects is that you may not fully understand how computers (or information systems) work. Hopefully knowing more about computers, networks, and information systems will help protect you.

THOUGHT QUESTIONS

1. How many people do you think are unaware that their emails may be unencrypted?
2. Why wouldn't email be encrypted by default?
3. Can you look at Web content just as easily as Web traffic?
4. Can you look at information being sent to/from your bank?

WIRESHARK IV (SIMPLE FILTERING)

It would be a shame not to show beginning users the filtering capabilities in Wireshark. Once you learn how to use all the functionality built into Wireshark your life will be much easier. By now you have noticed that there are a lot of packets flowing through a network. It takes a lot of mental energy to sift through all those packets to get the ones you are looking for.

Luckily, Wireshark can help us filter out some of the responses we are not interested in. Understanding how to use the built-in filtering functionality can reduce the amount of effort you put into using a packet sniffer. The filtering built into Wireshark is excellent and not that difficult once you understand the basics.

1. With Wireshark open click Capture, Options.
2. If you haven't already done so, select your Network Interface Card (NIC) in the Interface drop-down menu at the top of the screen. (Your NIC will undoubtedly have a different name.)
3. Leave the Capture Filter blank.
4. Click Start.
5. Open a Web browser and go to www.cnn.com.
6. Click Stop Capture.
7. Take a screenshot. (See Figure 4-10.)

8. Notice that you likely have a lot of packets that may not be intended for you. (In this example a lot of extra traffic was picked up from a router that wasn't intended for this computer.)

9. In the empty box next to Filter enter the following: ip.src == [enter your IP address without the brackets].

10. Press Enter after you finish typing the filter syntax.

11. The filter box will be green if you get the syntax correctly entered. (Mine was ip.src == 155.97.243.201.)

12. Take a screenshot. (See Figure 4-11.)

13. Note that you are now only getting packets where the source IP address is your own.

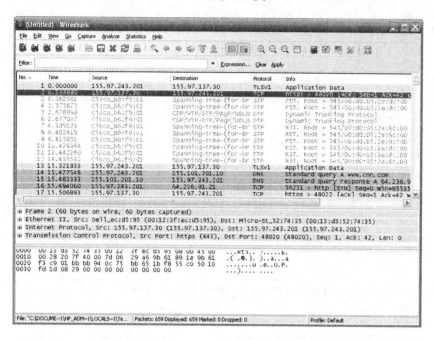

Figure 4-10: Captured packets.

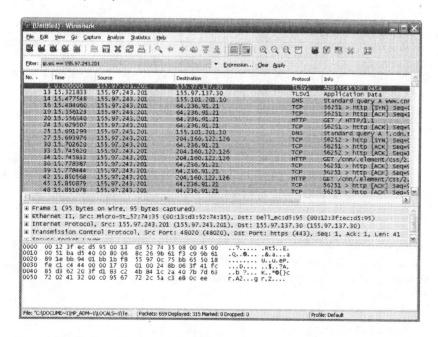

Figure 4-11: Filtering packets based on IP address.

14. Click on the Expression button to the right of the filter box.
15. Click on TCP to get the tcp.port field name.
16. Click == .
17. Enter 80 for the value (to view only Web traffic). (See Figure 4-12.)
18. Click OK.

Note: The filter box will be red indicating incorrect syntax. After you fix the syntax in the next step the box will turn green. (See Figure 4-13.)

19. Add an "and" to the syntax so that both the new filtering rule and the prior rule are applied together. (The filter box will turn green when you have the syntax correctly entered.)
20. Re-enter the correct syntax if you didn't get it to work correctly (tcp.port == 80 and ip.src == 155.97.243.201) replacing my IP address for your own.
21. Take a screenshot. (See Figure 4-14.)

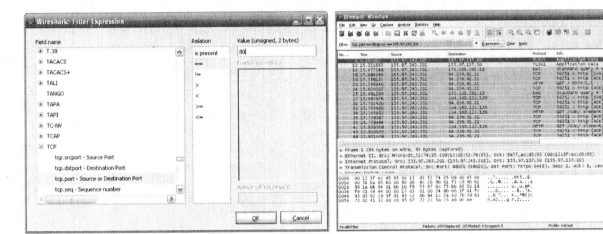

Figure 4-12: Creating a filter expression.   Figure4-13: Filter without "and" in the expression.

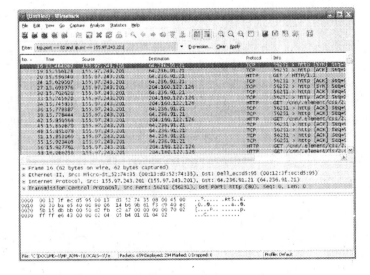

Figure 4-14: Filter packets by IP address and port 80.

You are now looking at only Web traffic that is coming from your computer. It's important to point out that we have only scratched the surface with these projects. Wireshark is a powerful program with a lot of features. It's highly recommended that you explore all of the functionality built into Wireshark. You may have to do some additional research and/or read the manual but it will be well worth it.

1. Could you filter the traffic based on IP address and packet type for a given person in your organization?
2. Why are there so many different field types to filter?
3. What protocols, other than TCP/IP, are used to manage traffic across networks?
4. What statistics are available about the data you picked up? (Hint: Look under the Statistics menu.)

CHAPTER 5: PORT SCANNERS

Port scanners are programs that determine how many possible open ports there are on your computer. It's like walking around a house and listing all the possible entry points. Ports allow information to flow in and out of your computer. Programs on your computer open ports when they want to send/receive information.

For example, when you open a Web browser your computer opens at least one port to send/receive information to/from the server at the other end of the connection (i.e., www.cnn.com). Any number of programs can open/close ports on your computer. It's important to know which ports are open and why they are sending and/or receiving information.

Just like doors or windows on your house, every port is a potential vulnerability point for hackers. There are a wide variety of port scanners available that have vastly different functionalities. Only a few free port scanners are shown below.

SUPERSCAN® 4.0

SuperScan is easy to use and has a lot of functionality. Foundstone produces SuperScan and is a great source of free IT security software. Their corporate software and professional services are also quite good. It is well worth spending an hour or so visiting their free downloads section (http://www.foundstone.com/us/resources-free-tools.asp) and trying all the tools. Foundstone deserves special recognition for providing so many useful free tools to the IT security community.

1. Download SuperScan from http://www.foundstone.com.
2. Click Resources, Free Tools, SuperScan.
3. Click Download this tool now (at the bottom of the page).
4. Click Download now.
5. Click Save.
6. Select the C:\security folder.
7. If the program doesn't automatically open, browse to C:\security.
8. Right-click superscan4.zip.
9. Select Extract All, Next, Next, Finish.
10. Browse to C:\security\superscan4\.
11. Right-click the SuperScan.exe program.
12. Select Copy.
13. Go to your desktop and paste a copy of the program (Right-click, Paste).
14. Double-click the SuperScan icon on your desktop.
15. Enter your IP address in the Hostname/IP address box. (Use the IPConfig command or go to http://whatismyipaddress.com/.)
16. If you can't figure out your IP address, enter: 127.0.0.1. (This is the default home address for every computer and I've used it in the examples to ensure that it works for those people that can't determine their IP address.)
17. Take a screenshot. (See Figure 5-1.)
18. Press the -> arrow next to the Hostname/IP address box to move the IP address into the adjacent box. (This tells SuperScan that you want to use this IP address.)
19. Click on the Host and Service Discovery tab.

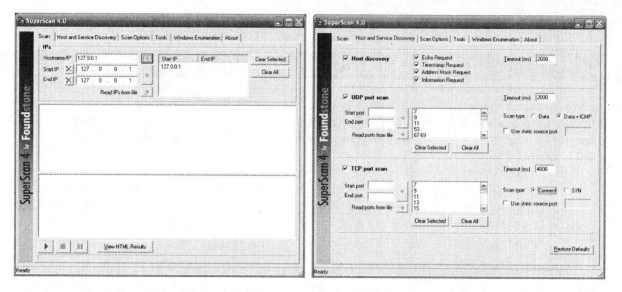

Figure 5-1: SuperScan configuration screen.   Figure 5-2: Host and discovery options.

20. Select Time Stamp Request, Address Mask Request, Information Request, the radio button Data+ICMP, and the radio button Connect.
21. Take a screenshot. (See Figure 5-2.)
22. Return to the Scan tab and click the Play button at the bottom of the screen.
23. If you see a Windows XP firewall message, click Unblock.
24. Take a screenshot once the scan is complete. (See Figure 5-3.)
25. Click the View HTML Results button at the bottom of the screen.
26. Take a screenshot of the SuperScan Report. (See Figure 5-4.)

Note: Foundstone reports "Windows XP Service Pack 2 has removed raw sockets support that now limits SuperScan and many other network scanning tools. Some functionality can be restored by running the following at the Windows command prompt before starting SuperScan." If your scan did not return any results, you should type this command at a DOS prompt: **net stop SharedAccess**

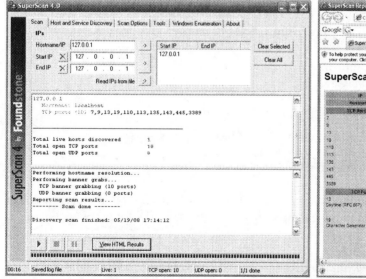

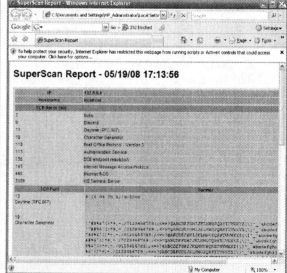

Figure 5-3: Results from port scan.   Figure 5-4: SuperScan report.

This computer has 10 ports open. The SuperScan Report tells you which ports are open and the results from an attempted port access. This computer doesn't actually have that many ports open. It's running a honeypot that is faking some of those ports and others. You'll learn how to install and configure a honeypot later. In general it's better to have fewer open ports because it makes life more difficult for hackers by limiting their potential entry points.

Port scanners are great because they can also be used to determine if your machine has been compromised. For example, if you see TCP port 80 open, then you most likely have a Web server running on your computer. If you know you aren't supposed to be running a Web server (or don't know what a Web server is) but the scan shows you have one running on your machine, then your computer might have been compromised by an intruder. Hackers use Web servers on compromised machines for various purposes (i.e. phishing, DOS attacks, etc.). Systems administrators "lose" servers more often than you'd think and more often than they'd like to admit.

WARNING Do not scan any networks without permission. Most good network/systems administrators watch who scans them and so does the U.S. federal government, large companies, law enforcement, the FBI, the CIA, and a host of other agencies. The safe bet is to just scan your own system/machines and/or the ones designated by your instructor.

THOUGHT QUESTIONS

1. How many ports are there on a single computer?
2. What programs (services) run over each port?
3. Can hackers use ports to spread malware?
4. How do you close ports that may already be open?

NMAP® (ZENMAP)

Another well-known port scanner that has been around for many years and is available on a variety of operating systems is Nmap. It also has a new GUI interface that makes it more user-friendly to introductory IT security students. Nmap can tell you which operating system a machine is running, which services are available, and can give you a graphical representation of a network. The GUI interface also gives a command-line option for those users that are accustomed to using the traditional CLI (command-line interface).

Nmap has long been an industry staple for IT security professionals. It's well worth the time to become familiar with Nmap. Insecure.org has a good reference by Gordon "Fyodor" Lyon that can help answer many questions about port scanning (http://nmap.org/book/toc.html). Let's look at a simple example using Nmap.

1. Download Nmap from http://nmap.org/download.html.
2. Click Download nmap-4.76-setup.exe.

Note: The version listed above will likely become outdated by the time this book is published. Make sure you get the latest stable release under the Windows section. Look for the version with the highest number. If you are uncertain which version to get, please ask your instructor.

3. Click Save.
4. Select the C:\security folder.
5. Browse to C:\security.

6. Double-click nmap-4.76-setup.exe.
7. Click Run, Run.
8. Click I Agree, Next, Install, Yes (if you are asked to replace WinPcap).
9. Click Next, Close, Next, Next, Finish.
10. Click I Agree, Install, Close.
11. Double-click the Nmap—Zenmap® icon on your desktop.
12. Take a screenshot. (See Figure 5-5.)
13. In the box named Target enter www.google.com.
14. In the Profile box select Regular Scan.
15. Press Scan.
16. Take a screenshot after the scan completes. (See Figure 5-6.)

Note: If you get an error you can get the latest version of WinPcap from http://www.winpcap.org/install/default.htm. Nmap should work correctly after you install WinPcap. You may have to close Nmap to get WinPcap to install correctly. You will need to restart Nmap once you have installed WinPcap.

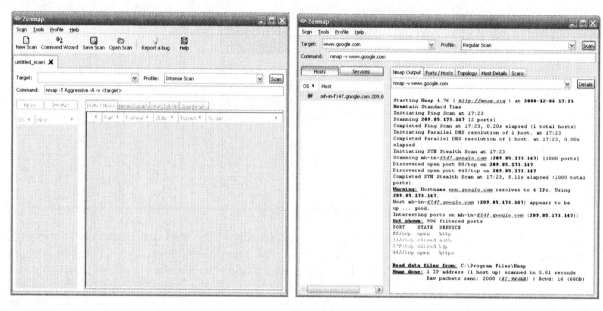

Figure 5-5: Zenmap configuration.   Figure 5-6: Results from a Zenmap scan.

17. Click on the Ports/Hosts tab.
18. Take a screenshot. (See Figure 5-7.)
19. Notice that there are four ports open including port 80 (for a Web server).
20. Click on the Host Details tab.
21. Take a screenshot. (See Figure 5-8.)
22. Swap IP addresses with a classmate/friend and scan his/her computer.
23. Take a screenshot.

Notice that you only port scanned one machine in this project. You can port scan entire blocks of IP addresses at one time. Nmap is a powerful tool with much more functionality than you have seen here. Additional documentation for Nmap can be found here: http://nmap.org/book/man.html.

Remember to scan only your own computers or machines designated by your instructor. Many organizations (corporations, governments, universities, etc.) have intrusion detection systems that will notice these scans. You will set up honeypots and IDSs later and test them with these port scanners.

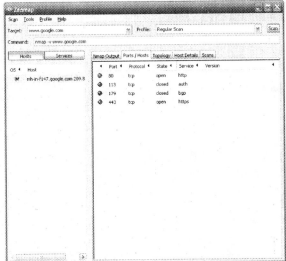
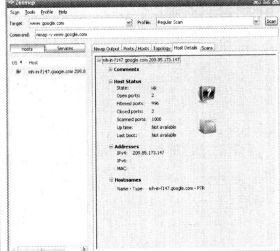

Figure 5-7: Ports identified from a port scan.   Figure 5-8: Host details from a port scan.

THOUGHT QUESTIONS

1. What is the difference between "Regular" and "Intense" scans?
2. Why does Nmap fail to identify some operating systems on certain machines?
3. Why does a port show up at all if it is closed?
4. Can you protect yourself from port scans? How?

ADVANCED LAN SCANNER 1.0

Another easy-to-use port scanner is Advanced LAN Scanner®. It can also yield more detailed results in some cases. If you are looking for an easy-to-use scanner this is it. You just enter the IP address or host name of the machine you want to scan and press the scan button.

Note: You need to be careful when you open Advanced LAN Scanner as it sets the target range as your entire C block of IP addresses. C blocks are groupings of about 255 IP addresses. You do NOT want to scan an entire C block of IP addresses because scanning multiple machines can make some network administrators nervous. Scan only those machines designated by your instructor.

1. Download Advanced LAN Scanner from
   http://www.radmin.com/products/utilities/lanscanner.php.
2. Click Download.
3. Click Save.
4. Select the C:\security folder.
5. Browse to C:\security.
6. Double-click lscan1b1.exe.
7. Click Run, Run, I Agree, Next, Start.
8. Right-click the Advanced LAN Scanner Icon select copy.
9. Right-click your desktop and select Paste Shortcut.
10. Enter your IP address in the box next to Scan.
11. Press Scan.
12. Take a screenshot. (See Figure 5-9.)

13. Clear your IP address from the Scan box and enter another IP address (e.g., a classmate's or friend's IP address).
14. Press Scan.
15. Take another screenshot. (See Figure 5-10.)

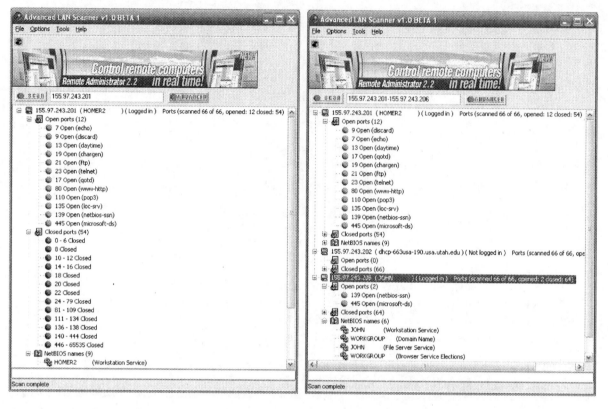

Figure 5-9: Results from a port scan.   Figure 5-10: Results from scanning multiple computers.

Again, you can see all ports open on your computer that are potential entry points for hackers. You may actually see more ports with this port scanner than you did with the other port scanners. You can also see that Advanced LAN Scanner shows your computer's name (this machine is named Homer2), network name (this network is named Simpsons), and possibly other users logged into your machine. Use these port scanners with caution.

THOUGHT QUESTIONS

1. Can you enter an IP address (209.85.173.99) in a Web browser and open a Web page directly without entering the domain name (www.google.com)?
2. Once hackers know which ports you have open what do they do next?
3. Which ports should you have open for your home PC, a Web server, an email server, etc.?
4. Web servers typically use port 80 to serve requests. Could they use a port other than port 80?

F-PORT

Foundstone (www.foundstone.com) has produced a handy command-line program called Fport® that lists all the ports you have open and which program opened it. It's important to know which programs are opening ports on your computer. You may not want some of them open.

Sometimes computers become infected with viruses/worms that open ports and send/receive information. This is not good. You need to be continually aware of which ports you have open and whether or not they are sending/receiving information. Fport can quickly give you an idea of which programs are sending/receiving information. Then you can take steps to remove the offending program(s).

1. Download Fport from http://www.foundstone.com. (There are a lot of other great tools to look at.)
2. Click Resources, Free Tools, Fport.
3. Click Download this Tool Now.
4. Click Download Now.
5. Click Save.
6. Select the C:\security folder.
7. If the program doesn't automatically open, browse to C:\security.
8. Right-click fport.zip.
9. Select Extract All, Next, Next, Finish.
10. Browse to C:\security\fport\.
11. Right-click the Fport.exe program and select Copy.
12. Right-click in the C:\security folder and select paste. (If you don't have a security folder on your C: drive, then create one at this time.)
13. Open a command prompt by clicking Start, Run, and typing CMD (or command).
14. Use the cd command to change directory to C:\security. (Feel free to review the DOS section for a refresher on DOS commands.)
15. Enter the DIR command to get a directory listing of all the files in the security folder.
16. Enter Fport.
17. Take a screenshot. (See Figure 5-11.)

Figure 5-11: Results from fport.

Figure 5-12: Process details for nfrbof.exe.

Note that you should see the following:

PID: Process Identifier
Process: the actual process name
Port: the port opened by the process
Proto: either TCP or UDP

For each open port on your machine you will see the path where the actual program is located. If you are not sure if a port should be open you can follow this link to Wikipedia for a complete list of ports (http://en.wikipedia.org/wiki/List_of_TCP_and_UDP_port_numbers). You can also Google the actual process/program name itself.

For example, you can see that the Fport results shown above list a program named nfrbof.exe. When you Google nfrbof.exe you find out that it is a Honeypot that fakes opening many different ports. (See Figure 5-12.) NFR BackOfficer Friendly is running on this machine to attract more hackers without actually making this machine more vulnerable.

THOUGHT QUESTIONS

1. Who decides which services should be on a given port?
2. Why are there multiple PIDs for a single program?
3. Can you force your operating system (Windows XP, Windows Vista, Linux, Leopard, etc.) to ask you before a program attempts to open a port and send/receive information?
4. Can you log which programs are opening/closing ports on your machine?

CHAPTER 6: VULNERABILITY SCANNERS

Vulnerability scanners have all the functionality of port scanners and a lot more. They give additional information regarding open ports and other operating system information. For example, a port scanner may tell you that a server has port 80 open. A vulnerability scanner will tell you the name of the Web server (Apache, IIS, etc.) running on that port and its specific version number. You typically won't get this information from a simple port scanner.

The additional information provided can be helpful to network administrators, penetration testers, and hackers alike. It tells you which machines have software running that may need to be patched and are currently vulnerable to attack. Many organizations run vulnerability scans on every single machine in the organization at least twice a year (if not monthly). Most users are completely unaware that these scans are being run. If you take your laptop to work and use the local network, you need to be aware that your company may run a vulnerability scan on your personal computer. Some organizations have mandatory vulnerability scans written into their IT security policies.

To illustrate the differences between port scanners and vulnerability scanners you will do a simple scan using Nessus. A two-minute demonstration conveys more meaning than 20 pages of ad nauseum instruction.

WARNING Remember, only scan your own computer or those designated by your instructor. Do NOT start randomly scanning computers. Network administrators are watching, and they will see you scan their machines. They will not be happy, and you may get in trouble.

Hopefully this was a strong enough warning. If you are still considering scanning a machine other than your own, please re-read the above paragraph until the desire goes away. If you want to scan another machine, ask a classmate for their permission and IP address.

NESSUS

Nessus® is a well-known vulnerability scanner that has been around for a long time. It is fast and thorough. Many companies, universities, organizations, and governments use it every day. A single scan can put 700+ entries on a single intrusion detection system with a single scan.

As previously mentioned, Nessus is like any other security tool. It can be used for good or bad. The good/bad part has nothing to do with the tool and everything to do with the person running the tool. Beginner and advanced user guides can be found at the following URLs. They are great recreational reading.

Installation Guide: http://www.nessus.org/documentation/nessus_4.0_installation_guide.pdf
User Guide: http://www.nessus.org/documentation/NessusClient_4.0_User_Guide.pdf
Advanced User Guide: http://www.nessus.org/documentation/nessus_3.2_advanced_user_guide.pdf

Let's install Nessus and do a simple scan of your local machine. As previously mentioned the scans are thorough and can take several minutes.

1. Download Nessus 4 from http://www.nessus.org/download/.
2. Select Nessus 4.0.0 for Microsoft Windows from the drop-down menu at the bottom of the page.

3. Click Download.
4. Click I Accept.
5. Click on the link labeled Nessus-4.0.0-386i.msi (or Nessus-4.0.0-amd64.msi if you have a 64-bit system).
6. Click Save.
7. Select the C:\security folder.
8. If the program doesn't automatically open, browse to C:\security.
9. Double-click Nessus-4.0.0-386i.msi.
10. Click Next, I Accept, Next, Next, Next, Install, Finish.
11. Click Start, All Programs, Tenable Network Security, Nessus, Nessus Server Manager.
12. Click Obtain an activation code.
13. Click on the link labeled "Register a HomeFeed."
14. Click I Accept.
15. Enter an email address. (You'll need to retrieve the access code to get Nessus to work.)
16. Click Register.
17. Open the email that Nessus.com just sent you and copy/paste the access code from the email to the Nessus Server Manager screen.
18. Click Register.
19. Wait for the plug-ins to update and then close the Nessus Server Manager window.

Note: The plug-in update and installation may take awhile. There were about 22,000 plug-ins when this test machine was updated. Plug-ins are what gives Nessus the ability to do an effective vulnerability scan. You only need a large update like this once. It's worth the wait.

20. Click Start, All Programs, Tenable Network Security, Nessus, Nessus Client.
21. Take a screenshot.
22. Click the "+" button on the bottom of your screen.
23. In the Host Name box enter your IP address. (Enter 127.0.0.1 if you don't know your IP address.)
24. Click Save.
25. Click Connect, Connect.

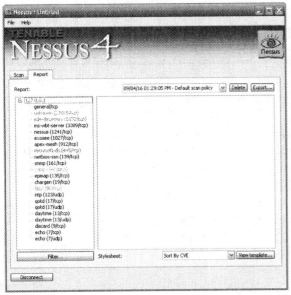

Figure 6-1: Ports shown from a Nessus scan.

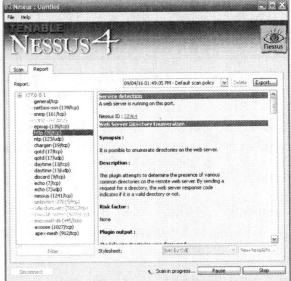

Figure 6-2: Details for specific a port and vulnerability.

26. Select Default Scan Policy in the right-hand pane.

27. Click Scan Now. (This scan drives honeypots and IDSs wild!)
28. On the Report tab press the "+" button to reveal the port information.
29. Take a screenshot. (See Figure 6-1.)
30. Click on any of the open ports on the left to see the detailed information.
31. Take a screenshot. (See Figure 6-2.)
32. Repeat the scan using one of your friend's/classmate's IP address. (Do NOT scan anyone else.)
33. Take a screenshot.

Notice that the Nessus scanner yields much more information than a port scanner. For example, Nessus can tell me that this machine has a medium risk factor related to port 161 using SNMP. Information about this system can be obtained including: network shares, users, system information, network interfaces, services, processes, and software installed on this computer. All of this can be obtained by anyone with a Nessus scanner and a network connection.

A nice feature of Nessus is that it tells you how to protect your machine from intruders. It gives you solutions to the weaknesses noted on your computer. Overall, a vulnerability scanner will give you a lot more information than a simple port scanner. Nessus is an easy-to-use scanner that is well worth getting acquainted with. Many people are unaware that this type of scanner is available to help them diagnose potential computer weaknesses.

THOUGHT QUESTIONS

1. Running the scan was fairly easy. Where could you go to get more information about understanding the results from the scan?
2. Who creates the plug-ins for Nessus and how do they decide which vulnerabilities to include?
3. How many vulnerabilities are reported each day?
4. Do all operating systems and applications have vulnerabilities? Which are less vulnerable?

APPSCAN

IBM's AppScan® is a vulnerability scanner specifically focused on testing Web sites. This is the only commercial (not free) piece of software in the book. It is included in this book because you probably work for a company/organization that has a Web site that needs to be secured. Securing your company's Web site is likely more important than securing your personal computer. Your company's Web site may be a major source of revenue and interact with mission-critical systems.

The AppScan demo shown below can help companies assess potential risks related to their Web server(s). At the writing of this book I could not find a totally free Windows-based vulnerability scanner for Web sites with all the features that are built into AppScan. There might be one available now.

You will use a fully functional version of AppScan but it will only run on a test Web site that IBM has set up. AppScan is advertized by online retailers for about $6,000. It's worth using the free version to get exposure to this type of software and see how it works. It has good documentation and is easy to use. It is a good idea for companies running mission-critical Web servers to consider buying a vulnerability scanner to secure their electronic storefronts.

WARNING The way IBM® hosts this application changes often. The instructions were accurate at the time this book was printed. You may have to follow slightly different instructions to get the download to work. Internet Explorer might be the best Web browser to use.

1. Download AppScan from http://www.ibm.com/developerworks/downloads/r/appscan/?S_TACT=105AGX15&S_CMP=LP.
2. Select Free Download Rational AppScan.
3. Click "register here."
4. Fill out their form with as many creative answers as you can dream up but the email address has to be real. (They send the download link to that email account.)
5. Click Continue.
6. Fill out more creative information (only where you see an asterisk).
7. Click Submit.
8. Log in using the email address you provided and your fake password.
9. Click Continue.
10. Fill out more creative information (only where you see an asterisk).
11. Click Submit.
12. Click Continue.
13. Finish filling out their survey and click submit. (That's a lot of work to get a demo.)
14. Click on the tab labeled Download using HTTP.
15. Right-click on I Agree for "**IBM Rational AppScan Developer Evaluation License Key File.**"
16. Click Save Target As.
17. Select the C:\security folder.
18. Click Save, Close.
19. Click on I Agree for "**IBM Rational AppScan Developer Edition 7.8 for Rational Application Developer 7.5/Eclipse 3.4 Windows English.**"
20. Select the C:\security folder.
21. Click Save, Close.
22. If the program doesn't automatically open, browse to C:\security.
23. Right-click C1X8GEN.zip.
24. Select Extract All, Next, Next, Finish.
25. Browse to C:\security\C1X8GEN\AppScanDE78_341\.
26. Double-click Launchpad.exe.
27. Click "Install IBM Rational AppScan Developer and Build Edition."
28. Click Next, I Accept, Next, Next, Next, Next, Install, Finish.

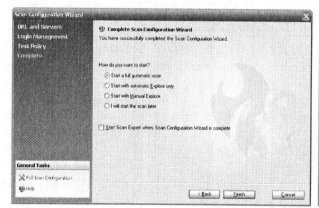

Figure 6-3: AppScan.

Figure 6-4: Installing additional packages.

29. Double-click the IBM Rational AppScan icon on your desktop.
30. Click Create New Scan.
31. Click demo.testfire.net under predefined templates.
32. Click Next, Next, Next, Next.
33. Uncheck the option for selecting "Start Scan Expert..."
34. Click Finish. (See Figure 6-3.)

35. Click "Yes" to save the scan and enter "test" for the scan name.
36. Click Enter.
37. Take a screenshot once the scan ends. (It will take several minutes but is fun to watch.) (See Figure 6-4.)

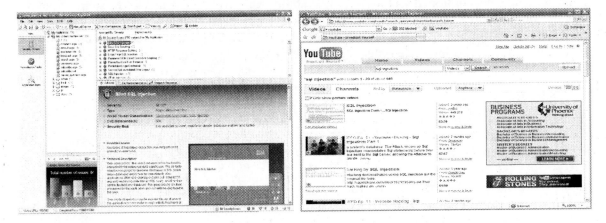

Figure 6-5: Results and details from a scan.   Figure 6-6: Youtube.com videos about SQL injection.

38. Click on the line that reads "Blind SQL Injection."
39. Take a screenshot. (See Figure 6-5.)
40. Click on the bottom right pane that tells you about Blind SQL Injection.
41. Read about the blind SQL injection issue and how it works.
42. Go to www.Youtube.com and search for "sql injection."
43. Click on the one that gives you a demo for eNorthwestern (http://www.youtube.com/watch?v=MJNJjh4jORY).
44. Take a screenshot when you are done viewing it. (See Figure 6-6.)

As you can see AppScan is a good tool that can analyze a large number of potential weaknesses in Web sites. If you are involved with e-commerce, it's probably worth the money to purchase a full copy. Not only does AppScan identify vulnerabilities in your Web site but it also tells you how they work and how to fix them.

For example, you may not have even known what SQL injection was before running this scan. Now that you are aware of what a SQL injection attack is you are in a much better position to protect yourself. You can see from the YouTube video that the information and knowledge surrounding SQL injection is commonplace.

AppScan also comes with several "power tools" that you can find in the Start menu. They are really useful if you take the time to understand how to use them. As this is an introductory book on information security software, we won't be using them. Please feel free to browse them (and hopefully learn them). These tools are fully functional and free.

THOUGHT QUESTIONS

1. What would it take to fix your Web site so it's not vulnerable to a SQL injection attack?
2. What background training would you need to be able to fully understand all the attacks listed in AppScan (e.g. databases, SQL, HTML, programming, networking, TCP/IP, etc.)?
3. Do you think companies actually see SQL injection attacks? How often?
4. If a hacker could get into your Web server could he/she subsequently gain access to the rest of your mission-critical systems through your Web server?

SHIELDS UP

Home users may benefit from a Web-based vulnerability scanner if they want to do a simple scan of potential vulnerabilities on their own personal computers. Shields Up® is a Web-based vulnerability scanner managed by Gibson Research Corporation® that will scan your computer without installing any additional software. The downside is that it doesn't have the ability to scan additional computers other than your own machine.

1. Go to the Shields Up main page at the following link: https://www.grc.com/x/ne.dll?bh0bkyd2. (If the link has been moved, please Google "Shields Up.")
2. Click Proceed.
3. Click Continue.
4. Click File Sharing.
5. Take a screenshot of the results. (See Figure 6-7.)
6. Click Common Ports.
7. Take a screenshot of the results.

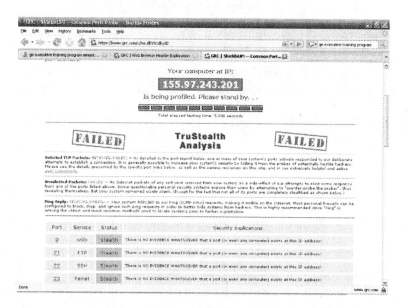

Figure 6-7: Results from a Shields Up scan.

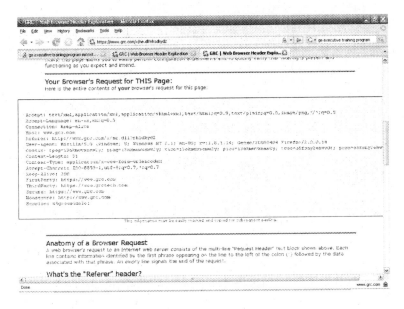

Figure 6-8: Contents from your Web browser request.

8. Click on any one of the ports that may have been open.
9. Take a screenshot of the explanation page.
10. Go back to the port results page.
11. Click on All Service Ports. (This may take a couple minutes.)
12. Take a screenshot of the results.
13. Scroll to the bottom of the page and click on Messenger Spam.
14. Take a screenshot.
15. Click Spam Me with this Note.
16. Take a screenshot if a note appears.
17. Scroll to the bottom and click on Browse Headers.
18. Take a screenshot of the box named "Your Browser's Request for THIS Page." (See Figure 6-8.)

Shields Up is an easy way to see common security vulnerabilities on your personal computer without installing or configuring new software. Running the scan is the easy part. The hard part is interpreting and understanding the results.

You also need to think about the eventual security implications from the page you see. Running the scan and looking at the results page only gives you an idea of how vulnerable your computer is. You need to make changes to your computer to actually make it safer.

Shields Up provides a good explanation about the scans and their results if you are willing to do a little more reading. Please feel free to take the time to read and understand the results from the scans. Once you understand what is going on you can run the scan on your friends' computers and dazzle them with your IT security understanding.

THOUGHT QUESTIONS

1. Why isn't this functionality built into your operating system?
2. Do you have any ports open that you know shouldn't be open?
3. Could this functionality be built into Web sites that you visit and be used by the Web administrator to compromise your computer?
4. Could other tools listed in this book be written as a Web-based application?

CHAPTER 7: MONITORING SOFTWARE

A keylogger is a piece of software (or hardware) that records all keystrokes on a computer. Over the years keyloggers have added functionality and become much more than just a tool to capture keystrokes. As a result, many people have tried to come up with new terms to convey the fact that these new products have added functionality. However, most people still use the term "keylogger" to mean a piece of software that monitors a person's activity on a computer.

Keyloggers can be hidden from users. A certain sequence of keys can be pressed to reveal the keylogger program and configuration screen. Information gathered from logging sessions can be stored in encrypted files and/or sent to a pre-specified email account at regular intervals. Keyloggers can also hide themselves from anti-virus scans.

Keyloggers can be used by concerned parents wanting to monitor Internet activity, spouses worried about infidelity, employers suspicious of employees, and hackers capturing passwords on compromised systems. Users can use keyloggers on their own computers to ensure that no one else is using their machine. Below is an example of a free Windows-based keylogger. It will give you an idea of the basic functionality provided by keyloggers.

Another example below (demo only) shows a larger enterprise monitoring suite that can be used at a corporation. Commercial versions have even greater functionality. They are currently being used by most large employers to monitor employees' desktops throughout the day. There are many employees that are fired each year for inappropriate behavior (i.e., looking at porn while at work). This example is included to give users an idea of the type of functionality available in corporate monitoring systems.

Anecdotal evidence from students and employees that have used this software has been surprising. They mention that they have effectively used keyloggers at home and at work with surprising results.

WARNING Do NOT load a keylogger on any computer that is not your own. You can get in trouble. It's not worth the risk of loading a keylogger onto a machine that is not your own.

Note: Your anti-virus may tell you that these keyloggers are a virus. Although these keyloggers are not viruses, it is actually comforting to see your anti-virus software doing its work. It's good to know that your computer could actually keep someone else from installing a keylogger without your knowledge.

If your anti-virus program recognizes these files as viruses, you will need to create an exception folder to store your files. Appendix A shows you how to create an exception folder using McAfee or Norton. Once you have an exception folder created, the anti-virus scanner will not scan that folder.

REFOG KEYLOGGER

Refog® is a really good keylogger with an easy-to-use interface. There are monitoring suites available that have more functionality but the downside is that they cost anywhere from $50 to +$100. Refog is one of the few GUI-based keyloggers that is completely free. Most keyloggers will be free to download but will require you to pay $20–$70 to get full functionality.

Refog can stay completely hidden until you press the specific key sequence to recall the main window. It can automatically load the keylogger and hide it from users. It also monitors programs, Web sites, chat, and can take screenshots.

1. Download Refog from http://www.refog.com/trial2.html.
2. Click Download Keylogger Free Version.
3. Click Save.
4. Select the C:\security folder.
5. If the program doesn't automatically open, browse to C:\security.
6. Double-click refog_setup_free_kl_514.exe. (The numbers may be slightly different depending on the version you download.)
7. Click OK, Next, Next, I Agree, Next, Next, Next, Install, Finish, OK.
8. Click the green play button to start monitoring.
9. Press the Hide button. (It has a little eye on it.)

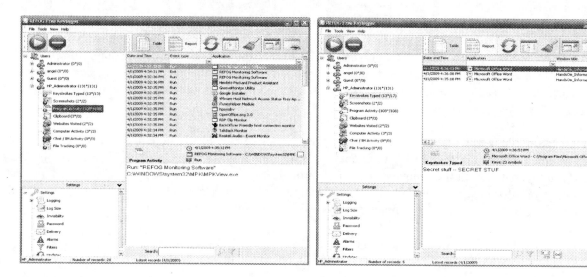

Figure 7-1: Monitoring program activity.   Figure 7-2: Results from monitoring keystrokes.

10. Remember you will need to press Shift+Ctrl+Alt+k to get the program to show again.
11. Make a Word document or Send yourself an email with the words "Credit card number, SSN, and Secret Stuff."
12. Open a Web browser and visit a couple of Web sites.
13. Press Shift+Ctrl+Alt+k to get the program to show again.
14. Click on Program Activity under your username.
15. Take a screenshot. (See Figure 7-1.)
16. Click on Keystrokes Typed under your username.
17. Take a screenshot. (See Figure 7-2.)
18. Scroll through the bottom window to see all the words you just typed.

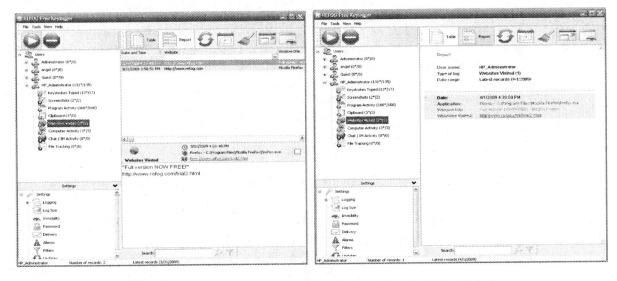

Figure 7-3: Web sites visited.

Figure 7-4: Details for Web sites visited.

19. Click on Web sites Visited.
20. Take a screenshot. (See Figure 7-3.)
21. Click on the Report button at the top of the screen.
22. Take a screenshot. (See Figure 7-4.)
23. Click the Clear Logs button.
24. Select Clear all logs.
25. Click Clear, Yes.

THOUGHT QUESTIONS

1. Does your employer/spouse/roommate monitor your activities with a keylogger? Are you sure?
2. What would happen if your employer/spouse/roommate found out you were using a keylogger to monitor their activities?
3. Why would someone want to install a keylogger on their own computer?
4. How would you know if you had a keylogger on your computer? How would you get rid of it?

SPECTOR 360

This book was written to give beginning students practical experiences with real-world security software. We have focused on free windows-based software that shows the range of functionality possible in each category. This project is going to be one of the few exceptions to that rule. Spector360® is commercial software that can monitor employees at the enterprise level. It can log all keystrokes, track Web sites visited, take real-time screenshots, etc. of all employees within a company.

Most people don't have a good understanding of the extent to which an employer can monitor their activities. Employers can monitor anything and everything that is done on their computers or goes across their networks. It's their system. They pay for it. They can do it. It's also perfectly legal to do so. Most large companies do watch their employees' computer usage on a daily basis. Many more employers are catching on to how easy, and relatively cheap, it is to monitor employees.

The purpose of this project is to give you an idea of what is possible. We won't install/run the software because it's $2,995 for 25 licenses. It would be nice if they had a free version but they don't. However, it is worth watching the demo.

1. Click "here" to view the Spector360 demo: http://www.spector360.com/OnlineDemos/index.htm#.
2. Click View Demo for the Product Overview Demonstration (8 minutes).
3. Take a screenshot while it's playing. (See Figure 7-5.)
4. Click View Demo for the Recording Tools Demonstration.
5. Click on one of the Recording Tools you find interesting.
6. Take a screenshot while it's playing. (See Figure 7-6.)
7. Click View Demo for the Internet Filtering and Employee Monitoring.
8. Take a screenshot while it's playing. (See Figures 7-7 and 7-8.)

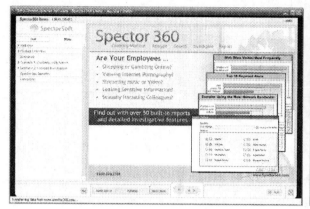

Figure 7-5: Spector 360.

Figure 7-6: Spector 360 menu.

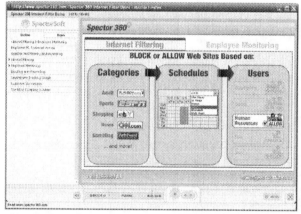

Figure 7-7: Spector 360 filtering options.

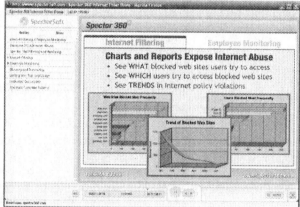

Figure 7-8: Spector 360 reports.

THOUGHT QUESTIONS

1. Would this software help reduce wasted time at work? How?
2. Could this software help protect the company from being sued? How?
3. Could this software hurt employee morale and lead to other negative behaviors?
4. What industries or types of companies would really benefit from this software?

CHAPTER 8: PORN & SPAM FILTERS

One of the increasingly important pieces of software people ask about is application layer filters (i.e., porn filters, spam filters, etc.). More specifically, individuals are seeing solutions to keep their children safe. Companies are looking for ways to keep their employees productive while on the clock. Application layer filters can solve both of these problems.

Talking about porn filters is not regular conversational fare. In fact, it makes some people uncomfortable to even talk about it. However, once you broach the subject people are interested and will likely want to implement a solution right away. The response from parents can be overwhelming. They want to protect their children but were just not sure how to do it.

Spam is easier to talk about, but people tend to be less motivated to devote resources to solve this problem. Employers are more likely to want a strong spam filter. The larger your organization is the more likely you are to need a spam filter. Spam, unlike porn, is illegal. However, the enforcement of the existing spam laws has been anemic at best. Companies have been forced to defend themselves against this electronic plague. There are some excellent commercial products available.

Companies are becoming aware that they can, and often are, held liable when one of their employees creates a hostile work environment by viewing porn at work or sending pornographic emails. In the past ten years companies have really started to crack down on employees that view porn at work. Not only is viewing porn at work illegal, but it also reduces employee productivity. We will only look at personal application filters in this book (e.g., porn and spam filters).

If your organization needs a commercial porn/spam filter, it's worth the time and effort to look at the variety of VM appliances (images) available for testing at http://www.vmware.com/appliances/. It's much easier to try out the virtual machine before you buy the product

K-9

K-9® is a free porn filter that allows parents/spouses to block Internet content that they feel is inappropriate. Users can make exceptions, block/unblock whole categories, and override any filtering. Only the administrator can make changes to the program settings and the account is locked with a password. If someone tries to access the administrator account (sometimes people foolishly try to guess passwords), it will send the administrator an email telling them that someone is trying to make changes to their account. This is a great feature for parents with persistent children.

Using a porn filter is great for adults too. It assures that you can avoid potentially embarrassing situations. For example, a business professional can feel confident that they won't accidentally hit a pornographic page during an important presentation. You only have to have one important meeting go badly to see the value of a good porn filter. You can always override it, but it's nice to know that it's there keeping you safe.

Parents are very interested in using a porn filter. Porn is prevalent and one of the most profitable industries on the Internet. We'll test the filter after we are done to see how effective it is at filtering porn. Let's walk through an installation.

1. Click on the following link: http://www1.k9webprotection.com/getk9/index.php.

2. Fill in a first name, last name, and a valid email address. (In this example we used John Doe.)

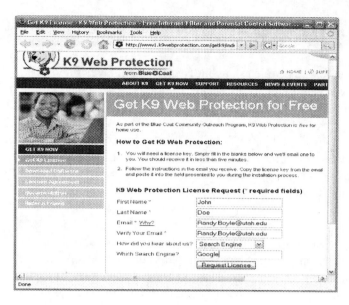

Figure 8-1: K9 sign-up page.

3. Click the Request License button and an email will arrive in about 5 minutes with the license code to activate the software. (See Figure 8-1.)
4. Click on the email link to get the download http://www1.k9webprotection.com/getk9/download-software.php.
5. Click on the Download for Windows XP button.
6. Click Run and Run again if prompted to do so.
7. Click Next, I Agree, Next.
8. Copy the license code from the email you received and paste it into the box labeled License. (One of the codes I got looked like K9USERFE43; this one is already used and won't work again.)
9. Enter a password that only you will know, or one given to you by your instructor if you are using a remote machine. (This password will allow you to override the Web filter and change its settings.)
10. Write this password down. (REMEMBER YOUR PASSWORD!!)
11. Enter the same password in both boxes.
12. Click Next, Next, Install, and Finish. (This completes the installation and will restart your computer.)

Figure 8-2: K9 administrator main menu.

13. Open K9 by clicking Start, All Programs, Blue Coat K9, Blue Coat K9.
14. Take a screenshot. (See Figure 8-2.)
15. Click Setup.
16. Enter your administrator password.
17. Feel free to select/deselect any categories.
18. Take a screenshot.
19. Click View Internet Activity at the top of the screen.
20. Take a screenshot.
21. Open your Web browser and test the porn filter to see if it is effective by entering www.playboy.com or www.sex.com.
22. Take a screenshot. (See Figure 8-3.) (Hopefully, it blocked the request.)
23. You can enter your password to temporarily override the block. (See Figure 8-4.)

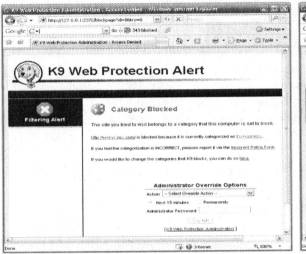

Figure 8-3: Internet request blocked.

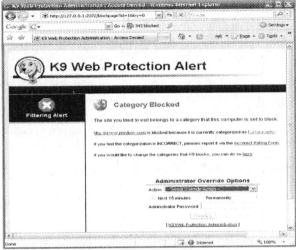

Figure 8-4: K9 override options.

24. Open K9 again and click on View Internet Activity.
25. Take a screenshot. (See Figure 8-5.)
26. Click on the Pornography link to view the details for that category.
27. Take a screenshot. (See Figure 8-6.)

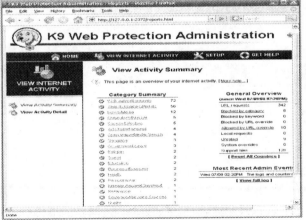

Figure 8-5: K9 activity summary.

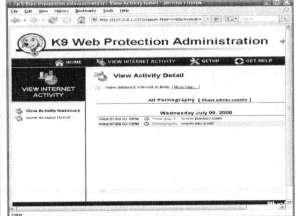

Figure 8-6: K9 activity detail.

1. Can you put in custom exceptions for specific pages that are blocked by default?
2. How do they make the list of "blocked" pages?
3. Does the filter work for foreign languages? Slang?
4. What other things would you want to block/filter? Could you filter IM, chat, specific photos, or songs?

EMAIL FILTER (OUTLOOK)

Corporations and homes are inundated with about 100 billion pieces of illegal spam emails every day (CAN-SPAM Act of 2003). Billions of dollars ($11–20B depending on the survey you look at) are lost each year from decreased productivity. Not to mention the fact that it is ABSOLUTELY annoying. Don't purchase anything from spam email. It just encourages more wasteful behavior.

Many large companies are using their own spam filters at the server level to reduce the workload on users. However, they don't want to accidently delete valid emails. Setting up spam filtering rules can be tricky. To solve this dilemma many companies add a special tag (e.g., [SPAM]) to the subject line of a potential spam email. This additional tag indicates that the email may be spam. Users can then make a custom filter using this [SPAM] tag to send offending emails to a "junk" folder. Ask your Admin if they are using a server-level spam filter with this capability.

Below are instructions to create a filtering rule in Microsoft Outlook®. We will take care of spam in a later project. It's important to learn how filters work so you can get an idea of what's possible. Most peoples' inboxes are wildly out of control and they need a lesson on filtering rules.

As a lot of people give out one email address to both work associates and friends, we will show you how to make a filter to separate them into different folders. First, we will create a Friends folder. Next, we will make a filtering rule to send all emails you receive from a friend to the Friends folder you're about to create.

Note: If you don't have access to Outlook, skip down to the Hotmail and/or Gmail examples.

1. Open Outlook.
2. Right-click on Mailbox.
3. Select New Folder.
4. Enter Friends in the Name text box. (See Figure 8-7.)
5. Click OK.

Figure 8-7: Manage Outlook mail folders.

6. Click Tools, Rules and Alerts.
7. Click New Rule. (See Figure 8-8.)
8. Select "Move messages from someone to a folder." (See Figure 8-9.)
9. Click Next.

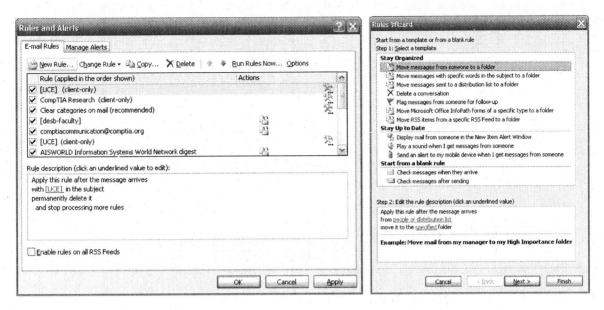

Figure 8-8: Manage Outlook rules and alerts   Figure 8-9: Outlook rules wizard.

10. Click on the highlighted text in the bottom pane (Step 2) labeled "people or distribution list." (See Figure 8-10.)
11. Double-click on anyone in your Address Book (preferably a friend). (See Figure 8-11.)

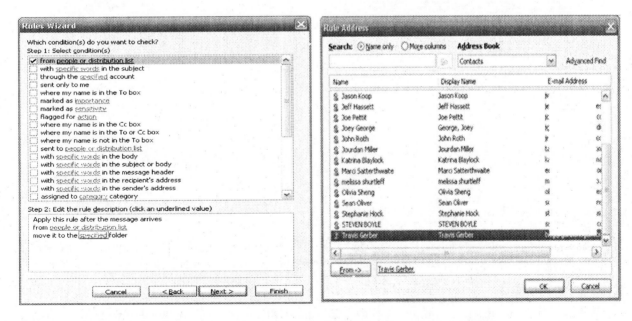

Figure 8-10: Select conditions to filter.   Figure 8-11: Select source contact to filter.

12. Click OK.
13. Click Next.
14. Click on the highlighted text in the bottom pane (Step 2) labeled "specified." (See Figure 8-12.)
15. Double-click on the Friends folder.

16. Take a screenshot. (See Figure 8-13.)

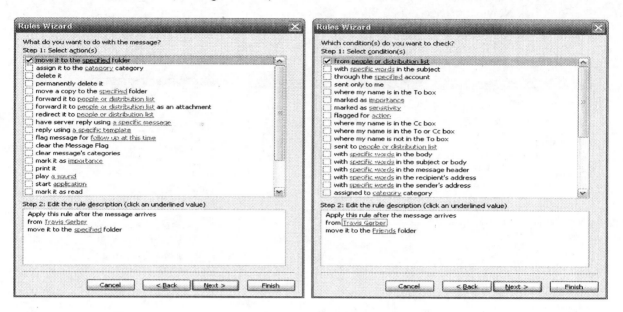

Figure 8-12: Action to take with email.

Figure 8-13: Conditions for filtering.

17. Click Next, Next, Next (no exceptions), Finish.
18. Take a screenshot. (See Figure 8-14.)
19. Click OK.

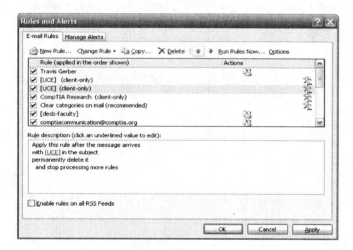

Figure 8-14: Rules and alerts listing.

The next time you get an email from the person you selected in the list the email should go into your Friends folder. You can repeat this procedure for all your friends. You can also create new folders for notices, bills, clients, or a specific organization.

Taking a few minutes to set up some basic email rules will help you take control of your Inbox and save you a lot of time in the future. Nothing is worse than seeing an Inbox with 1000+ emails in it. Seize the day and start taking control of your computer.

1. Is there a person in your organization that keeps sending you emails and you'd like to put them in a folder called "Annoying?"
2. Can you filter by more than just email address?
3. Can you filter emails if they contain a list of offensive words?
4. What is the criminal penalty for sending spam?

BLOCK SENDERS (OUTLOOK)

Poor people never get sued. They also don't get a lot of spam for the same reason. In general the higher your annual salary goes up the more spam you will likely get. Regardless of your income you will inevitably get a gaggle of annoying emails from individuals that believe they have the right to force you to accept their emails. Luckily technology can help us electronically isolate these petulant newbies.

Blocking people from sending you emails is quick and easy. However, if you are getting a lot of junk emails, you should consider changing to a different email provider. You don't have to sit there and waste your time blocking emails that the admin should be taking care of. Gmail and Hotmail have gotten a lot better since their inceptions. Let's look at an example of how to block a sender in Outlook.

1. Open Outlook.
2. Click on the Inbox folder.
3. Select an email or send yourself an email that we will block. (Don't worry; we will show you how to unblock it later.)
4. Take a screenshot. (See Figure 8-15.)
5. Click Actions, Junk E-mail, Add Sender to Blocked Senders List. (You can also right-click the email.) (See Figure 8-16.)
6. Click the Junk E-mail folder.
7. Take a screenshot.

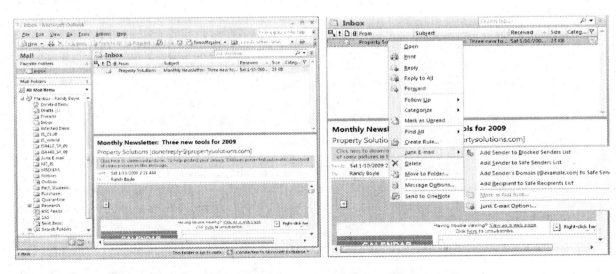

Figure 8-15: Select sender to block.   Figure 8-16: Junk email.

8. Click Actions, Junk E-mail, Junk E-mail Options.
9. Click on Blocked Senders tab.
10. Select the email address you just blocked.
11. Take a screenshot. (See Figure 8-17.)

12. If you blocked your own email address, select your email address and click Remove.
13. Click on the International tab.
14. Click Blocked Top-Level Domain List.
15. Select any three of the countries listed.
16. Take a screenshot. (See Figure 8-18.)

Note: Several countries are notorious for sending spam. Blocking emails from a given country is really easy. Unfortunately the spammers have caught on and now only send emails that look like they are coming from internal domains.

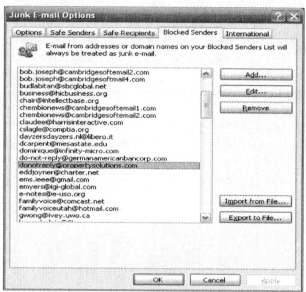

Figure 8-17: List of blocked senders.

Figure 8-18: Block emails from top-level domains.

THOUGHT QUESTIONS

1. Who is in charge of tracking down and arresting spammers?
2. Is sending spam from a fake email address possible? Easy?
3. How much does spam cost corporations each year?
4. Which countries send the most spam per capita?

JUNK EMAIL (HOTMAIL)

Most people should have at least three email addresses. You should have one for friends, one for work, and one for Internet usage (in case you need an authorization). It's a great idea to keep your personal emails from bouncing off work email servers. All the email going over company servers is considered company property and can be read anytime. Most email programs can check multiple email accounts at the same time so three accounts is not a big deal. They just take some time to set up.

Let's sign up for an online email account and set up some junk mail preferences. They use similar settings that you saw in the Outlook project. If you already have a Hotmail account, you can skip down to step 7.

1. Go to www.hotmail.com.
2. Click Sign up. (See Figure 8-19.)

3. In the Windows Live ID box enter your FirstNameLastName12345. (Mine was RandyBoyle12345.)
4. Click Check Availability.
5. Enter fake information for the rest of the text boxes. (See Figure 8-20.)
6. Click I Accept to log in.
7. Take a screenshot of your inbox showing your new email address. (See Figure 8-21.)

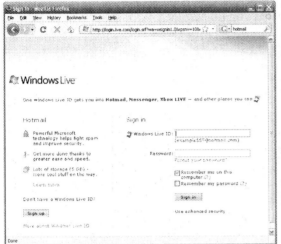

Figure 8-19: Hotmail sign-in.

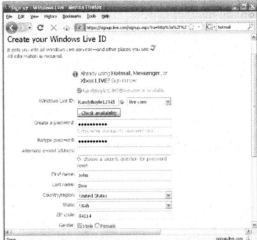

Figure 8-20: Creating a Windows Live ID.

8. Click Options on the right hand of the screen.
9. Click More options.
10. Under Junk email click Filters and reporting. (See Figure 8-22.)
11. Under Delete junk email select Immediately. (You'll likely never see spam.)
12. Under Report junk message select Report junk. (You'll help get rid of spam.)
13. Take a screenshot. (See Figure 8-23.)

Figure 8-21: Hotmail inbox.

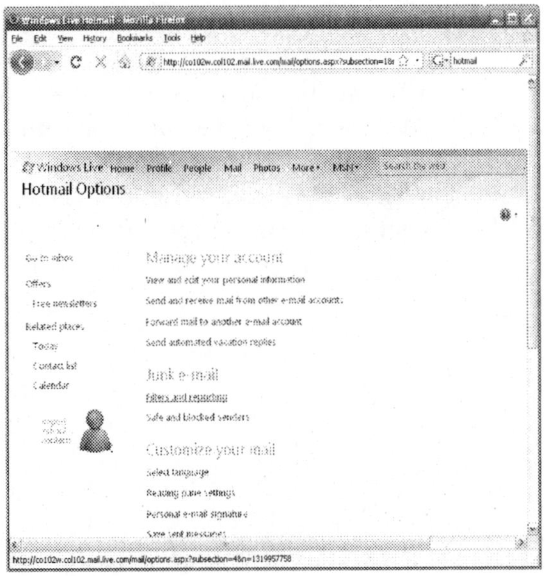

Figure 8-22: Hotmail configuration options.

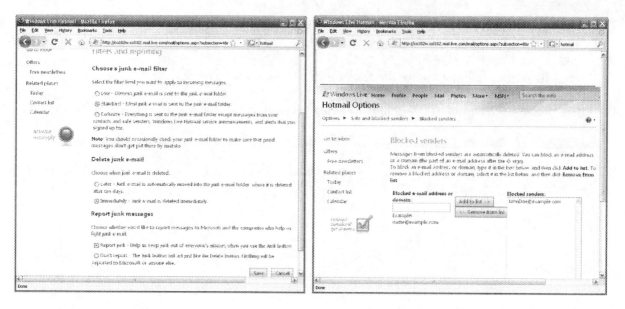

Figure 8-23: Junk email filter.　　　　　　　　Figure 8-24: Blocked senders configuration screen.

14. Click Save.
15. Under Junk email click Safe and Blocked Senders.
16. Click blocked senders.
17. In the Blocked e-mail address box enter JohnDoe@example.com.
18. Click Add to List.
19. Take a screenshot. (See Figure 8-24.)

If you use Gmail you will have even more control over filtering emails. Gmail has similar filtering mechanisms that you may have used in Outlook. You won't have to do another project using Gmail. If you were able to work through the prior two examples you are more than capable of setting up the Gmail email filters.

THOUGHT QUESTIONS

1. Can Hotmail or Gmail see who is sending spam and block them?
2. Could Hotmail or Gmail block an entire domain (like YourSchool.edu or YourCompany.com) from sending/receiving emails?
3. Can Hotmail or Gmail read your emails and/or turn them over to police without your permission?
4. Are all your messages sent through Hotmail or Gmail encrypted over your network?

CHAPTER 9: TRACING & INFORMATION GATHERING

To physically enter the United States you need a passport. However, you can enter it electronically without a passport of any kind. You can be the nastiest criminal mastermind in the world and enter the United States electronically without any questions asked. In some ways the cyber world is like the Old West. People can easily move between countries without documentation. Enforcement of existing electronic laws is scarce. In order to hold people accountable for their actions done over computer networks we need to know who they are and where they live.

Tracing tools may be some of the more useful tools you will learn about in this book. You will be able to actually determine the physical location of a person, a company, an internet site, etc. Sometimes users see a Web address (URL) like www.cnn.com and they have no idea where it's physically located. Just because the Web address sounds like an English word does not mean the Web site is physically hosted within the United States The Web site may be located in a country with completely different laws governing electronic communications (or worse… no laws at all). It can be valuable to know the actual physical location of an online company or hacker.

Email is also fairly anonymous to the uninformed computer user. They just don't know how email really works. IT security professionals are getting more and more requests to track down the source of an email. Typically the person got flamed, conned out of money, keeps getting spammed, or wants to verify the sender's identity. Anonymity does have its place in society. However, email is increasingly being used for deleterious purposes.

In general, getting information about the actual source of data is becoming much easier. Sites are tying data sources together and triangulating data to yield previously confidential information. This may be good or bad. Either way, it's accelerating at an increasing rate. Let's look at a few examples.

TRACE ROUTE TO SOURCE

Let's look at a hypothetical example using the author's alma mater (Florida State University). Suppose you are hard at work and all of a sudden your intrusion detection system (IDS) goes off. It turns out that someone from the IP address **128.186.6.14** just scanned your machine to see if you had port 25 open. You have no idea who it is or where they're located. You may also be unsure what service runs over port 25. (This didn't really happen; it's just an example.)

There is a great online trace route tool that maps the physical location of every computer between you and the IP address you enter. YouGetSignal.com® has several useful tools that are worth looking at. Having them online is also nice because the tools are not operating system dependent. You just need to make sure your Internet connection doesn't go down. Let's trace an IP address.

1. Go to the tracing tool hosted by You Get Signal at http://www.yougetsignal.com/tools/visual-tracert/.
2. Enter 128.186.6.14 in the Remote Address text box.
3. Click Host Trace (from yougetsignal.com to your target). (See Figure 9-1.)
4. Take a screenshot.
5. Click Proxy Trace (from you to yougetsignal.com to your target). (See Figure 9-2.)

6. Take a screenshot.

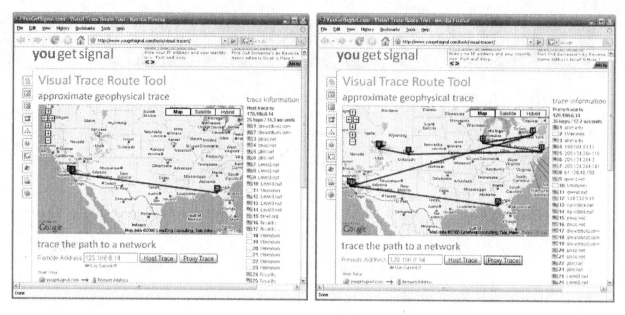

Figure 9-1: Tracing a route.   Figure 9-2: Tracing a route with a proxy.

Not only did you learn the actual physical location of the remote computer (Florida State University in Tallahassee, FL) but you can also see that information doesn't always take a straight line between hosts. The information between these two computers took what appears to be a wildly inefficient path from the University of Utah to Florida State University. This was likely the "best" path for the information to take depending on the metric used.

Information traveling through the Internet moves quickly and passes through many different computers. Trace route programs are also useful in diagnosing network problems (i.e., determining slow points in a network). It is worth the time and effort to become well acquainted with a trace route program. Network administrators use them every day.

THOUGHT QUESTIONS

1. Could any person along the route look at my information? How?
2. How could you keep someone from looking at your information as it is passed along the Internet?
3. Who owns the routers that forward your information?
4. How does the program map the IP addresses of the routers to their physical location?

TRACE A PHONE SOURCE

When students first see that it's possible to trace a phone number they are pleasantly surprised. It's highly likely that you have seen a number show up on your phone that you didn't know. This project will show you how to look up the number and see who is calling you before you answer the call. You don't have to blindly answer the phone and be forced to talk to someone. You can also get their general location mapped!

Some people find phones to be a nuisance. Once someone knows you are "good at computers" you'll likely be dogged by tech support calls from your intellectually lazy "friends" for the rest of your life. In general, it is a good idea not to answer a call unless you know who is calling. It's also smart to change your phone number every couple of years. Let's go through a simple example that will really help you screen your calls and give you some more free time.

1. Go to the tracing tool hosted by www.YouGetSignal.com at http://www.yougetsignal.com/tools/phone-location/.
2. Enter your home phone number in the Phone Number text box. (I entered my office phone number as an example.)
3. Click Locate. (See Figure 9-3.)
4. Take a screenshot.
5. Change area code to another random three-digit number and see where it takes you. (I did 507.)
6. Click Locate. (See Figure 9-4.)
7. Take a screenshot.
8. Go to the tracing tool hosted by www.WhitePages.com® at http://www.whitepages.com/.
9. Click on People Search.
10. Enter your first name, last name, city, and state. (I did Randy Boyle, Ogden, UT.)
11. Click Find. (See Figure 9-5.)
12. Take a screenshot.

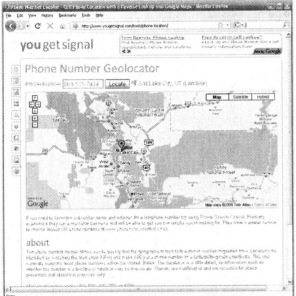

Figure 9-3: Locating the source of a phone number.

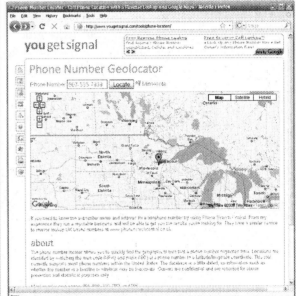

Figure 9-4: Locating a random phone number.

13. Go to the search tool hosted by PrivateEye.com at http://www.privateeye.com/.
14. Enter your first name, last name, city, and state.
15. Click Continue.
16. Take a screenshot.

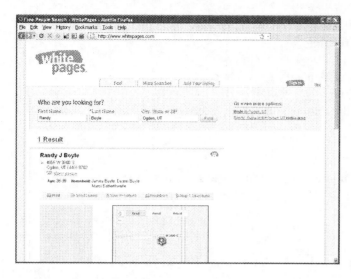

Figure 9-5: Locating a person.

Not only did you find out who called but you also know where they live and who their relatives are. There are many other tools that are used to collect information but we will stop here. If we showed you all the tools used to gather information, and the implications of that information, it might surprise you. Most hackers/crackers spend quite a bit of time and energy just gathering information as a first step. It's easy and no one notices.

The integration of these information sources is disconcerting from a security point of view. For example, Web site A may be restricted by law from giving out a certain piece of information. However, Web site B can take the information from Web sites A, C, and D to triangulate, calculate, or estimate the prohibited information. Laws governing information use are still in the dark ages.

You need to take steps to protect yourself until all the old technologically illiterate politicians are replaced by more tech savvy individuals. If the example of information triangulation didn't make sense you may have to re-read it or wait for the advanced edition of this book to see a real-world example.

The following are some useful guidelines to help you keep your privacy:

✓ Don't give personal information to anyone unless you absolutely have to.

✓ Learn the phrase "**I don't give that information out**" and repeat it every time you are asked for your phone number, SSN, zip code, address, etc.

✓ If you ever consider giving out your Social Security Number put a metal bucket on your head and continually hit it with wooden spoon until you realize it's a really bad idea.

THOUGHT QUESTIONS

1. Why doesn't your cell phone have an application just like this?
2. Can someone fake their phone number to make it appear that it is coming from a different number?
3. Who controls the exchange of information between different private companies?
4. How could you get your information taken out of other companies' directories? (Do you own your information?)

WHOIS LOOKUP TO SOURCE NETWORK

Oftentimes an IP Address will show up in an IDS or honeypot log and you don't know exactly which individual caused the log entry. The reason you can't see a specific person associated with the log entry is because currently we don't have a lookup service to resolve an IP address into a specific person's name (though it's possible that there will be one in the future).

IP addresses can be "loaned" out to several individuals throughout the day. We really need to know who had which IP address at a given time. Without cooperation from the network administrator we can't tell who was using the computer at the time of the log entry. However, we can tell who the network administrator is (the person in charge of managing that range of IP addresses), and get a copy of his/her contact information.

Hackers do questionable things to IT security professionals' computers all the time. In general, you can email the network administrators about the incidents but you will typically get an automated response in return. Once in a while you will get an actual email from the administrator in charge of a particular address range. If you get a log entry for a network outside the United States you'll likely be wasting your time trying to contact the network administrator about it. They'll probably get a good laugh out of your email.

Once in a while you will get an IDS log entry, email the network admin, and get a thank you email back. It turns out that the network administrator didn't even know that a certain machine had been "lost" (i.e., hacked). They walk down, shut it off, and send you an email thanking you for bringing it to their attention. However, this turns out to be the exception, not the rule. Let's see how to find out who is in charge of an IP address range.

1. Go to the WHOIS Lookup Tool hosted by You Get Signal® at http://www.yougetsignal.com/tools/whois-lookup/.
2. Enter your IP address in the Remote Address text box.
3. Click Check. (See Figure 9-6.)
4. Take a screenshot.
5. Enter this IP address (155.97.243.201).
6. Click Check.
7. Take a screenshot.

Figure 9-6: Looking up an IP address.

Now you have the contact information for the network administrator for the University of Utah. If you get an IP address in the 155.97.X.X range that tries to break into your machine you can email the administrator. Just don't email them too often. If they keep getting flooded with emails, they will implement an automated response system.

This is another good project that reiterates the need to be cautious when using IT security software. Your actions may alarm your administrator and cause him/her to take legal action against you. Your network administrator will likely know which computer has a specific IP address at any given time. Your network administrator knows who you are and has your home address.

THOUGHT QUESTIONS

1. If we can trace the IP addresses of people trying to break into our computers, why is it so hard to catch hackers?
2. Can someone fake an IP address?
3. Who decides ownership over a given IP address range?
4. What can you do if the hacker is coming from outside the United States?

LOCATE AN IP ADDRESS SOURCE

One of the most common tasks that IT security professionals perform on a daily basis is to track down an external IP address. IDS and honeypot logs are slowly being filled with IP addresses of individuals doing things they shouldn't be doing. A good tool that can trace their physical location is necessary. If they are outside the United States, there is little you can do. However, if they are from the network of a competing company or from an internal network you do have some recourse. It's fun to see where these people are coming from.

Most IT security professionals have seen log entries from almost every single country in the world. (If you get one from Antarctica, you should feel extremely lucky.) You will also see log entries from all major U.S. universities and a surprising number of local/state governments. It's understandable that students are bored and/or curious, but the number of local and state government log entries is surprising. You will load your own honeypot in the next section and you'll be able to start recognizing possible scans/attacks. Let's do a couple of examples.

1. Go to the IP address lookup tool hosted by WhatIsMyIpAddress® at http://whatismyipaddress.com/.
2. Enter your IP address in the Remote Address text box.
3. Click Check. (See Figure 9-7.)
4. Take a screenshot.
5. Enter the IP address (155.97.243.201).
6. Click Check.
7. Take a screenshot.
8. Change the first octet (155) to a random number less than 255 and see where the network is located. (In this example we used 140 and got London.) (See Figure 9-8.)
9. Take a screenshot.

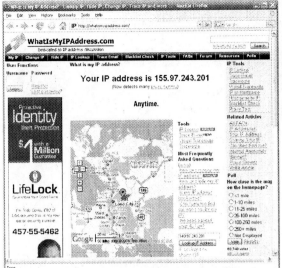

Figure 9-7: Finding your location based on IP address.

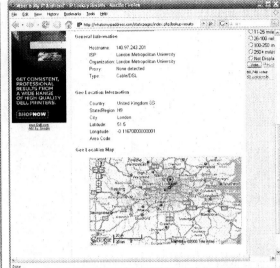

Figure 9-8: Locating the source of an IP address.

THOUGHT QUESTIONS

1. What is a proxy server and can it really hide my identity?
2. How does a proxy server work?
3. Can someone (company, law enforcement, government) track everything that is sent to/from my computer?
4. Do I have to have an IP address to send/receive information?

LOCATE AN EMAIL SOURCE

Occasionally IT security professionals will have an individual come to them and ask if it is possible to trace an email back to its source. It's hard not to laugh. Almost 99% of the time they have gotten a nasty email from someone that was unhappy with them and they want to find out who it was. Whether or not they deserved it is another story. There are other reasons for wanting to track down the source of an email but this is a fairly common occurrence.

It's surprisingly easy to get most of the information. Let's look at an example that uses the email's header to trace it back to the source. The header, which is typically hidden, contains all the routing information for that specific email. Finding the header information will be the hardest part. Most people are unaware that emails even have header information. Below is a really good tool by www.ip-adress.com®. There are other Web sites that have similar tools. We've tried to use a variety of Web sites in this book to encourage readers to explore the Web for other valuable tools.

1. Open Outlook. (Hotmail and Gmail also have header information.)
2. Open any email message (preferably from someone that lives in another state/country). (See Figure 9-9.)
3. Click on Message Options.

Note: If you're using the MS ribbon feature you need to click on the little arrow next to the word Options. Yes, this is confusing. Before Office 2007 it was much easier to view an email header. If you are using another email program you may have to look around for some option that allows you to view the email header. Most online email accounts like Hotmail and Gmail have this option too.

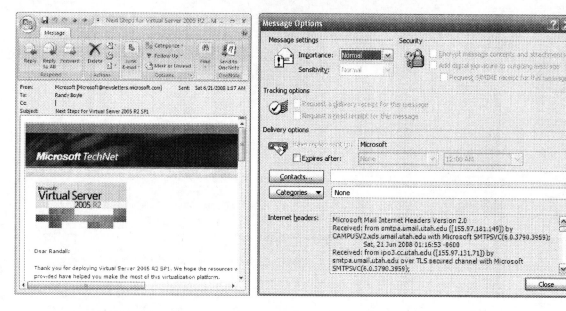

Figure 9-9: Email to trace.

Figure 9-10: Header from an email.

4. Select ALL of the header information in the bottom text box (Ctrl-A). (See Figure 9-10.)
5. Copy all the information you just selected (Ctrl-C).
6. Go to the Email Trace tool hosted by IP-Address.com at http://www.ip-adress.com/trace_email/.
7. Paste all the information you just copied from Outlook into the text box at the bottom of the page. (See Figure 9-11.)
8. Take a screenshot.
9. Click Trace Email Sender. (See Figure 9-12.)
10. Take a screenshot.

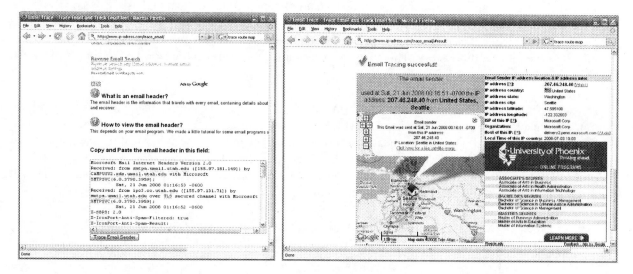

Figure 9-11: Copy and paste the email header.

Figure 9-12: Finding the source location of an email.

As you can see the email I received from Microsoft originated from Seattle. They were also kind enough to give me the IP address of the computer that sent the email. Although I still don't know the actual name of the person that sent the email, I do have their IP address. Knowing a person's IP address can be better than knowing their name. As you've seen from prior examples once you have one piece of information you can gather any additional information quickly.

The moral of this story is simple. Don't send "flaming" emails. Most people don't really have a strong grasp of the IP addressing system, how routers work, how mail servers work, or how email works. These are unknowns that can get you into trouble. Nowadays almost all electronic messages are copied, logged, and tracked.

There are many information gathering tools that could be demonstrated but as this book takes an introductory approach to information security it is best to stop here. It might shock you to learn the types and quantities of information available on the Internet.

THOUGHT QUESTIONS

1. Do all emails have headers?
2. Why do emails have headers?
3. How does the email trace program convert the header information to a physical address?
4. Can you modify and/or fake header information?

SAM SPADE

Sam Spade® is an easy-to-use tool that has been around for a fairly long time (since 1997). It incorporates several of the tools you just used into a single program that can be run from your local machine. It also has some additional functionality that is worth exploring. The benefit of a locally installed application like Sam Spade is that you don't have to worry about the remote Web site being down and the tools being unavailable. Let's click some buttons and look at the functionality built into Sam Spade.

1. Download Sam Spade from http://www.softpedia.com/get/Network-Tools/Network-Tools-Suites/Sam-Spade.shtml.
2. Click Download.
3. Click on Softpedia Mirror.
4. Click Save File.
5. Select the C:\security folder.
6. If the installation program doesn't automatically start, browse to C:\security.
7. Double-click the spade114.exe program to install Sam Spade.
8. Click Run, Next, Next, Next, Install.
9. Click "Yes" to update HTML help.
10. Click OK, Finish.
11. Click Start, All Programs, Blightly Design, Sam Spade 1.14.
12. Enter your IP address in the text box in the upper left-hand corner.
13. Press enter (or the purple arrow next to the text box). (See Figure 9-13.)
14. Take a screenshot.
15. Enter www.google.com into the text box in place of your IP address.
16. Click the Ping, DNS, Whois, and IP Block buttons on the left-hand side of the screen. (See Figure 9-14.)
17. Take a screenshot.
18. Click Trace. (See Figure 9-15.)
19. Take a screenshot.

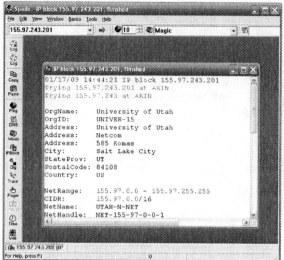

Figure 9-13: Sam Spade reverse lookup.

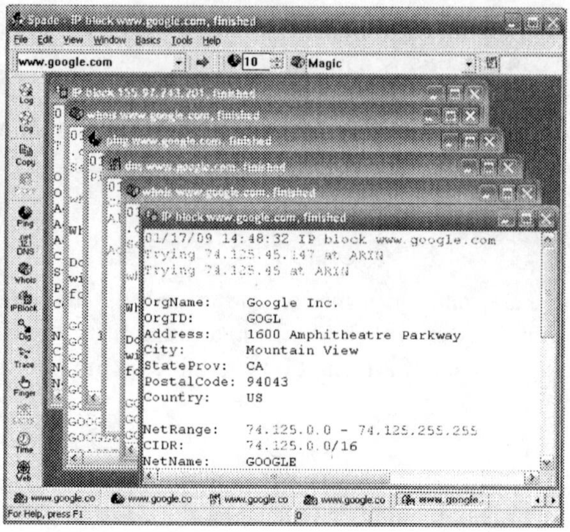

Figure 9-14: Sam Spade utilities.

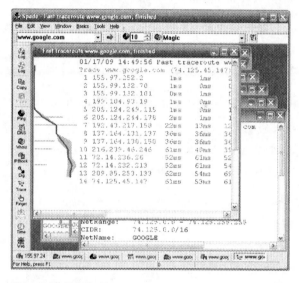

Figure 9-15: Sam Spade trace route.

Sam Spade has several other useful built-in tools. Feel free to test all of Sam Spade's functionality. For a tool that has been around for over a decade, Sam Spade is still quite useful for getting information about a specific URL or IP address.

THOUGHT QUESTIONS

1. What does the Whois tool do?
2. What does the Crawl Web site command do?
3. What legitimate uses would a network administrator have for the tools in Sam Spade?
4. How could a hacker use the information provided by Sam Spade for illegal purposes?

CHAPTER 10: HONEYPOTS AND INTRUSION DETECTION SYSTEMS

Honeypots are fun because they can attract hackers and log/record what they do to your computer without putting it at additional risk. For example, a hacker would like to break into a computer with a Web server running because it might serve as a potential launching platform for a future denial-of-service attack. A hacker might also want to store stolen software, host a phishing scheme, deface the Web site, steal valuable information, etc. A hacker will look for a computer with port 80 open because Web servers use that port to serve Web pages.

A honeypot will trick outsiders by making it look like port 80 is open on your computer. In reality you won't be running a real Web server. It will be the equivalent of painting a door on a brick wall. A better way to think of honeypots is to remember back to the old Roadrunner cartoons. The Roadrunner would paint a picture of a tunnel on a rock wall and the Coyote would run right into it. The same basic principle applies here. It appears that you have a Web server running but you really just painted a door on a brick wall.

Hackers waste a lot of time and clock cycles on honeypots. Honeypots are helpful in determining the real threat level for a given network, computer, and IP address range. It can give upper management an idea about the appropriate level of funding needed for IT security.

Intrusion detection systems (IDS) are notoriously difficult to setup, configure, and maintain. They watch computers (and the network) to see what is happening. They are difficult to run because of the sheer number of programs/processes, protocols, ports, logs, attack signatures, etc. There are a lot of different balls to keep bouncing to keep things running properly. IT security professionals must have a strong background in networking, databases, and programming just to understand the basics of what is going on inside an IDS. If you find someone that can run an IDS properly, it would be wise to pay them well and hold on to them.

Let's look at a couple examples of a honeypot and an IDS. You'll find that IT security professionals have little regard for people who try to break into other people's computer systems. Hackers create headaches, problems, and make administrators look bad. Curiosity and testing one's skills is perfectly acceptable. But individuals should explore and test their own systems, not poke around someone else's critical infrastructure.

HONEYBOT

HoneyBOT® is a simple tool for beginning IT security people to use. Since this might be the first time you have seen a honeypot, it's good to start out with a honeypot that is easy to use. Honeypots can give you a good idea of how many people are probing your machine for weaknesses. Without a honeypot you may not be able to tell if anyone is scanning your machine. It turns out that there is an active community of hackers interested in gaining access to a variety of computers.

Once the honeypot (or IDS) records the IP address of the remote machine that scanned your computer you can use the previously mentioned tracing tools to see who they are. If you run a honeypot long enough, you will likely see scanning attempts from several continents, all of the countries in Europe and Asia, all 50 states, and every university in the United States. Let's look at a simple example of how HoneyBOT works. We will use both a port scanner (SuperScan) and a vulnerability scanner (Nessus) and look at the results from HoneyBOT.

1. Download HoneyBOT from http://www.atomicsoftwaresolutions.com/download.php.
2. Click Download.
3. Click Save.
4. Select the C:\security folder.
5. Browse to C:\security.
6. Double-Click HoneyBOT_013.exe.(The version number may be different.)
7. Click Run, Next, I accept, Next, Next, Next.
8. Check Create desktop icon.
9. Click Next, Install, Finish.

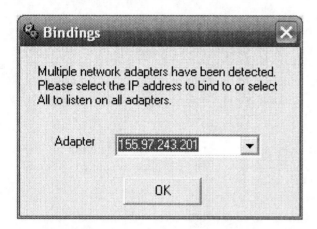

Figure 10-1: Designating an IP address.

10. Press the Start button or click File, Start.
11. HoneyBOT may ask you to select an adapter if you have multiple NICs in your computer; select your current IP address. (See Figure 10-1.)
12. Click OK.
13. Take a screenshot showing the total number of sockets loaded in the bottom status bar. (See Figures 10-2 and 10-3.)

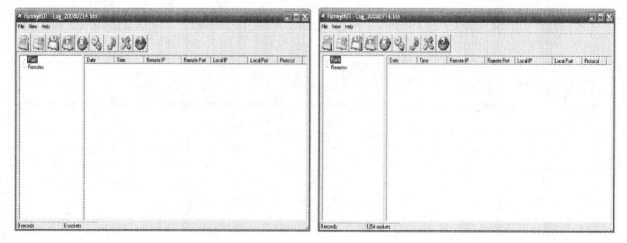

Figure 10-2: No sockets selected.   Figure 10-3: Multiple sockets selected.

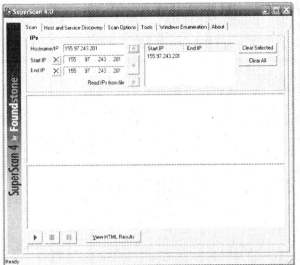

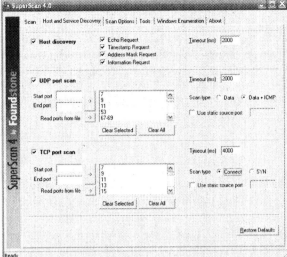

Figure 10-4: Port scanner to test HoneyBOT.

Figure 10-5: Selecting host and service discovery options.

14. Open up SuperScan4 (used in a prior example) by double clicking the SuperScan icon on your desktop.
15. Enter your IP address in the Hostname/IP address box. (Use the IPConfig command at the DOS prompt or go to http://whatismyipaddress.com/.)
16. If you can't figure out your IP address, enter: 127.0.0.1. (This is the default home address for every computer, and I've used it in the examples to ensure that it works for those people that can't determine their IP address.)
17. Press the -> arrow next to the Hostname/IP address box to move the IP address into the adjacent box. (This tells SuperScan that you want to use this IP address.) (See Figure 10-4.)
18. Click on the Host and Service Discovery tab.
19. Select Time Stamp Request, Address Mask Request, Information Request, the radio button Data+ICMP, and radio button Connect. (See Figure 10-5.)
20. Return to the Scan tab and click the Play button at the bottom of the screen.
21. If you see a Windows XP firewall message, click Unblock.
22. Take a screenshot of the SuperScan window after the scan completes. (See Figure 10-6.)

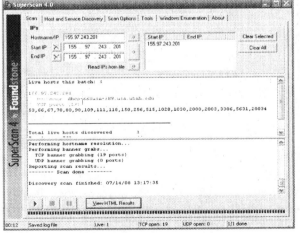

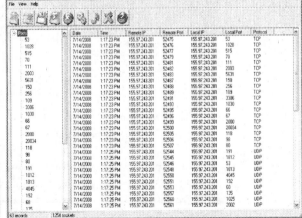

Figure 10-6: Results from port scan with HoneyBOT active.

Figure 10-7: HoneyBOT logs from port scan.

23. Take a screenshot of the HoneyBOT window with the new log entries you just created. (See Figure 10-7.)
24. Click on port 21 in the left-hand pane to show just the scans on port 21. (See Figure 10-8.)
25. Double-click the last entry in the list.
26. Take a screenshot of the scan details. (See Figure 10-9.)

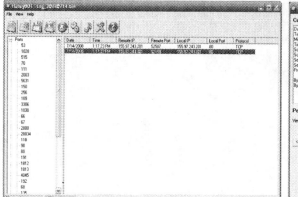

Figure 10-8: Results for a specific port.

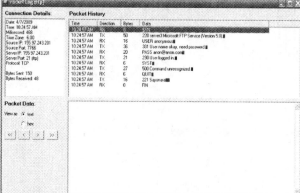

Figure 10-9: Details from an entry.

27. Click on Remotes in the left-hand pane to see which remote hosts scanned you.
28. Take a screenshot.

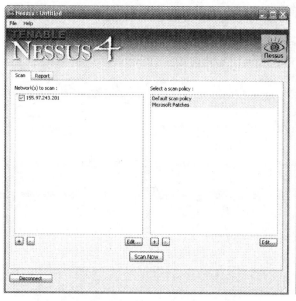

Figure 10-10: Nessus scan for target computer with HoneyBOT.

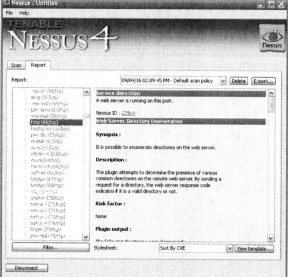

Figure 10-11: Results from Nessus scan.

29. Open Nessus 4.
30. Click the "+" button in the bottom of your screen.
31. In the Host Name box enter your IP address. (Enter 127.0.0.1 if you don't know your IP address.) (See Figure 10-10.)
32. Click Save.
33. Click Connect, Connect.
34. Select Default Scan Policy in the right-hand pane.
35. Click Scan Now. (This scan will log about 700+ entries in HoneyBOT.)

36. Take a screenshot as the scan is running. (The whole scan takes about 2 minutes.) (See Figure 10-11.)
37. Take a screenshot of the HoneyBOT results from the Nessus scan. (See Figure 10-12.)

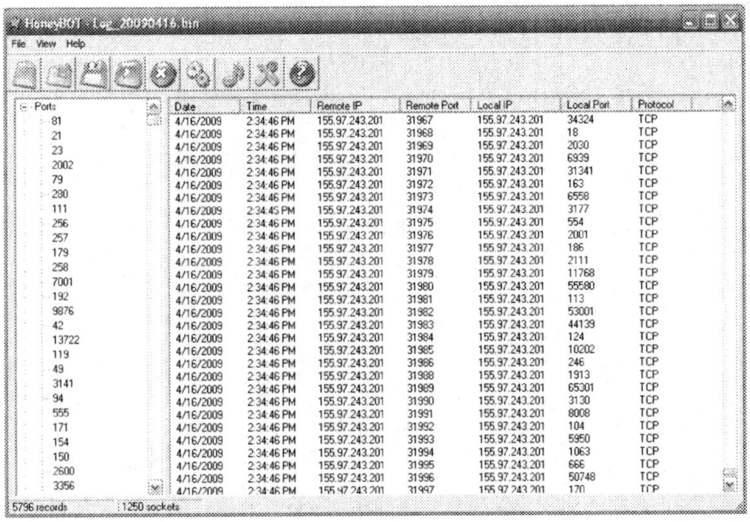

Figure 10-12: HoneyBot log from a Nessus scan.

As you can see HoneyBOT is able to "fake" a lot of ports and applications. It is also able to provide detailed logging features. HoneyBOT is simple to use and gives users an idea of the extent to which external hackers/bots are scanning their machines. They also allow non-technical users to estimate the probability of any given attack. This is a great way to show non-technical people (such as a business manager) how honeypots really work. They are usually amazed at the results.

The log entry for the scan (recorded on July 11, 2008) is shown on pages 91 and 92. (See Figure 10-13.) The log is copied using font size 6 to fit it on two pages. This partial log entry is shown to give you an idea of how thorough some of these automated scans are.

This individual tried quite a few default usernames and passwords in an attempt to gain access to this fake Web server. It's likely that he has tried to access other Web servers on other networks. This log also gives you an idea of why IT security professionals really dislike hackers. They cause a lot of additional work and trouble. How would you feel if someone stood in front of your house and kept shaking the door knob to see if the door was open?

THOUGHT QUESTIONS

1. What impact would more open ports have on the ability of your honeypot to attract hackers?
2. Can hackers tell that you have a honeypot running?
3. Do they have honeypots for spammers to keep them from harvesting emails from your Web pages?
4. Do you think law enforcement agencies (e.g., CIA, FBI, NSA, etc.) in the United States run honeypots to track criminal behavior?

Fri Jul 11 12:43:08   HTTP empty request from 221.8.61.69
Fri Jul 11 13:03:31   HTTP request from 221.8.61.69: GET /manager/html
Fri Jul 11 13:03:31   HTTP authorization attempt from 221.8.61.69: user: , password:
Fri Jul 11 13:03:32   HTTP request from 221.8.61.69: GET /manager/html

Fri Jul 11 13:03:32   HTTP authorization attempt from 221.8.61.69: user: admin, password: admin

Fri Jul 11 13:03:32   HTTP request from 221.8.61.69: GET /manager/html
Fri Jul 11 13:03:32   HTTP authorization attempt from 221.8.61.69: user: admin, password: 147258369
Fri Jul 11 13:03:32   HTTP request from 221.8.61.69: GET /manager/html
Fri Jul 11 13:03:32   HTTP authorization attempt from 221.8.61.69: user: admin, password: 369258147
Fri Jul 11 13:03:32   HTTP request from 221.8.61.69: GET /manager/html
Fri Jul 11 13:03:32   HTTP authorization attempt from 221.8.61.69: user: admin, password: 258147
Fri Jul 11 13:03:32   HTTP request from 221.8.61.69: GET /manager/html
Fri Jul 11 13:03:32   HTTP authorization attempt from 221.8.61.69: user: admin, password: 147258
Fri Jul 11 13:03:32   HTTP request from 221.8.61.69: GET /manager/html
Fri Jul 11 13:03:32   HTTP authorization attempt from 221.8.61.69: user: admin, password: 258369
Fri Jul 11 13:03:32   HTTP request from 221.8.61.69: GET /manager/html
Fri Jul 11 13:03:32   HTTP authorization attempt from 221.8.61.69: user: admin, password: 369258
Fri Jul 11 13:03:32   HTTP request from 221.8.61.69: GET /manager/html
Fri Jul 11 13:03:32   HTTP authorization attempt from 221.8.61.69: user: admin, password: 159357
Fri Jul 11 13:03:32   HTTP request from 221.8.61.69: GET /manager/html
Fri Jul 11 13:03:32   HTTP authorization attempt from 221.8.61.69: user: admin, password: 12
Fri Jul 11 13:03:32   HTTP request from 221.8.61.69: GET /manager/html
Fri Jul 11 13:03:33   HTTP authorization attempt from 221.8.61.69: user: admin, password: 123
Fri Jul 11 13:03:33   HTTP request from 221.8.61.69: GET /manager/html
Fri Jul 11 13:03:33   HTTP authorization attempt from 221.8.61.69: user: admin, password: 1234
Fri Jul 11 13:03:33   HTTP request from 221.8.61.69: GET /manager/html
Fri Jul 11 13:03:33   HTTP authorization attempt from 221.8.61.69: user: admin, password: 12345
Fri Jul 11 13:03:33   HTTP request from 221.8.61.69: GET /manager/html
Fri Jul 11 13:03:33   HTTP authorization attempt from 221.8.61.69: user: admin, password: 123456
Fri Jul 11 13:03:33   HTTP request from 221.8.61.69: GET /manager/html
Fri Jul 11 13:03:33   HTTP authorization attempt from 221.8.61.69: user: admin, password: 1234567
Fri Jul 11 13:03:33   HTTP request from 221.8.61.69: GET /manager/html
Fri Jul 11 13:03:33   HTTP authorization attempt from 221.8.61.69: user: admin, password: 12345678
Fri Jul 11 13:03:33   HTTP request from 221.8.61.69: GET /manager/html
Fri Jul 11 13:03:33   HTTP authorization attempt from 221.8.61.69: user: admin, password: 123456789
Fri Jul 11 13:03:33   HTTP request from 221.8.61.69: GET /manager/html
Fri Jul 11 13:03:33   HTTP authorization attempt from 221.8.61.69: user: admin, password: 1234567890
Fri Jul 11 13:03:33   HTTP request from 221.8.61.69: GET /manager/html
Fri Jul 11 13:03:33   HTTP authorization attempt from 221.8.61.69: user: admin, password: 9876543210
Fri Jul 11 13:03:33   HTTP request from 221.8.61.69: GET /manager/html
Fri Jul 11 13:03:33   HTTP authorization attempt from 221.8.61.69: user: admin, password: 987654321
Fri Jul 11 13:03:33   HTTP request from 221.8.61.69: GET /manager/html
Fri Jul 11 13:03:33   HTTP authorization attempt from 221.8.61.69: user: admin, password: 98765432
Fri Jul 11 13:03:33   HTTP request from 221.8.61.69: GET /manager/html
Fri Jul 11 13:03:33   HTTP authorization attempt from 221.8.61.69: user: admin, password: 9876543
Fri Jul 11 13:03:33   HTTP request from 221.8.61.69: GET /manager/html
Fri Jul 11 13:03:33   HTTP authorization attempt from 221.8.61.69: user: admin, password: 987654
Fri Jul 11 13:03:33   HTTP request from 221.8.61.69: GET /manager/html
Fri Jul 11 13:03:33   HTTP authorization attempt from 221.8.61.69: user: admin, password: 98765
Fri Jul 11 13:03:33   HTTP request from 221.8.61.69: GET /manager/html
Fri Jul 11 13:03:33   HTTP authorization attempt from 221.8.61.69: user: admin, password: 9876
Fri Jul 11 13:03:33   HTTP request from 221.8.61.69: GET /manager/html
Fri Jul 11 13:03:33   HTTP authorization attempt from 221.8.61.69: user: admin, password: 987
Fri Jul 11 13:03:33   HTTP request from 221.8.61.69: GET /manager/html
Fri Jul 11 13:03:33   HTTP authorization attempt from 221.8.61.69: user: admin, password: 0123
Fri Jul 11 13:03:33   HTTP request from 221.8.61.69: GET /manager/html
Fri Jul 11 13:03:33   HTTP authorization attempt from 221.8.61.69: user: admin, password: 01234
Fri Jul 11 13:03:33   HTTP request from 221.8.61.69: GET /manager/html
Fri Jul 11 13:03:33   HTTP authorization attempt from 221.8.61.69: user: admin, password: 012345
Fri Jul 11 13:03:33   HTTP request from 221.8.61.69: GET /manager/html
Fri Jul 11 13:03:33   HTTP authorization attempt from 221.8.61.69: user: admin, password: 0123456
Fri Jul 11 13:03:33   HTTP request from 221.8.61.69: GET /manager/html
Fri Jul 11 13:03:34   HTTP authorization attempt from 221.8.61.69: user: admin, password: 01234567
Fri Jul 11 13:03:34   HTTP request from 221.8.61.69: GET /manager/html

Fri Jul 11 13:03:35   HTTP request from 221.8.61.69: GET /manager/html
Fri Jul 11 13:03:35   HTTP authorization attempt from 221.8.61.69: user: admin, password: administrator
Fri Jul 11 13:03:35   HTTP request from 221.8.61.69: GET /manager/html

Fri Jul 11 13:03:35   HTTP authorization attempt from 221.8.61.69: user: admin, password: administrators

Fri Jul 11 13:03:35   HTTP request from 221.8.61.69: GET /manager/html
Fri Jul 11 13:03:35   HTTP authorization attempt from 221.8.61.69: user: admin, password:
Fri Jul 11 13:03:35   HTTP request from 221.8.61.69: GET /manager/html
Fri Jul 11 13:03:35   HTTP authorization attempt from 221.8.61.69: user: admin, password: tomcat
Fri Jul 11 13:03:35   HTTP request from 221.8.61.69: GET /manager/html
Fri Jul 11 13:03:35   HTTP authorization attempt from 221.8.61.69: user: admin, password: tomcatcat
Fri Jul 11 13:03:35   HTTP request from 221.8.61.69: GET /manager/html
Fri Jul 11 13:03:35   HTTP authorization attempt from 221.8.61.69: user: admin, password: tomcattomcat
Fri Jul 11 13:03:35   HTTP request from 221.8.61.69: GET /manager/html
Fri Jul 11 13:03:36   HTTP authorization attempt from 221.8.61.69: user: admin, password: manager
Fri Jul 11 13:03:36   HTTP request from 221.8.61.69: GET /manager/html
Fri Jul 11 13:03:36   HTTP authorization attempt from 221.8.61.69: user: admin, password: tomcatadmin
Fri Jul 11 13:03:36   HTTP request from 221.8.61.69: GET /manager/html
Fri Jul 11 13:03:36   HTTP authorization attempt from 221.8.61.69: user: admin, password: tomcatmanager
Fri Jul 11 13:03:36   HTTP request from 221.8.61.69: GET /manager/html
Fri Jul 11 13:03:36   HTTP authorization attempt from 221.8.61.69: user: admin, password: fackyou
Fri Jul 11 13:03:36   HTTP request from 221.8.61.69: GET /manager/html
Fri Jul 11 13:03:36   HTTP authorization attempt from 221.8.61.69: user: admin, password: fack
Fri Jul 11 13:03:36   HTTP request from 221.8.61.69: GET /manager/html
Fri Jul 11 13:03:36   HTTP authorization attempt from 221.8.61.69: user: admin, password: 1qaz
Fri Jul 11 13:03:36   HTTP request from 221.8.61.69: GET /manager/html
Fri Jul 11 13:03:36   HTTP authorization attempt from 221.8.61.69: user: admin, password: 1qaz2wsx
Fri Jul 11 13:03:36   HTTP request from 221.8.61.69: GET /manager/html
Fri Jul 11 13:03:36   HTTP authorization attempt from 221.8.61.69: user: admin, password: 1qaz2wsx3edc
Fri Jul 11 13:03:36   HTTP request from 221.8.61.69: GET /manager/html
Fri Jul 11 13:03:36   HTTP authorization attempt from 221.8.61.69: user: admin, password: 3edc4rfv
Fri Jul 11 13:03:36   HTTP request from 221.8.61.69: GET /manager/html
Fri Jul 11 13:03:36   HTTP authorization attempt from 221.8.61.69: user: admin, password: 5tgb6yhn
Fri Jul 11 13:03:36   HTTP request from 221.8.61.69: GET /manager/html
Fri Jul 11 13:03:36   HTTP authorization attempt from 221.8.61.69: user: admin, password: 7ujm8ik,
Fri Jul 11 13:03:36   HTTP request from 221.8.61.69: GET /manager/html
Fri Jul 11 13:03:36   HTTP authorization attempt from 221.8.61.69: user: admin, password: !@#!@#
Fri Jul 11 13:03:36   HTTP request from 221.8.61.69: GET /manager/html
Fri Jul 11 13:03:36   HTTP authorization attempt from 221.8.61.69: user: admin, password: !@#$%^&*()
Fri Jul 11 13:03:36   HTTP request from 221.8.61.69: GET /manager/html
Fri Jul 11 13:03:36   HTTP authorization attempt from 221.8.61.69: user: admin, password: !@#
Fri Jul 11 13:03:36   HTTP request from 221.8.61.69: GET /manager/html
Fri Jul 11 13:03:36   HTTP authorization attempt from 221.8.61.69: user: admin, password: !@#$
Fri Jul 11 13:03:36   HTTP request from 221.8.61.69: GET /manager/html
Fri Jul 11 13:03:36   HTTP authorization attempt from 221.8.61.69: user: admin, password: !@#$%^
Fri Jul 11 13:03:36   HTTP request from 221.8.61.69: GET /manager/html
Fri Jul 11 13:03:36   HTTP authorization attempt from 221.8.61.69: user: admin, password: !@#$%^&*
Fri Jul 11 13:03:36   HTTP request from 221.8.61.69: GET /manager/html
Fri Jul 11 13:03:36   HTTP authorization attempt from 221.8.61.69: user: admin, password: !@#$%^&*(
Fri Jul 11 13:03:36   HTTP request from 221.8.61.69: GET /manager/html
Fri Jul 11 13:03:36   HTTP authorization attempt from 221.8.61.69: user: admin, password: ~!@
Fri Jul 11 13:03:36   HTTP request from 221.8.61.69: GET /manager/html
Fri Jul 11 13:03:36   HTTP authorization attempt from 221.8.61.69: user: admin, password: ~!@#
Fri Jul 11 13:03:36   HTTP request from 221.8.61.69: GET /manager/html
Fri Jul 11 13:03:36   HTTP authorization attempt from 221.8.61.69: user: admin, password: ~!@#$
Fri Jul 11 13:03:36   HTTP request from 221.8.61.69: GET /manager/html
Fri Jul 11 13:03:36   HTTP authorization attempt from 221.8.61.69: user: admin, password: ~!@#$%
Fri Jul 11 13:03:36   HTTP request from 221.8.61.69: GET /manager/html
Fri Jul 11 13:03:36   HTTP authorization attempt from 221.8.61.69: user: admin, password: ~!@#$%^
Fri Jul 11 13:03:36   HTTP request from 221.8.61.69: GET /manager/html
Fri Jul 11 13:03:37   HTTP authorization attempt from 221.8.61.69: user: admin, password: ~!@#$%^&
Fri Jul 11 13:03:37   HTTP request from 221.8.61.69: GET /manager/html
Fri Jul 11 13:03:37   HTTP authorization attempt from 221.8.61.69: user: admin, password: ~!@#$%^&*

Fri Jul 11 13:03:34   HTTP authorization attempt from 221.8.61.69: user: admin, password: 012345678
Fri Jul 11 13:03:34   HTTP request from 221.8.61.69: GET /manager/html
Fri Jul 11 13:03:34   HTTP authorization attempt from 221.8.61.69: user: admin, password: 0123456789
Fri Jul 11 13:03:34   HTTP request from 221.8.61.69: GET /manager/html
Fri Jul 11 13:03:34   HTTP authorization attempt from 221.8.61.69: user: admin, password: 112233
Fri Jul 11 13:03:34   HTTP request from 221.8.61.69: GET /manager/html
Fri Jul 11 13:03:34   HTTP authorization attempt from 221.8.61.69: user: admin, password: 223344
Fri Jul 11 13:03:34   HTTP request from 221.8.61.69: GET /manager/html
Fri Jul 11 13:03:34   HTTP authorization attempt from 221.8.61.69: user: admin, password: 334455
Fri Jul 11 13:03:34   HTTP request from 221.8.61.69: GET /manager/html
Fri Jul 11 13:03:34   HTTP authorization attempt from 221.8.61.69: user: admin, password: 445566
Fri Jul 11 13:03:34   HTTP request from 221.8.61.69: GET /manager/html
Fri Jul 11 13:03:34   HTTP authorization attempt from 221.8.61.69: user: admin, password: 778899
Fri Jul 11 13:03:34   HTTP request from 221.8.61.69: GET /manager/html
Fri Jul 11 13:03:34   HTTP authorization attempt from 221.8.61.69: user: admin, password: 123123
Fri Jul 11 13:03:34   HTTP request from 221.8.61.69: GET /manager/html
Fri Jul 11 13:03:34   HTTP authorization attempt from 221.8.61.69: user: admin, password: 456456
Fri Jul 11 13:03:34   HTTP request from 221.8.61.69: GET /manager/html
Fri Jul 11 13:03:34   HTTP authorization attempt from 221.8.61.69: user: admin, password: 789789
Fri Jul 11 13:03:34   HTTP request from 221.8.61.69: GET /manager/html
Fri Jul 11 13:03:34   HTTP authorization attempt from 221.8.61.69: user: admin, password: 147123
Fri Jul 11 13:03:34   HTTP request from 221.8.61.69: GET /manager/html
Fri Jul 11 13:03:34   HTTP authorization attempt from 221.8.61.69: user: admin, password: 321321
Fri Jul 11 13:03:34   HTTP request from 221.8.61.69: GET /manager/html
Fri Jul 11 13:03:34   HTTP authorization attempt from 221.8.61.69: user: admin, password: 654654
Fri Jul 11 13:03:34   HTTP request from 221.8.61.69: GET /manager/html
Fri Jul 11 13:03:34   HTTP authorization attempt from 221.8.61.69: user: admin, password: 987987
Fri Jul 11 13:03:34   HTTP request from 221.8.61.69: GET /manager/html
Fri Jul 11 13:03:34   HTTP authorization attempt from 221.8.61.69: user: admin, password: 654654
Fri Jul 11 13:03:34   HTTP request from 221.8.61.69: GET /manager/html
Fri Jul 11 13:03:34   HTTP authorization attempt from 221.8.61.69: user: admin, password: 456456
Fri Jul 11 13:03:34   HTTP request from 221.8.61.69: GET /manager/html
Fri Jul 11 13:03:34   HTTP authorization attempt from 221.8.61.69: user: admin, password: 789789
Fri Jul 11 13:03:34   HTTP request from 221.8.61.69: GET /manager/html
Fri Jul 11 13:03:34   HTTP authorization attempt from 221.8.61.69: user: admin, password: 987987
Fri Jul 11 13:03:34   HTTP request from 221.8.61.69: GET /manager/html
Fri Jul 11 13:03:34   HTTP authorization attempt from 221.8.61.69: user: admin, password: 258369
Fri Jul 11 13:03:34   HTTP request from 221.8.61.69: GET /manager/html
Fri Jul 11 13:03:34   HTTP authorization attempt from 221.8.61.69: user: admin, password: 369147
Fri Jul 11 13:03:34   HTTP request from 221.8.61.69: GET /manager/html
Fri Jul 11 13:03:35   HTTP authorization attempt from 221.8.61.69: user: admin, password: 234567
Fri Jul 11 13:03:35   HTTP request from 221.8.61.69: GET /manager/html
Fri Jul 11 13:03:35   HTTP authorization attempt from 221.8.61.69: user: admin, password: 345678
Fri Jul 11 13:03:35   HTTP request from 221.8.61.69: GET /manager/html
Fri Jul 11 13:03:35   HTTP authorization attempt from 221.8.61.69: user: admin, password: 678910
Fri Jul 11 13:03:35   HTTP request from 221.8.61.69: GET /manager/html
Fri Jul 11 13:03:35   HTTP authorization attempt from 221.8.61.69: user: admin, password: 147369
Fri Jul 11 13:03:35   HTTP request from 221.8.61.69: GET /manager/html
Fri Jul 11 13:03:35   HTTP authorization attempt from 221.8.61.69: user: admin, password: 369369
Fri Jul 11 13:03:35   HTTP request from 221.8.61.69: GET /manager/html
Fri Jul 11 13:03:35   HTTP authorization attempt from 221.8.61.69: user: admin, password: 258258
Fri Jul 11 13:03:35   HTTP request from 221.8.61.69: GET /manager/html
Fri Jul 11 13:03:35   HTTP authorization attempt from 221.8.61.69: user: admin, password: 147147
Fri Jul 11 13:03:35   HTTP request from 221.8.61.69: GET /manager/html
Fri Jul 11 13:03:35   HTTP authorization attempt from 221.8.61.69: user: admin, password: admin3388
Fri Jul 11 13:03:35   HTTP request from 221.8.61.69: GET /manager/html
Fri Jul 11 13:03:35   HTTP authorization attempt from 221.8.61.69: user: admin, password: admin8888
Fri Jul 11 13:03:35   HTTP request from 221.8.61.69: GET /manager/html
Fri Jul 11 13:03:35   HTTP authorization attempt from 221.8.61.69: user: admin, password: admin3388

Fri Jul 11 13:03:37   HTTP request from 221.8.61.69: GET /manager/html
Fri Jul 11 13:03:37   HTTP authorization attempt from 221.8.61.69: user: admin, password: ~!@#$%^&*(
Fri Jul 11 13:03:37   HTTP request from 221.8.61.69: GET /manager/html
Fri Jul 11 13:03:37   HTTP authorization attempt from 221.8.61.69: user: admin, password: ~!@#$%^&*()
Fri Jul 11 13:03:37   HTTP request from 221.8.61.69: GET /manager/html
Fri Jul 11 13:03:37   HTTP authorization attempt from 221.8.61.69: user: admin, password: ^*$%^&#$%^@
Fri Jul 11 13:03:37   HTTP request from 221.8.61.69: GET /manager/html
Fri Jul 11 13:03:37   HTTP authorization attempt from 221.8.61.69: user: admin, password: asdfasdf
Fri Jul 11 13:03:37   HTTP request from 221.8.61.69: GET /manager/html
Fri Jul 11 13:03:37   HTTP authorization attempt from 221.8.61.69: user: admin, password: asdfg
Fri Jul 11 13:03:37   HTTP request from 221.8.61.69: GET /manager/html
Fri Jul 11 13:03:37   HTTP authorization attempt from 221.8.61.69: user: admin, password: qwer
Fri Jul 11 13:03:37   HTTP request from 221.8.61.69: GET /manager/html
Fri Jul 11 13:03:37   HTTP authorization attempt from 221.8.61.69: user: admin, password: qwertyuiop
Fri Jul 11 13:03:37   HTTP request from 221.8.61.69: GET /manager/html
Fri Jul 11 13:03:37   HTTP authorization attempt from 221.8.61.69: user: admin, password: asdfghjkl
Fri Jul 11 13:03:37   HTTP request from 221.8.61.69: GET /manager/html
Fri Jul 11 13:03:37   HTTP authorization attempt from 221.8.61.69: user: admin, password: zxcvbnm
Fri Jul 11 13:03:37   HTTP request from 221.8.61.69: GET /manager/html
Fri Jul 11 13:03:37   HTTP authorization attempt from 221.8.61.69: user: admin, password: 123qweasdzxc
Fri Jul 11 13:03:37   HTTP request from 221.8.61.69: GET /manager/html
Fri Jul 11 13:03:37   HTTP authorization attempt from 221.8.61.69: user: admin, password: 123qweasd
Fri Jul 11 13:03:37   HTTP request from 221.8.61.69: GET /manager/html
Fri Jul 11 13:03:37   HTTP authorization attempt from 221.8.61.69: user: admin, password: 123qwe
Fri Jul 11 13:03:37   HTTP request from 221.8.61.69: GET /manager/html
Fri Jul 11 13:03:37   HTTP authorization attempt from 221.8.61.69: user: admin, password: 1234qwer
Fri Jul 11 13:03:37   HTTP request from 221.8.61.69: GET /manager/html
Fri Jul 11 13:03:37   HTTP authorization attempt from 221.8.61.69: user: admin, password: 1234qwerasdf
Fri Jul 11 13:03:37   HTTP request from 221.8.61.69: GET /manager/html
Fri Jul 11 13:03:37   HTTP authorization attempt from 221.8.61.69: user: admin, password: 1234qwerasdfzxcv
Fri Jul 11 13:03:37   HTTP request from 221.8.61.69: GET /manager/html
Fri Jul 11 13:03:37   HTTP authorization attempt from 221.8.61.69: user: admin, password: 159753
Fri Jul 11 13:03:37   HTTP request from 221.8.61.69: GET /manager/html
Fri Jul 11 13:03:37   HTTP authorization attempt from 221.8.61.69: user: admin, password: microsoft
Fri Jul 11 13:03:37   HTTP request from 221.8.61.69: GET /manager/html
Fri Jul 11 13:03:37   HTTP authorization attempt from 221.8.61.69: user: admin, password: Microsoft
Fri Jul 11 13:03:37   HTTP request from 221.8.61.69: GET /manager/html
Fri Jul 11 13:03:37   HTTP authorization attempt from 221.8.61.69: user: admin, password: Server
Fri Jul 11 13:03:37   HTTP request from 221.8.61.69: GET /manager/html
Fri Jul 11 13:03:37   HTTP authorization attempt from 221.8.61.69: user: admin, password: server
Fri Jul 11 13:03:37   HTTP request from 221.8.61.69: GET /manager/html
Fri Jul 11 13:03:37   HTTP authorization attempt from 221.8.61.69: user: admin, password: Service
Fri Jul 11 13:03:37   HTTP request from 221.8.61.69: GET /manager/html
Fri Jul 11 13:03:37   HTTP authorization attempt from 221.8.61.69: user: admin, password: service
Fri Jul 11 13:03:37   HTTP request from 221.8.61.69: GET /manager/html
Fri Jul 11 13:03:37   HTTP authorization attempt from 221.8.61.69: user: admin, password: 2008
Fri Jul 11 13:03:37   HTTP request from 221.8.61.69: GET /manager/html
Fri Jul 11 13:03:38   HTTP authorization attempt from 221.8.61.69: user: admin, password: 2003
Fri Jul 11 13:03:38   HTTP request from 221.8.61.69: GET /manager/html
Fri Jul 11 13:03:38   HTTP authorization attempt from 221.8.61.69: user: admin, password: webserver
Fri Jul 11 13:03:38   HTTP request from 221.8.61.69: GET /manager/html
Fri Jul 11 13:03:38   HTTP authorization attempt from 221.8.61.69: user: admin, password: sqlserver
Fri Jul 11 13:03:38   HTTP request from 221.8.61.69: GET /manager/html
Fri Jul 11 13:03:38   HTTP authorization attempt from 221.8.61.69: user: admin, password: adminserver
Fri Jul 11 13:03:38   HTTP request from 221.8.61.69: GET /manager/html
Fri Jul 11 13:03:38   HTTP authorization attempt from 221.8.61.69: user: admin, password: 5201314
Fri Jul 11 13:03:38   HTTP request from 221.8.61.69: GET /manager/html
Fri Jul 11 13:03:38   HTTP authorization attempt from 221.8.61.69: user: admin, password: 1314520
Fri Jul 11 13:03:38   HTTP request from 221.8.61.69: GET /manager/html
Fri Jul 11 13:03:38   HTTP authorization attempt from 221.8.61.69: user: admin, password: 7758520

Figure 10-13: Honeypot log excerpt.

NST, SNORT (IDS), & BASE

We mentioned at the start of this chapter that intrusion detection systems (IDS) can be difficult to install, configure, and maintain because they look at more than just changes in local files. Intrusion detection systems also look at network traffic and use complex rules that try to identify attacks/scans that may be occurring on your network. Configuring an IDS to catch ALL intruders based on specific attack signatures is extremely difficult. Many new types of threats appear each day.

We are going to look at an IDS called Snort® that uses a GUI front-end called BASE® to analyze the log entries. Both of these tools are part of a larger suite of tools named Network Security Toolkit® (NST). NST incorporates many of the tools we have already looked at including some advanced tools that we will not cover. It's worth the time to explore the NST image or download a bootable CD image from their Web site (http://networksecuritytoolkit.org/nst/index.html).

We will download a virtual image of the NST and run it inside VMPlayer®. We will do an example of how virtual machines work later, but essentially you will be running a computer (Linux®) within your existing computer (Windows). This might seem foreign at first but you will quickly see how easy virtual machines are to use.

Snort is one of the most well known free intrusion detection systems available. Most students are excited to learn Snort but quickly realize that it can be difficult to use if they are not familiar with Linux/Unix. Snort, like most security tools, was initially developed to run on Linux/Unix operating systems. There are many security tools available for Linux that cannot be run under Windows. Visit www.snort.org and take a look around. Let's do a quick example to get set up.

1. Download VMware Player from http://www.vmware.com/download/player/download.html.
2. Click Download for VMware Player for Windows.
3. Click Save.
4. Select the C:\security folder.
5. If the program doesn't automatically, open browse to C:\security.
6. Double-click the VMware-player-2.0.4-93057.exe program. (Some of the version numbers may change.)
7. Click Run, Run, Next, Next, Next, Install, Next, Finish.

Note: You have just installed VMPlayer. We will now download and start the virtual machine for NST.

8. Download the NST VM image from http://networksecuritytoolkit.org/nst/index.html.
9. Click Download Virtual Machine on the right-hand side.
10. Click Save.
11. Select the C:\security folder. (This may take a couple of minutes to download.)
12. Right-click nst-vm-1.8.1.zip.
13. Select Extract All, Next, Next, Finish.
14. Browse to C:\security\nst-vm-1.8.1\.
15. Double-click the VMware icon on your desktop.
16. Click the Open button. (See Figure 10-14.)

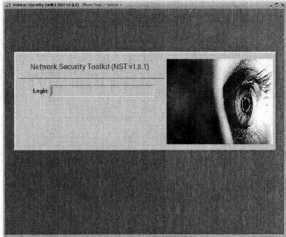

Figure 10-14: VMPlayer main menu.   Figure 10-15: NST login.

17. Navigate to the C:\security\nst-vm-1.8.1 folder where the VM image is located.
18. Select the file labeled nst-vm-windows-1.8.1.vmx.
19. Click Open and wait for the virtual machine to completely open. (You should see a login screen like the one above.) (See Figure 10-15.)
20. Enter "root" for the login and "nst2003" for the password.
21. Click OK. (You should see a screen like the one below after it has finished opening.)

Note: You won't see asterisks when you enter the password. This is normal and safer than the Windows convention of showing asterisks because someone standing behind you won't be able to tell the length of your password. Remember that the system you are going to use is Web-based. You will move forward and backward just like you do when you browse the Internet.

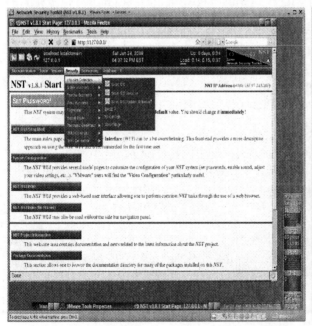

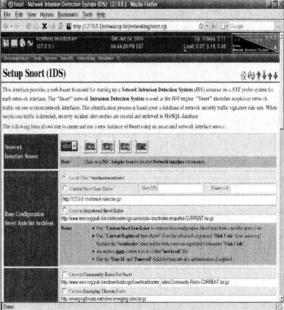

Figure 10-16: NST start page.   Figure 10-17: Snort setup page.

22. On the navigation bar click Security, Intrusion Detection, Snort IDS. (See Figure 10-16.)

23. Check the option labeled "Startup this instance of Snort immediately after setup." (See Figure 10-17.)
24. Scroll to the bottom of the page and click Setup/Start Snort.
25. Click the Check Status button.
26. Check to see that the mysqld and snortd services are running. (If not, press the corresponding "start" buttons.) (See Figure 10-18.)
27. Take a screenshot.

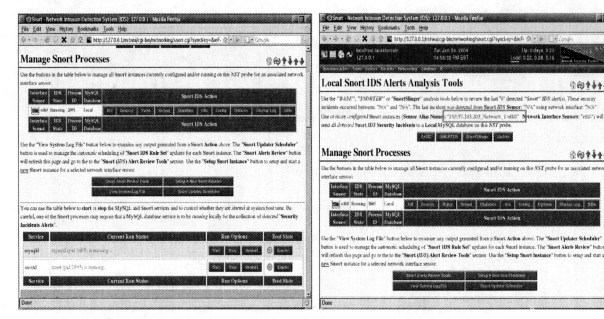

Figure 10-18: Snort management page.   Figure 10-19: Snort analysis tool.

28. Scroll up to see the IP address associated with the virtual network adapter (shown in green letters) set up by VMPlayer. (See Figure 10-19.)
29. Write down the virtual IP address you see because you'll need it later.

Note: In this example the IP address was 155.97.243.205. Your IP address will not be the same but may appear like 192.168.X.X (where the Xs' represent any number between 0 and 255). Make sure and write your IP address down.

30. Double-click the SuperScan 4.0 icon on your Windows Desktop.
31. Enter the IP address you just wrote down into the Hostname/IP text box.
32. Click the right-arrow button next to the Hostname/IP text box to move the IP address over.
33. Click the start scan button in the bottom left-hand corner of the window to start the scan. (If it doesn't recognize a "live" host, you have entered an incorrect IP address.)
34. Return to your NST virtual machine.
35. Click on the button labeled Base located just below the IP address you wrote down. (See Figure 10-20.)
36. Click on the link labeled "listing" under Today's Alerts. (See Figure 10-21.)
37. Take a screenshot.

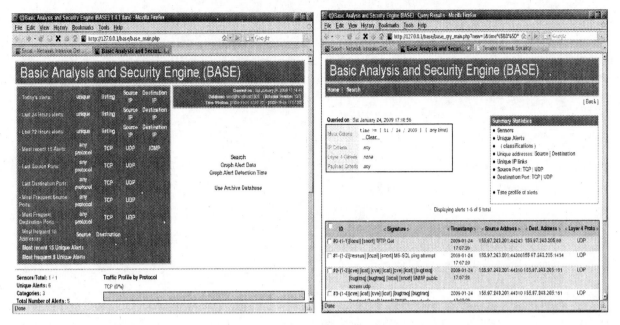

Figure 10-20: BASE main page.　　　　Figure 10-21: BASE results from scan.

You can see that Snort recorded a lot of information about the scan you just did. BASE provides excellent reporting and analysis tools to handle large numbers of log entries. Take some time and explore the graphical front-end to BASE. If you want to see a large number of log entries run a Nessus scan on that same IP address.

It would also be worthwhile to look over the tools that are included with NST. There are several tools included in NST that are not currently ported for Windows. Also, if you plan on leaving NST installed you should reset the password. We will look at a couple of other IT security suites similar to NST later.

THOUGHT QUESTIONS

1. Why are tools like Snort initially developed for Linux/Unix if there are more Windows users and potentially more customers?
2. Who makes the "rules" used by Snort?
3. What is the difference between Snort and a packet sniffer like Ethereal?
4. What would you do with the information you get from Snort/Base?

CHAPTER 11: FILE INTEGRITY CHECKERS & SYSTEM MONITORS

There are a couple of different ways to determine if someone is breaking into, or has already broken into, your home. You can see someone trying to get into your home (IDS) or you can come home and notice that things are missing or have been changed (file integrity checkers). Intrusion detection systems are more complicated to operate but file integrity checkers are fairly straightforward and easy to run.

File integrity checkers basically take a snapshot of a file and then compare it to a later snapshot to see if anything has changed. There are several good file integrity checker programs on the market. We will start with the basics and move up from there. We will also look at software that monitors and logs system activity.

HASHCALC

HashCalc® is a program that will compute a checksum or message digest for any given file. Hashes can be confusing for beginners. You can think of a hash as a unique number that is generated based on the contents of a file or program. If any part of the file or program changes, then the unique number (the hash) will also change.

SlavaSoft® has produced a GUI hash calculator that will demonstrate the basic principles of how hashes work. It's important to understand the basics of how hash calculation works before you move on to more advanced concepts. Let's look at an example.

1. Download HashCalc from http://www.slavasoft.com/hashcalc/index.htm.
2. Click Download.
3. Click Save.
4. Select the C:\security folder.
5. Browse to C:\security\.
6. Right-click hashcalc.zip.
7. Select Extract All, Next, Next, Finish.
8. Browse to C:\security\hashcalc\.
9. Double-click the setup.exe program.
10. Click Next, I accept, Next, Next, Next, Next, Install, Finish. (See Figure 11-1.)
11. Open Windows Explorer.
12. In the C:\security folder right-click and select New, Text Document. (See Figure 11-2.)
13. Name the new txt document your FirstnameLastname.txt.
14. In the HashCalc window click on the Find File button to the right of the Data text box.
15. Browse until you select the file you just created in C:\security named YourName.txt.
16. Click Open.
17. In the HashCalc window click the Calculate button. (See Figure 11-3.)
18. Take a screenshot.
19. Back in Windows Explorer open the YourName.txt file and type your name in the txt file. (See Figure 11-4.)

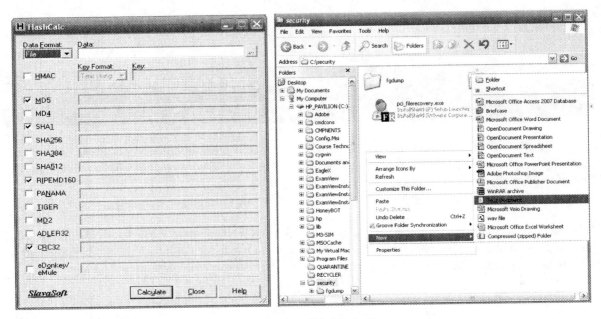

Figure 11-1: HashCalc.

Figure 11-2: Select a file.

Note: We now need to create a test file to determine if HashCalc really works. You are going to create a basic text file in the C:\security folder called YourName.txt. (In this case it was RandyBoyle.txt.)

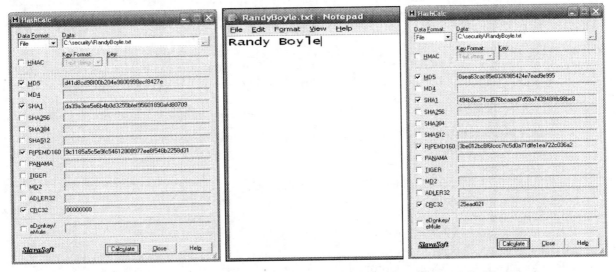

Figure 11-3: Hash calculated for file.

Figure 11-4: Change contents of file.

Figure 11-5: Hash is changed.

20. Click File, Save to save the changes in the YourName.txt file.
21. Click File, Exit to close the text file.
22. Back in the HashCalc window click Calculate again. (See Figure 11-5.)
23. Take a screenshot.

You can clearly see that the MD5 hash is different after you changed the text file. You can do the same thing for any file or program on your computer. We can use programs that will automatically note any/all changes made to files on your computer. This can be useful when you need to know which files have been changed after a possible intrusion.

You may have downloaded programs before and noticed that the authors posted an MD5 number for the download. The authors of the program post this MD5 so you can be sure that your download is authentic, not corrupted, and not infected with spyware/viruses. There are other hash and message digest standards used depending on your specific security needs.

THOUGHT QUESTIONS

1. Why are there so many different hashing methods?
2. Is it possible to get the exact same hash out of two different files?
3. Is hashing the same thing as encrypting?
4. Can you de-hash?

PROCESS MONITOR (FILEMON)

Now that you have seen how hashes work we will get an idea of how often files are changed on your computer. This will give you an idea of why IDS are so difficult to configure. You will see that thousands of files are changed on your computer every day. Most users have no idea that this volume of activity is occurring on their computers. It's good to know which files are changing and which program is making the changes.

Process Monitor® is a collection of tools available from Microsoft (developed by Sysinternals®) that give you real-time monitoring capabilities for your local machine. It will show you any changes made to files, the registry, network activities, and/or process activity. This is a useful tool for tracking down malicious programs that may be lurking on your computer.

This program can be overwhelming for many users due to the number of events shown. We will start with the component that tracks file changes (Filemon).

1. Download Process Monitor from http://technet.microsoft.com/en-us/sysinternals/bb896645.aspx.
2. Click Download Process Monitor.
3. Click Save.
4. Select the C:\security folder.
5. Browse to C:\security\.
6. Right-click ProcessMonitor.zip.
7. Select Extract All, Next, Next, Finish.
8. Browse to C:\security\ProcessMonitor\.
9. Double-click the procmon.exe program.
10. As it opens, click Cancel to close the smaller window.

Note: Process Monitor will start collecting large amounts of data immediately. It's collecting a variety of changes including changes to or by the registry, processes, and files. We need to stop all these log entries and only collect information about changes in files. You will see that there are a large number of entries. Knowing how to use filters will be a useful skill at this point. Let's stop everything before we move on.

11. In Process Monitor click File, Capture Events. (This should stop Process Monitor from capturing events.)
12. Click Edit, Clear Display. (You can use the icons if you can decipher their symbolic meaning.)
13. Click Filter, Reset Filter. (This will show all captured events.)
14. Click File, Capture Events. (This will start capturing MANY events.) (See Figure 11-6.)

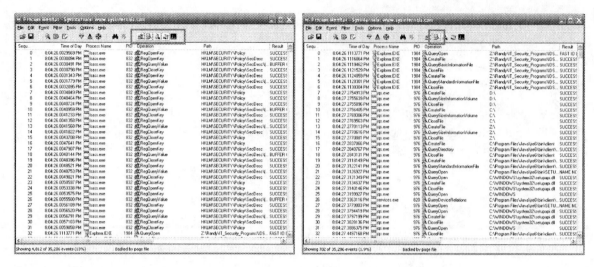

Figure 11-6: Process Monitor.　　　　　　　　　　　Figure 11-7: Filter only file system activity.

15. After about 10 seconds click File, Capture Events to stop capturing events.
16. Deselect all of the depressed buttons in the middle of the Process Monitor Screen that act as basic filters. (This should make your screen blank.)
17. Press the icon labeled Show File System Activity. (It looks like a file cabinet with a magnifying glass.) (See Figure 11-7.)
18. Take a screenshot.
19. Open a Web browser (Internet Explorer, Firefox, Chrome®, etc.) behind Process Monitor.
20. Make sure Process Monitor is reduced and your Web browser is maximized in the background as shown in the screenshot. (See Figure 11-8.)

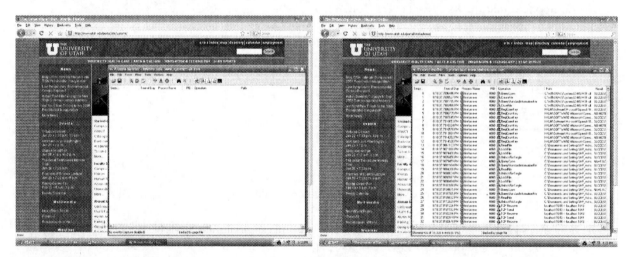

Figure 11-8: Process Monitor and Web browser.　　　　　Figure 11-9: Events recorded for Web browser activity.

21. Click Edit, Clear Display.
22. Click-and-drag the icon labeled Include Process From Window (it looks like a cross-hair) from the Process Monitor window onto the Web browser window.
23. Click File, Capture Events (to start capturing events).
24. In your Web browser click on any link or reload the page.
25. In Process Monitor click File, Capture Events (to stop capturing events). (See Figure 11-9.)
26. Take a screenshot.

In the first part of this project you captured events and filtered out all events happening on your computer except those that dealt with file system activity. In the second example you directed Process Monitor to capture events but only show those events that were associated with your Web browser (Firefox.exe in this case).

Process Monitor is an excellent piece of software that can help you identify changes/events due to malware. The intrusion into your computer or system may have already happened. You may have a virus, spyware, a keylogger, etc. and not even know it. This program can help you find those rogue programs and stop them. It may help prevent future intrusions.

THOUGHT QUESTIONS

1. Why do programs make so many read/writes to the hard drive?
2. Can you stop programs from running or starting up?
3. Why are there so many entries for the registry? What is the registry?
4. What is the difference between a process and a thread?

SENTINEL

Sentinel® is a file integrity checker that automatically scans all your critical system files and executables to see if there have been any changes. It will tell you which files were changed and (the best part) automatically direct your anti-virus program to scan the changed file for a virus. Sentinel will not scan for changes in file types other than those listed (DLL, DRV, SYS, 386, OCX, EXE, COM, PIF, and SCR).

Sentinel will also allow you to create custom folders and tell you if certain file types (listed above) have been changed. This can tell you if your executables have been infected but won't tell you if your documents were changed. This is a fairly good tool that is worth exploring. Let's look at a simple example.

1. Download Sentinel from http://www.runtimeware.com/sentinel.html.
2. Click Download Sentinel Now.
3. Click Save.
4. Select the C:\security folder.
5. Browse to C:\security\.
6. Double-click sentinelsetup.exe.
7. Click Next, I accept, Next, Next, Install, Finish.
8. If it asks you to run the scan for the first time click "Yes."
9. Click OK.
10. Click the Scan tab. (See Figure 11-10.)
11. Click the Add/Remove Custom Folders button.

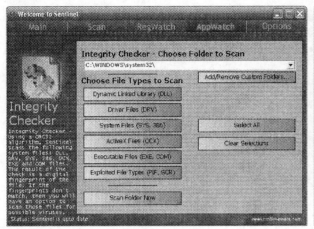

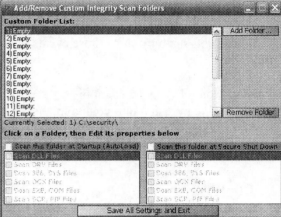

Figure 11-10: Sentinel integrity checker.

Figure 11-11: Custom integrity checker.

12. Click on the first line.
13. Click the Add Folder button. (See Figure 11-11.)
14. Select the C:\security folder, click OK, OK.
15. Click Save All Settings and Exit button.
16. Click OK.
17. In the drop-down window select C:\security.
18. Click "Yes" (to perform the scan).
19. Click OK.
20. Click Select All. (See Figure 11-12.)
21. Take a screenshot.
22. Click Scan Folder Now. (See Figure 11-13.)

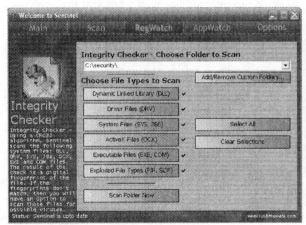

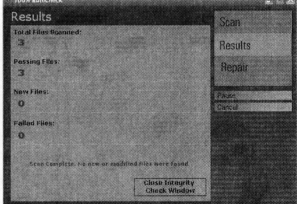

Figure 11-12: Scanning to see changes.

Figure 11-13: Results from a Sentinel scan.

23. Take a screenshot.
24. Click Close Integrity Check Window.
25. Open Windows Explorer to C:\security.
26. Select any.exe program in the folder.
27. Click Edit, Copy (or Ctrl-C).
28. Click Edit, Paste (or Ctrl-V). (This will put a copy of one of your programs in that same folder.)

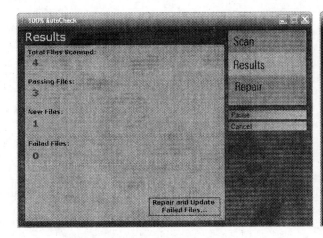

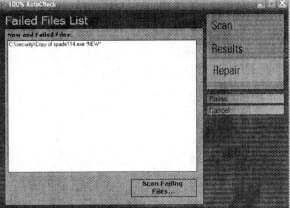

Figure 11-14: Results showing one new file.

Figure 11-15: Details showing new file found.

29. Back in Sentinel click Scan Folder Now (again).
30. Take a screenshot. (You should see one new file.) (See Figure 11-14.)
31. Click Repair and Update Failed Files. (See Figure 11-15.)
32. Click Scan Failing Files.
33. Click OK.
34. Click Close Integrity Window.

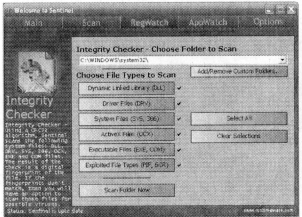

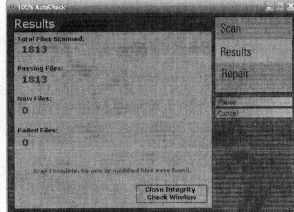

Figure 11-16: Chose folder to Scan.

Figure 11-17: Results from scan.

35. In the drop-down window select C:\WINDOWS\system32\. (See Figure 11-16.)
36. Click Select All (just to make sure).
37. Click Scan Folder Now.
38. Take a screenshot. (See Figure 11-17.)

THOUGHT QUESTIONS

1. Why would this integrity checker only be concerned with certain types of file extensions (DLL, SYS, EXE, COM, etc.)?
2. What does the RegWatch feature do?
3. What advantage would an integrated virus scanner give a file integrity checker?
4. Does Sentinel use MD5 hashes too? How do you know?

FileVerifier++® is an excellent tool that will compute hashes on any single file, or all of your files at once. It can also automatically check to see if there have been any changes to those files. It is intuitive and easy to use. Prior examples showed software that only checked system files or individual files one at a time. FileVerifier++ can check the integrity of a large number of files at a single time.

FileVerifier++ could come in handy if you needed to verify that a given set of files has not been changed or altered in any way. Certain professionals and vocations might find this tool to be useful if they are dealing with information-based products. You may have to use your imagination to see where you would use this tool.

If you find that your files are continually being changed, you may need third party encryption software. Encryption software will help ensure the integrity and confidentiality of your data. We will discuss encryption options in a later section. Let's look at a quick example.

1. Download File Verifier from http://www.programmingunlimited.net/siteexec/content.cgi?page=fv.
2. Scroll down to the Download section and click on the link labeled Available on SourceForge.net.
3. Click on the FileVerifier link.
4. Clink on the link labeled fv-0.6.1.5643W.msi. (Note that this link may change with time.)
5. Click Save.
6. Select the C:\security folder.
7. If the program doesn't automatically open, browse to C:\security\.
8. Double-click fv-0.6.1.5643W.msi.
9. Click Next, I agree, Typical, Install, Finish.
10. Start, All Programs, FileVerifier++, FileVerifier++.
11. In FileVerifier click the Options button.
12. Change the Default Algorithm to MD5. (See Figure 11-18.)
13. Click OK.

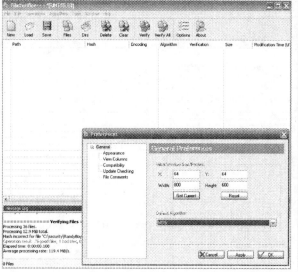

Figure 11-18: FileVerifier++ preferences.　　　　Figure 11-19: Hashes calculated for files.

14. Click on the Dirs button to select the directories you want. (You can also select individual files.)
15. Browse to and select the C:\security directory.
16. Click OK.
17. Take a screenshot.
18. Click the Verify All button.
19. Click OK. (See Figure 11-19.)
20. Take a screenshot.
21. Open the text file labeled YourName.txt you created earlier in C:\security.
22. Add your name one more time to that text file. (See Figure 11-20.)
23. Save your changes to that text file by clicking File, Save.

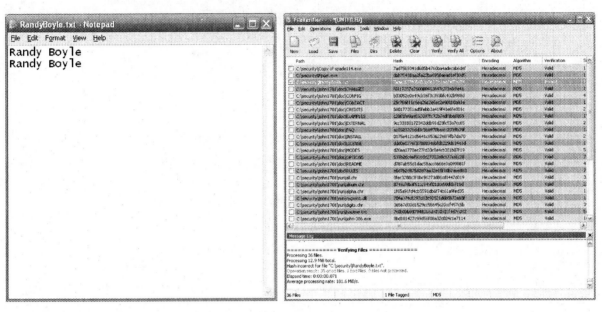

Figure 11-20: Text file to change.   Figure 11-21: FileVerifier++ showing file changed.

24. In the FileVerifier++ window click Verify All again.
25. Take a screenshot. (See Figure 11-21.)
26. Go to C:\security.
27. Select four or five files. (See Figure 11-22.)
28. Right-click the selected files.
29. Select FileVerifier++, Create Hash File (using default options).
30. Click Close.
31. Take a screenshot.

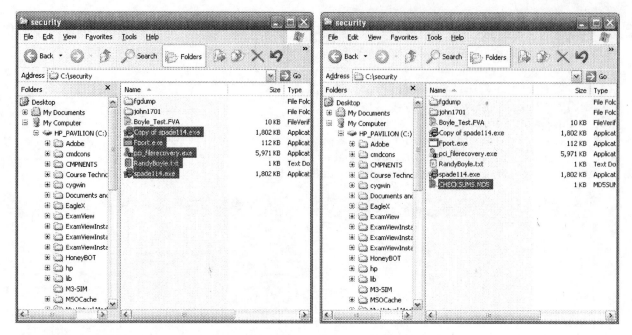

Figure 11-22: Select files to estimate hashes.　　　　　Figure 11-23: Result hash file.

32. Right-click the CHECKSUMS.MD5 file you just created. (See Figure 11-23.)
33. Select Verify Hash Files (using default options).
34. Take a screenshot of the results window.
35. Click Close.

Note that the file you changed is now marked as "invalid" in red. Any change in a document or file will be recognized due to a non-matching hash. You can do this to any or all files on your system. This is a handy tool you can use to see which, if any, files were changed on your computer. The ability to create automatic hash files through a point-and-click program is nice.

This is one way IT security professionals can detect a possible intrusion. They can see which files an intruder may have changed. The trick is in knowing which files are changed due to the normal operation of your computer and which files were changed due to an intrusion.

THOUGHT QUESTIONS

1. How could a top-notch hacker keep you from knowing which files were changed?
2. Can you calculate a hash for a single file?
3. From the hash could you tell what was changed in the file?
4. Should you use the longest hash possible? How long is good enough?

WINDOWS EVENT VIEWER (LOGS)

Good administrators check their logs as soon as they get to work. They need to know what went on when they were away. They need to look for intruders, compromised machines, stolen or deleted files, etc. The list of things to look for can be long depending on your role in the organization.

Windows Event Viewer® is a simple program that organizes these logs in a way that makes them easy to view. Learning how Event Viewer works is a great training platform for beginners. You need to understand how all the pieces fit together and how important it is to look at your logs every day. It's also a great way to diagnose problems on your machines.

Let's look at an example where you enable logging of security events, log in and out of your machine, and then look up the event in Event Viewer.

1. Click Start, Control Panel.
2. Double-click Administrative tools.
3. Double-click Local Security Policy. (See Figure 11-24.)
4. Click on Local Policies, Audit Policy.
5. Double-click on the policy labeled "Audit account logon events." (See Figure 11-25.)
6. Select both Success and Failure.
7. Click OK.
8. Double-click on the policy labeled "Audit logon events."
9. Select both Success and Failure.
10. Click OK.
11. Take a screenshot.

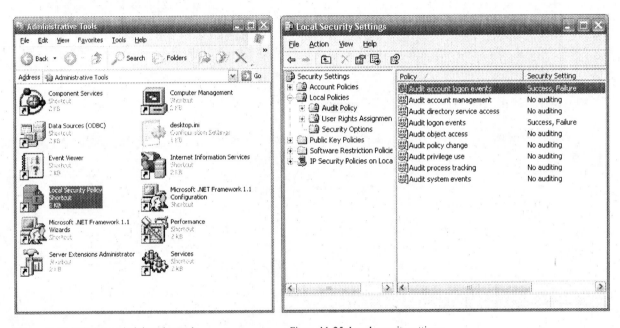

Figure 11-24: Windows administrative tools.   Figure 11-25: Local security settings.

12. In the control panel double-click Administrative tools.
13. Double-click Computer Management.
14. Click Event Viewer.
15. Click Security.
16. Take a screenshot.
17. Log off your computer (you don't need to shut down) by clicking Start, Log Off, Log Off.
18. Log onto your computer by clicking your username and entering your password.
19. In the control panel double-click Administrative tools.
20. Double-click Computer Management.
21. Click Event Viewer.
22. Click Security. (See Figure 11-26.)
23. Take a screenshot.
24. Double-click on the Logon/Logoff event that was just recorded. (See Figure 11-27.)
25. Take a screenshot.

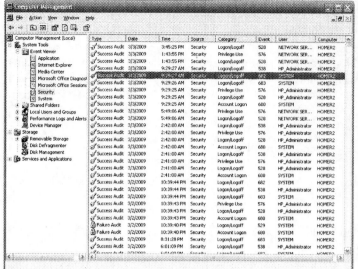

Figure 11-26: Security logs.

Figure 11-27: Details for logged security event.

26. Click OK.
27. Click on Microsoft Office Sessions. (See Figure 11-28.)
28. Take a screenshot.
29. Double-click on any event. (See Figure 11-29.)
30. Take a screenshot.

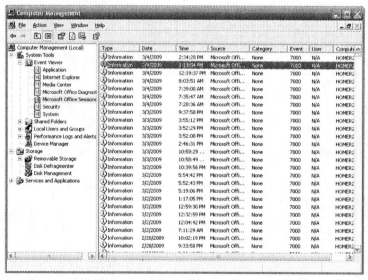

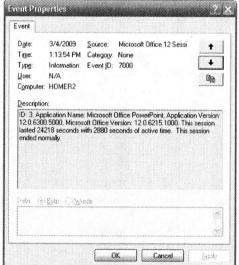

Figure 11-28: Log for Microsoft Office sessions.

Figure 11-29: Details for a specific event.

THOUGHT QUESTIONS

1. Will these security logs track failed logon attempts? From remote machines too?
2. Will it track security events other than just logon/logoff events?
3. Can you use event viewer to view other logs?
4. Why is there a log that tracks which Microsoft office programs you use and how long you use them?

SNARE FOR WINDOWS

Snare® for Windows is a service that takes events from Windows Eventlog subsystem and presents them in an easy-to-use interface through your Web browser. It gives you real-time custom event logging. You also have a remote administration feature that makes watching a large number of machines much easier.

It can filter events from your Security, Application, and System logs that we looked at earlier. It can provide you with custom rankings of the severity of logged events. This makes administering your computers much easier because you can automatically filter all logged events and only look at the ones that interest you. Let's look at a quick example.

1. Download Snare for Windows from http://www.intersectalliance.com/.
2. Click on Snare Agents & Tools.
3. Scroll down to the Snare Agent for Windows section and click on Download.
4. Click Snare installation package.
5. Click Save.
6. Select the C:\security folder.
7. If the program doesn't automatically open, browse to C:\security\.
8. Double-click SnareSetup-3.1.4-MultiArch.exe.
9. Click Next, Next, Next, Next, Next, Install, Next, Finish.
10. Start, All Programs, InterSect Alliance, Snare for Windows.
11. Click Latest Events. (See Figure 11-30.)
12. Take a screenshot.

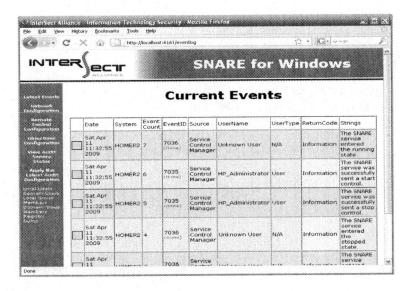

Figure 11-30: Current events.

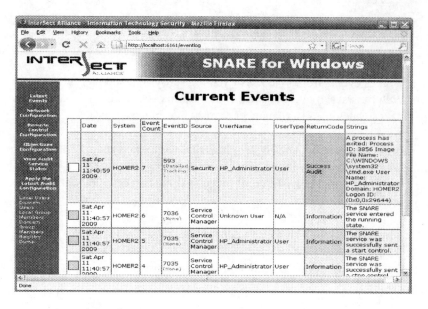

Figure 11-31: Events showing CMD run.

13. Click Latest Events again.
14. Take a screenshot.
15. Click Start, Run, CMD, OK.
16. Back in Snare for Windows press F5 or refresh. (See Figure 11-31.)
17. Take a screenshot.

THOUGHT QUESTIONS

1. Can you view the events happening on your machine from a remote computer? How?
2. Can you add custom filters?
3. How can Snare for Windows help a network administrator manage a network?
4. How can Snare for Windows help secure a machine or network?

CHAPTER 12: FORENSICS

Computer forensics is not exactly like it's portrayed in the movies and on TV. Performing a computer forensic investigation requires significant levels of technical skill, patience, organization, and the ability to follow specific procedures. You need to be able to follow very specific instructions and protocols to work in the field of computer forensics.

In this section you will see a few basic forensic tools and a forensic suite (which includes a variety of tools). The forensic suite (CAINE) is actually a Linux distribution that we will run as a virtual machine. This book has tried to focus on free Windows-based software. However, at this time there aren't many free pieces of Windows-based software available with the same functionality included in this CAINE distribution. The Windows-based versions are quite good and expensive.

The following projects are intended to give introductory exposure to computer forensics and get students excited about the field of computer forensics. You will not be ready, or qualified, to complete a forensics investigation after reading this book. You will need a great deal more experience and certified training in order to be qualified to initiate a real investigation. Again, these projects are just an introduction to the IT security field.

BGINFO

In general, computer forensics gathers information (artifacts) from a computer system while trying to explain what information is present and its origin. When people first hear the word "forensics" they put up mental road blocks and just assume that they won't understand what is going on. We are going to start slowly with basic software that gathers general information from a computer. Then we will move on to tools with more functionality.

The first tool we will look at is BgInfo® developed at Sysinternals by Bryce Cogswell. It shows basic system information on the computer background. Systems administrators are always running multiple DOS commands or clicking through a series of windows to get basic information that they need about the local computer. Having it displayed in the background saves administrators time and effort. Let's look at a quick example using BgInfo.

1. Download BgInfo from http://technet.microsoft.com/en-us/sysinternals/bb897557.aspx.
2. Click Download BgInfo at the bottom of the page.
3. Click Save.
4. Select the C:\security folder.
5. If the program doesn't automatically open, browse to C:\security.
6. Right-click Bginfo.zip.
7. Select Extract All, Next, Next, Finish.
8. Browse to C:\security\BgInfo.
9. Double-click Bginfo.exe.
10. Click anywhere on the text to stop the ten-second timer. (It will close the program if you don't.)

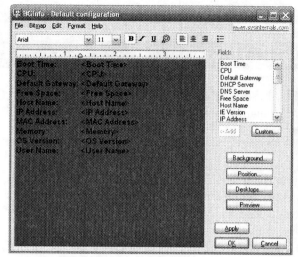

Figure 12-1: BgInfo configuration screen.

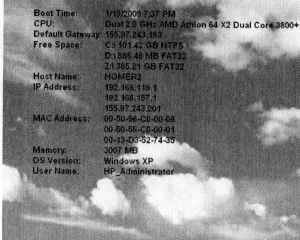

Figure 12-2: Desktop showing system details.

11. Remove any fields you don't want to see by editing the text directly (i.e., select and delete lines).
12. Take a screenshot. (See Figure 12-1.)
13. Click OK.
14. Take a screenshot of your computer background with the system information showing. (See Figure 12-2.)

THOUGHT QUESTIONS

1. What DOS commands would you have to enter to get the information shown by BgInfo?
2. Why would an administrator need to know the IP and MAC addresses for a given computer?
3. Why does this computer have three IP addresses and three MAC addresses?
4. Can you change your MAC address?

NIGILANT32

Let's look at a tool that has more functionality and is closer to being a true forensic tool. Nigilant32® is more of an incident response tool than a complete forensic suite. Nigilant32 will produce a full report showing current system information including all processes, services, users, and network ports. These basic facts may provide investigators with information about what is happening on the system and who is making it happen. It will help direct the investigation.

Nigilant32 will also produce a complete physical memory (RAM) dump. Oftentimes there is information held in RAM that may not be written to the hard drive. This will produce an image file as large as the amount of RAM installed on the local machine. You can also inspect existing files and/or deleted files directly without changing them.

1. Download Nigilant32 from http://www.agilerm.net/publications_4.html.
2. Click Nigilant32 Download Now! at the bottom of the page.
3. Click Download Nigilant32 Now! at the bottom of the next page.
4. Click Save.
5. Select the C:\security folder.
6. If the program doesn't automatically open, browse to C:\security.
7. Right-click Nigilant32-0.1beta.zip.

8. Select Extract All, Next, Next, Finish.
9. Browse to C:\security\Nigilant32-0.1beta.
10. Double-click Nigilant32.exe.
11. Click Run.
12. Click on the Nigilant32 screen.
13. Click File, Preview Disk. (See Figure 12-3.)

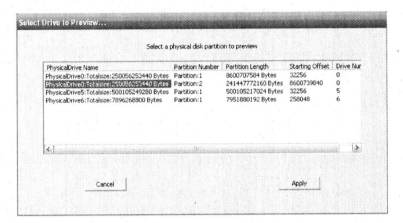

Figure 12-3: Selecting a drive to preview.

14. Select the largest drive. (This will likely be your hard drive.)
15. Click Apply.
16. Scroll down until you see the Security folder you made on C:\security. (See Figure 12-4.)
17. Double-click the security folder.
18. Select the YourName.txt file you created earlier (or any other file). (See Figure 12-5.)
19. Take a screenshot.

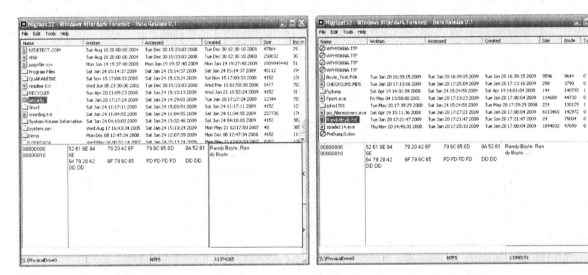

Figure 12-4: Selecting files to preview.　　　Figure 12-5: Previewing contents of a file.

20. Click Tools, Snapshot Computer. (See Figure 12-6.)
21. Take a screenshot.
22. Click Tools, Image Physical Memory. (This will take a couple of minutes; we will use this image later.) (See Figure 12-7.)

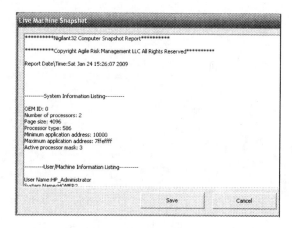

Figure 12-6: System information details.

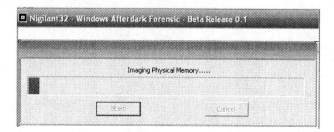

Figure 12-7: Memory imaging progress.

THOUGHT QUESTIONS

1. Why are investigators so concerned about preserving the times a file was written, accessed, and created?
2. What types of information would be in the RAM memory dump that wouldn't be on the hard drive?
3. Why does the program show the file in hexadecimal?
4. What does the Extract File feature in Nigilant32 do?

CAINE

CAINE® is a distribution focused on IT forensics. It is a good learning environment for beginning users. CAINE has intuitive interfaces, a variety of functionality, and good reporting/documentation tools. Most IT forensics suites are quite expensive and require a fair amount of training. A free tool like CAINE that has good collection, analysis, and reporting tools is invaluable for someone just starting out in the field.

In this exercise you will download a Live version of CAINE and load it on a virtual machine using Sun xVM Virtual Box. You'll then take a partial image of the virtual hard drive using the Air tool and search for specific file types using SFDumper® and Scalpel®. This is one of the longer projects in this book. The imaging and analysis components may each take several minutes. You can take breaks and come back as needed.

1. Download CAINE from http://www.caine-live.net/page5/page5.html.
2. Click CAINE LiveCD v0.5.
3. Click Save.
4. Select the C:\security folder.

Note: You will need Sun's Virtual Box to load CAIN on a virtual machine. We will install it first and then create the CAINE virtual machine.

5. Download Virtual Box from http://www.virtualbox.org/wiki/Downloads.
6. Click on the "x86" link next to VirtualBox 2.1.4 for Windows hosts.
7. Click Save.
8. Select the C:\security folder.
9. Browse to the C:\security folder.
10. Double-click VirtualBox-2.1.4-42893-Win_x86.msi.
11. Click Next, I Accept, Next, Next, Next, Yes, Install, Finish.
12. Click Cancel on the registration window.

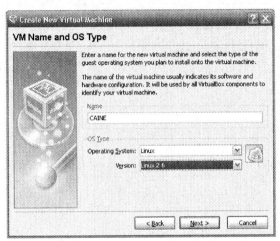

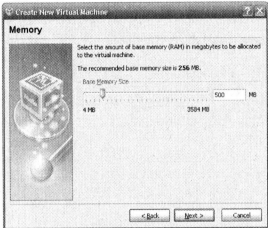

Figure 12-8: Creating virtual machine.　　　Figure 12-9: Setting the amount of RAM.

13. Open Sun xVM VirtualBox by clicking Start, All Programs, Sun xVM VirtualBox, VirtualBox.
14. Click New, Next.
15. Enter CAINE for the Name.
16. Enter Linux for the Operating System.
17. Enter Linux 2.6 for the Version. (See Figure 12-8.)
18. Click Next.
19. Increase the amount of memory to 500MB. (See Figure 12-9.)
20. Click Next, New, Next, Next.
21. Increase the hard drive space to 10GB.
22. Click Next, Finish.
23. Click Next, Finish.
24. Select the Virtual machine labeled CAINE. (See Figure 12-10.)
25. In the right-hand pane click CD/DVD-Rom.
26. Select Mount CD/DVD Drive.
27. Select ISO Image File.
28. Click the Browse button.
29. Click Add.
30. Browse to the C:\security folder.
31. Select the ISO image labeled caine05.iso. (See Figure 12-11.)
32. Click Open, Select, OK.
33. Click Start.
34. Select Install Cain Live CD.
35. Press Enter.

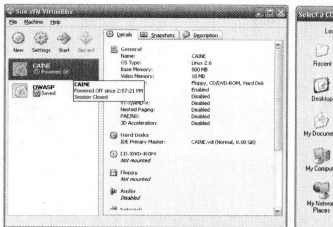

Figure 12-10: Virtual machine created.

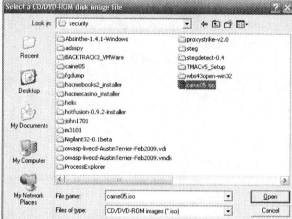

Figure 12-11: Loading the CAINE image.

36. Click Forward.
37. Select your time zone.
38. Click Forward, Forward.
39. Enter your login information. (Feel free to make up anything you can remember.) (See Figure 12-12.)
40. Click Forward, Install. (This will take several minutes to finish installing. Remember: hold the right Ctrl key to escape out of the virtual machine.)
41. Wait—this will take several minutes.
42. Click Restart Now.
43. Press Enter (when the boot process asks you to remove the disk).
44. Enter your username/password and press Enter.

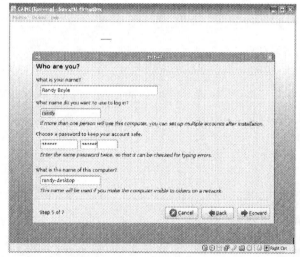

Figure 12-12: Installing CAINE.

Figure 12-13: CAIN menu.

45. Click the Main Menu button, Forensic Tools, Air. (See Figure 12-13.)
46. Enter the password you entered at installation.
47. Click Cancel if asked to delete the previous log.
48. Click on the icon labeled SDA.
49. Click Set as Source.
50. Click the browse button for the Destination device/file.

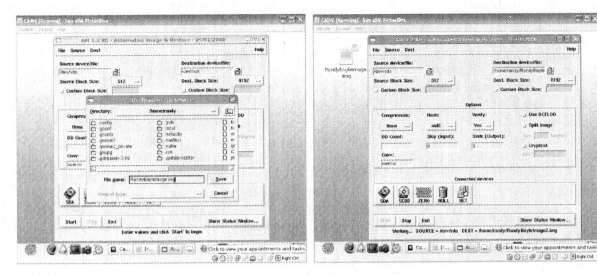

Figure 12-14: Designating destination file.

Figure 12-15: Creating image.

51. Enter YourNameImage.img for the file name (in this case RandyBoyleImage.img). (See Figure 12-14.)
52. Click Save.
53. Click Start. (See Figure 12-15.)
54. Click Show Status Window. (See Figure 12-16.)
55. Press and hold the right Ctrl key.
56. Take a screenshot.
57. Wait—this will take several minutes. (Take a break and come back in ten minutes.)
58. Click Stop when you get to about 2 GB. (Get at least 1GB.) (See Figure 12-17.)

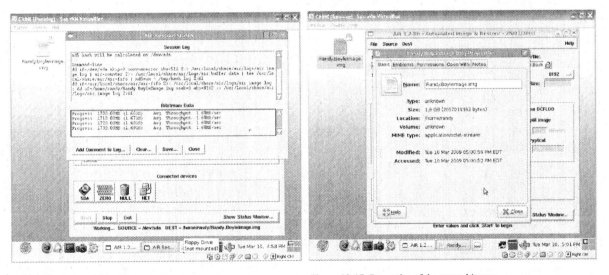

Figure 12-16: Acquiring data.

Figure 12-17: Properties of the created image.

59. Click the Main Menu button (the Start button in Windows), Forensic Tools, CAINE interface.
60. Enter your password.
61. Click Create Report.
62. Enter YourNameCase as the case name (in this case RandyBoyleCase).
63. Click OK.
64. Enter YourName as the name of the investigator.

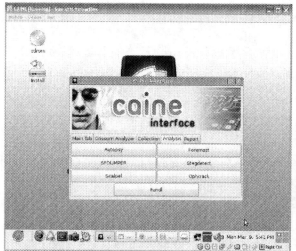

Figure 12-18: CAINE analysis tools.

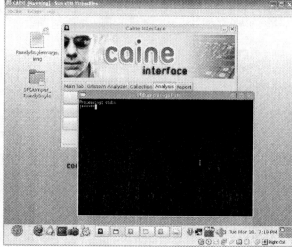

Figure 12-19: SFDumper processing a file.

65. Click on Analysis, SFDUMPER. (See Figure 12-18.)
66. Select Run.
67. Click OK.
68. Enter YourName for the investigator's name (in this case RandyBoyle).
69. Click OK.
70. Click Create Folder.
71. Enter SFDumper_YourName in the text box (in this case SFDumper_RandyBoyle).
72. Press Enter. (Don't click OK before you press the Enter key or you will have to start this part over.)
73. Click OK, OK.
74. Select the file labeled YourNameImage.img.
75. Click OK, OK, OK.
76. Enter txt for the file type to do data carving.
77. Click OK.
78. Wait—this will take several minutes so you can move on and come back for the screenshot later. (See Figure 12-19.)

Figure 12-20: Foremost.

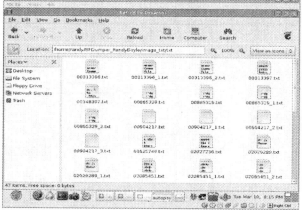

Figure 12-21: Files recovered.

79. When SFDumper finishes click Cancel, Cancel, OK.
80. Select Quit.
81. Click OK.

82. Double-click the folder on your Caine desktop labeled SFDumper_YourName.
83. Double-click the folder labeled image_txt.
84. Double-click the file labeled audit.txt. (See Figure 12-20.)
85. Click Display.
86. Take a screenshot. (This is the list of the txt files it recovered.) (See Figure 12-21.)
87. Close audit.txt.
88. Double-click on the folder labeled "txt." (These are the actual files or file fragments it recovered.)
89. Take a screenshot.
90. Close this file browser.
91. At the Caine interface click on Analysis, Scalpel.
92. Click on Open input file.
93. Select YourNameImage.img (in this case RandyBoyleImage.img). (See Figure 12-22.)
94. Click OK.

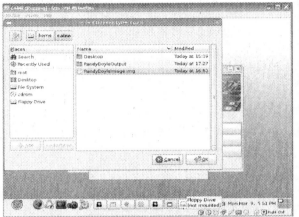

Figure 12-22: Select file to be used by Scalpel.

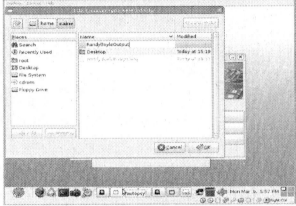

Figure 12-23: Select a target directory.

95. Click Select directory.
96. Click Create Folder.
97. Enter Scalpel in the text box.
98. Press Enter. (Don't click OK yet.) (See Figure 12-23.)
99. Click OK.

Note: You are going to remove the "#" from the beginning of several lines in this configuration file. Removing the "#" from each line allows Scalpel to search for this file type. You can remove all the "#" from the appropriate lines if you want to search for multiple file types. Just make sure not to remove the "#" from any lines that are just descriptive text. If you have questions, please ask your instructor.

100. Click Edit to edit the configuration file. (This file will configure Scalpel to search for specific file types.)
101. Remove all the "#" from the lines with extensions for Graphics files, Microsoft Office, HTML, and Adobe PDF. (This will allow Scalpel to find these file types.) (See Figure 12-24.)
102. Click File, Save As.
103. Browse to /home/YourUserName (in this case /home/randy).
104. Click Save. (See Figure 12-25.)

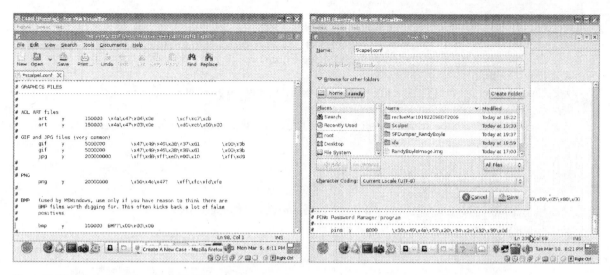

Figure 12-24: Edit the Scalpel configuration file.   Figure 12-25: Save the modified configuration file.

105. Click Run Scalpel. (See Figure 12-26.)
106. Click Quit.
107. Click Open Output Directory.
108. Take a screenshot. (These are the folders that may contain recovered files.)
109. Double-click a folder with recovered files (in this case the bmp folder). (See Figure 12-27.)
110. Take a screenshot of the contents of the folder you opened.

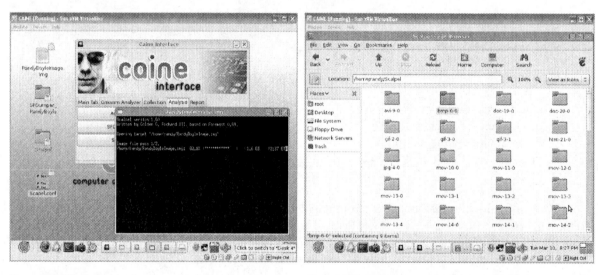

Figure 12-26: Scalpel processing data.   Figure 12-27: Folders that may contain recovered data.

THOUGHT QUESTIONS

1. Could you run Autopsy on the image you used in this exercise?
2. What advantage would the Live CD have in a forensic investigation?
3. What does the Report tab allow you to do?
4. Which programs are included in the Grissom Analyzer tab?

CHAPTER 13: ALTERNATE DATA STREAMS

Alternate data streams (ADS) are memory spaces linked to files. One of the purposes of an ADS is to store metadata about a file (i.e., file type, icon, etc.). However, they can be used to store more than just information specific to a file. You can store entire files within an ADS.

The problem IT security professionals have with ADS is that they can be used to store malicious content. It's extremely easy to store a variety of files within an ADS belonging to a non-descript text file. In fact, viruses can be stored inside an ADS making them difficult to detect.

In this section you will learn how to create an ADS. You will also use software to detect the ADS you just created. You can scan your computer to see if you have any other hidden alternate data streams on your computer. An example will help you understand alternate data streams.

CREATE A SIMPLE ADS

This is a simple example showing you how to create an ADS. You won't need to download any additional software. You can create the new ADS within a DOS prompt. Alternate data streams are pretty easy to work with after you've played with them for a while. You just need to understand the syntax.

1. Click Start, All Programs, Accessories, Windows Explorer.
2. Browse to C:\security on your computer.
3. Right-click inside the C:\security folder.
4. Select New, Text Document.
5. Name the text document YourNameADS.txt. (See Figure 13-1.)
6. Double-click the text file you just created to open it.
7. Type your name twice in the text file. (This is done to increase the file size.)
8. Click File, Save.
9. In the C:\security folder right-click the YourNameADS.txt file you just made. (In this example it was named RandyBoyleADS.txt.)
10. Click Properties. (See Figure 13-2.)

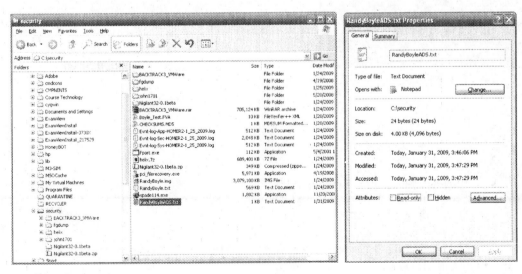

Figure 13-1: Create text file.

Figure 13-2: Properties of text file.

11. Take a screenshot and note the exact file size. (In this example it was 24 bytes.)
12. Click Start, All Programs, Accessories, Command Prompt.
13. In the DOS prompt navigate to the C:\security folder. (Refer to the Dir & CD section in the DOS Prompt section if you need a review.)
14. In the C:\security folder type **dir** to get a directory listing. (Make sure you see YourNameADS.txt.) (See Figure 13-3.)
15. Type **notepad YourNameADS.txt**

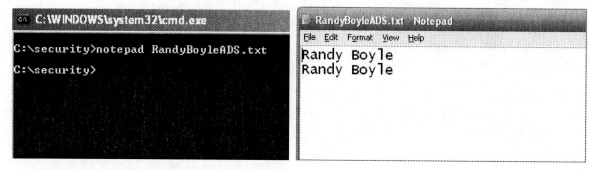

Figure 13-3: Opening the text file from the command prompt.   Figure 13-4: Modifying your original text file.

16. Note that it opened the YourNameADS.text file. (See Figure 13-4.)
17. Close the notepad document that just opened.
18. Type **notepad YourNameADS.txt:SecretStuff.txt**
19. Take a screenshot of the DOS prompt showing this command. (See Figure 13-5.)
20. Click "Yes" if prompted to create a new file.
21. Type "Secret Stuff" a few times in the new text document. (See Figure 13-6.)
22. Click File, Save.
23. Click File, Exit (to close this text document).

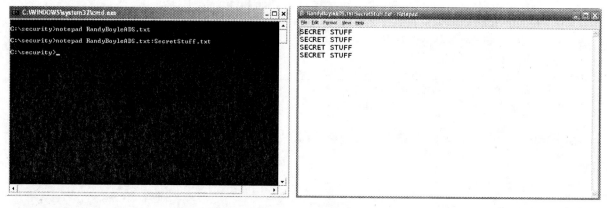

Figure 13-5: Make the ADS.   Figure 13-6: Enter text into the ADS.

24. In Windows Explorer right-click the YourNameADS.txt file in C:\security.
25. Select Properties. (See Figure 13-7.)

Note: It's worth noticing that the file size of YourNameADS.txt did not change. If you look in Windows Explorer you will also see that there is not a new text file named SecretStuff.txt. In fact, if you search the entire C:\ drive you will not find a "SecretStuff.txt" file at all.

26. In the command prompt type **notepad YourNameADS.txt:SecretStuff.txt** to show the ADS with the SecretStuff.txt file again.

27. Take a screenshot of this SecretStuff.txt text document. (See Figure 13-8.)

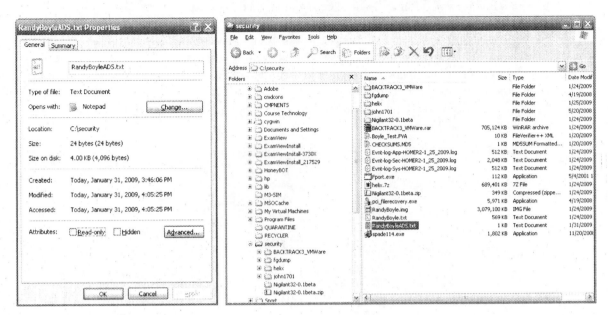

Figure 13-7: Check the properties of the text file.

Figure 13-8: Only the original text file appears to exist.

THOUGHT QUESTIONS

1. Why do alternate data streams (forks) exist?
2. Where does the operating system store them on the hard drive?
3. Can you store more than just text in an ADS? How?
4. If you move/copy the file to your USB, will you still be able to open the SecretStuff.txt ADS?

ADS PART 2

In the prior example you created a simple ADS by hiding some text in another text document. In this example we will hide a program (FreeCell.exe) inside a text file. It's important to understand that even executables can be hidden in files because virus writers can, and do, hide their malware in alternate data streams.

Let's look at a simple example of how to hide freecell.exe inside a text file. We will see how to search for and delete ADS in the next project.

1. Click Start, All Programs, Accessories, Windows Explorer.
2. Browse to C:\security on your computer.
3. Right-click inside the C:\security folder.
4. Select New, Text Document.
5. Name the text document YourNameExecutableADS.txt. (See Figure 13-9.)
6. Double-click the text file you just created to open it.
7. Enter the words "Executable" several times just to give the file some size. (This step is not necessary to make the ADS, but it's done to show that the file size will not change when the ADS is created.) (See Figure 13-10.)
8. Click File, Save.
9. Click File, Exit.

10. In the C:\security folder right-click the YourNameExecutableADS.txt file you just made. (In this example it was named RandyBoyleExecutableADS.txt.)
11. Click Properties.
12. Note the exact file size. (In this example it was 46 bytes.)
13. Click Start, All Programs, Accessories, Command Prompt.
14. In the DOS prompt navigate to the C:\security folder. (Refer to the Dir & CD section in the DOS Prompt section if you need a review.)
15. In the C:\security folder type **dir** to get a directory listing. (Make sure you see YourNameExecutableADS.txt.)

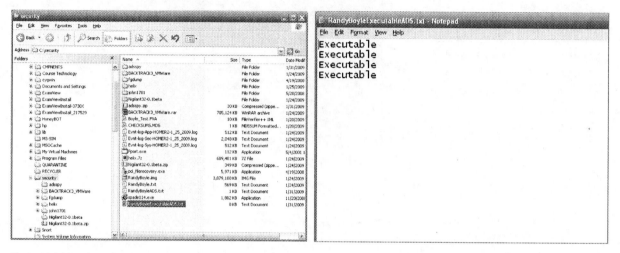

Figure 13-9: Creating a text file.   Figure 13-10: Entering text into your original text file.

16. Enter the following command including the word "type" (See Figure 13-11.):

```
Type C:\windows\system32\freecell.exe >C:\security\YourNameExecutableADS.txt:FREECELL.exe
```

17. Enter **Start C:\security\YourNameExecutableADS.txt:FREECELL.exe**
18. Take a screenshot of the command prompt showing both commands. (See Figure 13-12.)
19. Take a screenshot of the FreeCell window open.

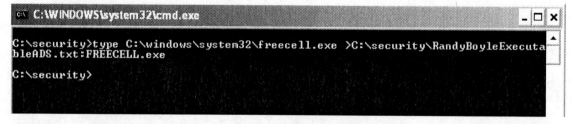

Figure 13-11: Hiding freecell.exe in the ADS.

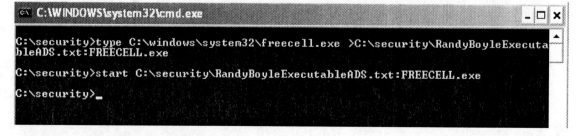

Figure 13-12: Starting freecell.exe that was hidden in the ADS.

1. Did creating the ADS change the size of the YourNameExecutableADS.txt file? (FreeCell.exe is 55,296 bytes.)
2. How could a virus use alternate data streams to hide its payload?
3. Can you create an ADS for an executable file (i.e., hide a program within a program)?
4. Could criminals hide illicit material in alternate data streams? Could you get it out?

ADS SPY

As you saw in the prior examples creating alternate data streams is quite easy. You can also hide a variety of different file types in alternate data streams. Hidden files with dangerous payloads can be detrimental to a computer system. They are also potentially large security risks. It's good for systems administrators to know if anyone is hiding files within alternate data streams.

ADS Spy® is a program that will find any ADS on your computer. It won't open the file or decrypt it if it has been encrypted prior to being put in the ADS. You can easily open the ADS yourself from the command prompt. Let's see if ADS Spy will find the ADS we just created in the prior example.

1. Download ADS Spy from http://www.bleepingcomputer.com/files/adsspy.php.
2. Click ADS Spy Download Link.
3. Click Save.
4. Select the C:\security folder.
5. If the program doesn't automatically open, browse to C:\security.
6. Right-click adsspy.zip.
7. Select Extract All, Next, Next, Finish.
8. Browse to C:\security\adsspy.
9. Double-click ADSSpy.exe.

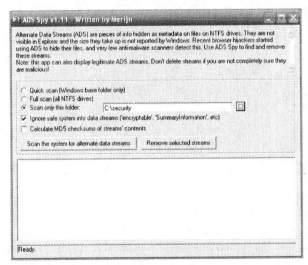

Figure 13-13: Select the folder or drive to scan.

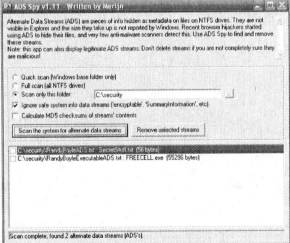

Figure 13-14: Files with ADS are shown.

10. Select the radio button labeled "Scan only this folder:"
11. Browse to C:\security. (See Figure 13-13.)
12. Click OK.
13. Click Scan the system for alternate data streams.

14. Take a screenshot. (See Figure 13-14.)

1. Do you have additional alternate data streams anywhere on your computer?
2. Why would ADS Spy have the option for calculating MD5 checksums for the stream's contents?
3. Are alternate data streams being used by legitimate system files?
4. Would law enforcement be interested in using ADS Spy? Why?

CHAPTER 14: CRYPTOGRAPHY AND STEGANOGRAPHY

Maintaining your privacy is increasingly difficult due to innovations in tracking, monitoring, and recording. Technology has enabled us to monitor just about everything done on a computer. With administrator-level permissions systems administrators can look at any file on a given computer regardless of ownership (including your computer). Although many of these monitoring tools can be beneficial, they can also be used in malicious ways.

As people learn more about the extent to which they are being monitored, they search out ways to maintain their privacy. They don't necessarily have anything to hide but are just trying to maintain their privacy. In a business setting there may be confidential information that must be kept secret to maintain a competitive advantage. There are many legitimate reasons for wanting privacy.

In the following section we will look at some simple tools that can help you keep your information private. We will also look at an Enigma simulator that works just like the original Enigma machines used in WWII. We will then look at a simple steganography example.

There are many excellent books written about cryptography (e.g., *Practical Cryptography* by Bruce Schneier). We could fill this entire book with modern cryptography examples and fun projects. Cryptographers spend their entire lives studying cryptography and implementing cryptographic systems. However, as this is an introductory IT security book, we will look at a just a few basic examples. Hopefully they will inspire you to learn more about the subject and how it really works.

LOCKNOTE

Users often keep a list of their usernames and passwords written on a piece of paper near their computer. Even worse, they may keep them on a yellow sticky note under their keyboard. This is not a good idea. Anyone with a modicum of computer knowledge will look for your passwords under your keyboard or in the drawer right next to your computer. There is a simple tool that can help you remember all those usernames and passwords.

LockNote® by Steganos® is a basic program that will encrypt any amount of text with a password. The great thing about LockNote is how simple it is. You don't have to install or configure anything. Even the newest of computer users can pick it up right away. It uses 256-bit AES so you don't have to worry about it being cracked. Let's look at a simple example.

1. Download LockNote from https://www.steganos.com/us/products/data-security/locknote/overview/.
2. Click Download via HTML.
3. Click Save.
4. Select your Desktop.

Note: In this example we saved LockNote to your desktop to make it easier for you to access your usernames and passwords when you need them. You can also download LockNote to the C:\security folder if you prefer.

5. Double-click the LockNote icon on your desktop.
6. Click Run.
7. Delete the text in the LockNote window.
8. Enter YourName and the words "username and password." (In this example it was Randy Boyle.) (See Figure 14-1.)
9. Click File, Exit, Yes.
10. Enter a password you can remember. (In this example we entered "tiger1234" for the password.) (See Figure 14-2.)
11. Double-click the LockNote icon on the desktop again to see the text we just entered.

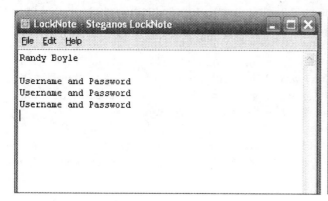

Figure 14-1: Entering text into LockNote.

Figure 14-2: Choose a password.

12. Enter the password you used (in this example "tiger1234" without quotes). (See Figure 14-3.)
13. Take a screenshot of the unlocked LockNote screen.
14. Click File, Save As.
15. Enter YourNameLockNote and leave the file type blank. (In this example it was RandyBoyleLockNote.)
16. Save it to your desktop.
17. Enter the same password you used in the prior example when prompted.
18. Take a screenshot of your desktop showing both the original LockNote.exe program and the new YourNameLocknote file. (See Figure 14-4.)

Figure 14-3: Enter your password.

Figure 14-4: New LockNote file.

Figure 14-5: New LockNote file.

19. Right-click your desktop.
20. Select New, Text Document.
21. Name the new text file YourNameSecrets.txt. (In this case the file name was RandyBoyleSecrets.txt; don't forget to add the .txt extension.)
22. Double-click the text document you just created.
23. Enter YourName and the words Secret Stuff in the text document.

24. Click File, Save.
25. Click File, Exit.
26. Drag-and-drop the YourNameSecrets.txt file on top of the LockNote.exe icon.
27. Click Run, Yes.
28. Enter the same password again (in this case "tiger1234" without quotes).
29. Click OK, OK.
30. Take a screenshot showing all three LockNote files you have on your desktop. (See Figure 14-5.)

THOUGHT QUESTIONS

1. How many usernames and passwords do you have to remember?
2. If someone "discovered" your password how many logins could they access?
3. If you lost the paper with all your passwords on it, could you remember them all?
4. Do people other than yourself have physical access to your computer?

AXCRYPT

In the prior example we looked at encrypting simple text. What do you do if you have to encrypt more than just text? Do you have sensitive files such as databases, documents, spreadsheets, images, programs, logs, etc., that you need to keep confidential? Most individuals and businesses have files on their computer that they know need to be encrypted. They just don't know how to encrypt them. Once you show someone how easy encryption can be they may start using it on a regular basis.

AxCrypt® is a great 3rd-party encryption tool. You just select the files you want encrypted, enter your password, and you're done. It is even available as an option when you right-click a file. AxCrypt will automatically encrypt the file after you are done modifying it and will permanently shred a file. It uses 128-bit AES to keep your files safe and it is open source. Let's look at some of the functionality built into AxCrypt.

1. Download AxCrypt from http://www.axantum.com/AxCrypt/.
2. Click Download AxCrypt.
3. Click Save.
4. Select the C:\security folder.
5. If the program doesn't automatically open, browse to C:\security.
6. Right-click AxCrypt-Setup.exe.
7. Click Run, I Agree.
8. Select "I do not wish to receive update notifications."
9. Click Next, Yes, Next.
10. Select "I want to manually reboot later."
11. Click Finish.

Note: At this point you will need to save all your work, exit all other programs, and reboot your computer. Once your computer is rebooted you can continue on to the next step.

12. Open Windows Explorer.
13. Browse to C:\security.
14. Right-click the file named YourName.txt. (You can create it if necessary.) (See Figure 14-6.)
15. Select AxCrypt, Encrypt.
16. Enter the password "tiger1234" (without quotes).
17. Click OK.

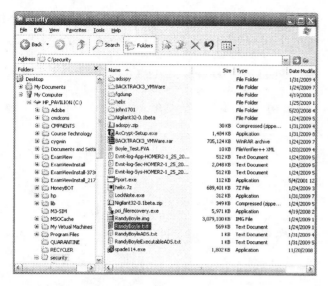

Figure 14-6: Select file to encrypt.

18. Double-click the new YourName-txt.axx file you just created.
19. Enter the password "tiger1234" (without quotes).
20. Click OK.
21. Close the text file that you just opened.
22. In Windows Explorer highlight the YourName-txt.axx file. (See Figure 14-7.)
23. Take a screenshot.

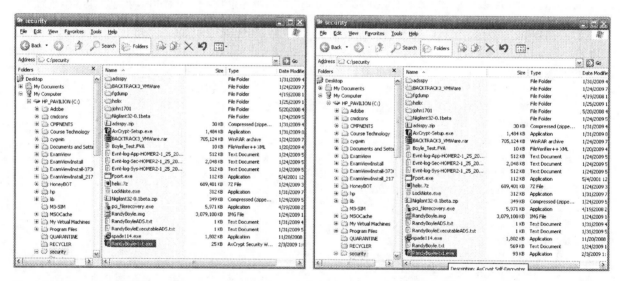

Figure 14-7: New encrypted file.   Figure 14-8: Executable encrypted file.

24. Right-click the file named YourName-txt.axx.
25. Select AxCrypt, Decrypt.
26. Enter the password "tiger1234" (without quotes).
27. Click OK.
28. Right-click the file named YourName.txt. (Again; this time you're going to make an executable.)
29. Select AxCrypt, Encrypt copy to .EXE.
30. Enter the password "tiger1234" (without quotes).
31. Click OK.

32. In Windows Explorer highlight the YourName-txt.exe file. (See Figure 14-8.)
33. Take a screenshot.

THOUGHT QUESTIONS

1. Why would you need an encrypted file that self-extracts (.EXE)?
2. Will AxCrypt work on multiple files or entire directories (folders)?
3. Even if you encrypted a file with AxCrypt, wouldn't someone be able to recover a previous version of the file with a file recovery program? (Hint: AxCrypt has a built-in shredder.)
4. Could your network administrator open these files after you encrypted them with AxCrypt? Why not?

ENIGMA

Below is an Enigma® machine simulator. It functions exactly like the Enigma machines used during WWII. This example has been included to help you better understand how encryption actually worked in the early days and to inspire you to learn more about cryptography.

This project is more for learning, entertainment, and historical purposes. It's a great learning tool when you first start exploring the subject of cryptography and how it actually works. Younger children find this project fairly interesting after you show them how they can send messages to their friends (as long as they both have copies of the simulator, of course).

Enigma machines provided fairly good encryption strength for their day. Modern cryptographic systems are much more secure than Enigma machines. However, Enigma machines are more fun to watch. Let's look at the basic functionality of an Enigma machine.

1. Download the M3 Enigma simulator from http://cryptocellar.org/simula/m3/.
2. Click "Here" to download the simulator.
3. Click Save.
4. Select the C:\security folder.
5. If the program doesn't automatically open, browse to C:\security.
6. Right-click M3101.zip.
7. Select 7zip, Extract to "\M3101\".
8. Browse to the C:\security\M3101\ folder.
9. Double-click the Install.exe program.
10. Click Continue, OK, Yes, OK.
11. Click Start, All Programs, Enigma M3 Simulator, M3 Enigma.
12. Write down the three-letter sequence you see next to the rotors (in this case AAA) that you will need in a later step. (See Figure 14-9.)
13. Type your first name and last name (in this case RandyBoyle). (See Figure 14-10.)

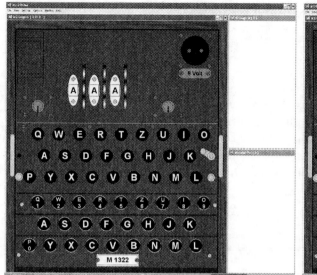

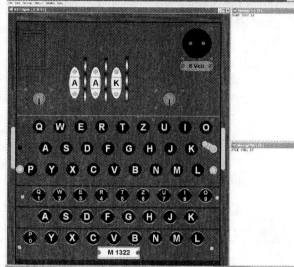

Figure 14-9: Start Enigma with "AAA" settings.

Figure 14-10: Your name encrypted.

Note: You can use your regular keyboard or click the keys on the screen. The text in the top box is what you typed and the text in the bottom box is what you would send. You are now going to reset the dials to their original position (in this case AAA) and type the encrypted text you produced in the bottom box. You should see your name reproduced in the bottom box. This is the equivalent of decrypting the message.

It is critical that you have the dials reset to the exact position when you first typed in your name. The black and white bars to the left of the starting letter sequence allow you to dial back the letters until you get back to where you started (AAA).

14. Click on the black and white bar (the rotor) to reset the starting letter sequence so it shows the same three-letter sequence you started with (in this case AAA). (See Figure 14-11.)
15. Look at the encrypted text in the bottom box and key in the sequence of letters you see.

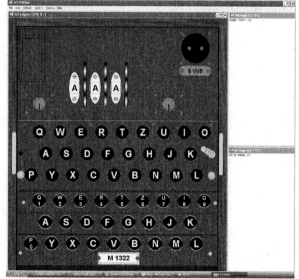

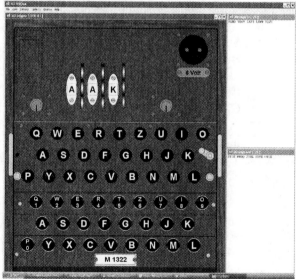

Figure 14-11: Reset dials to "AAA" settings.

Figure 14-12: Your name decrypted by entering encrypted text.

16. Take a screenshot showing your name in both the top and the bottom panes. (See Figure 14-12.)
17. Click View, Scrambler.
18. Slowly press the A key ten times and notice how a different encrypted letter is chosen as output even though you are hitting the exact same key each time. (See Figure 14-13.)
19. Take a screenshot.

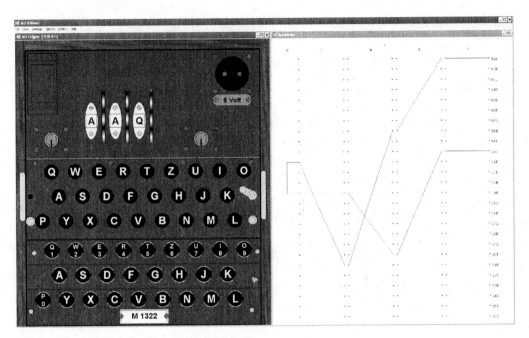

Figure 14-13: Mapping of keys with encrypted characters.

THOUGHT QUESTIONS

1. How does an Enigma machine compare with modern cryptographic systems? (Hint: If the wiring scheme is known, the number of possible combinations is 10^{23} (about 76 bits).)
2. Could modern computers crack a message sent using an Enigma machine?
3. What factor(s) determines how long a computer would take to crack a cryptographic system?
4. Why is a different letter chosen each time even though you keep hitting the same key?

HIDE TEXT

Cryptography makes messages unreadable to unintended users. Steganography goes one step further and hides the encrypted message itself. Throughout the past two thousand years messages were hidden in a variety of different media including images, tattoos, an innocuous-looking message, etc. More recently digital media, email, and the Internet have allowed steganography to blossom.

Individuals can hide covert messages in a variety of different digital media (e.g., images, video, text, music, etc). They can then be posted to the web or sent by email. The receiver can download the image/video/text/music and extract the message using a secret password. Not only is the covert message encrypted but it is also hidden. To the casual observer it doesn't even appear to be a covert message.

The use of steganography has some IT security professionals concerned. Criminals, terrorists, disgruntled employees, drug dealers, and other nefarious individuals could use these tools for a variety of illegal acts. It's not hard to think up a list of ways steganography could be used inappropriately. Luckily there are ways to search for and decrypt messages hidden using steganography.

Below is an example using a simple tool called Hide Text®. Hide Text hides text in specific types of images. It won't hide covert messages in ALL types of digital media. Other steganography software will accommodate a variety of media types.

1. Download Hide Text from http://members.lycos.co.uk/wuul/texthide/readme.html.
2. Click on the link labeled "program and full Delphi source code" to download the program.
3. Click Save.
4. Select the C:\security folder.
5. If the program doesn't automatically open, browse to C:\security.
6. Right-click texthide.zip.
7. Select 7zip, Extract to "\texthide\".
8. Browse to the C:\security\texthide\ folder.
9. Double-click the texthide.exe program.
10. Click Load.
11. Select any .bmp image or use the globe image in the C:\security\texthide\ folder. (See Figure 14-14.)

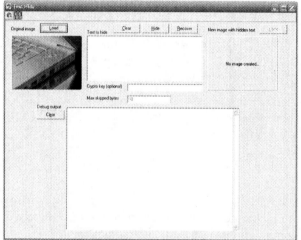

Figure 14-14: Load original image.

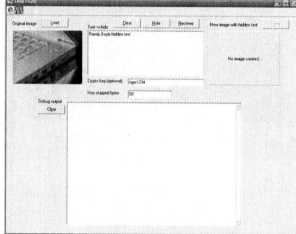

Figure 14-15: Enter text to hide.

12. Enter "YourName hidden text" in the text to hide text box.
13. Enter "tiger1234" for the passphrase (without quotes). (See Figure 14-15.)
14. Click Hide.
15. Select Save.
16. Enter YourNameSTEG.bmp (in this case RandyBoyleSTEG.bmp).
17. Click Save.
18. Take a screenshot.

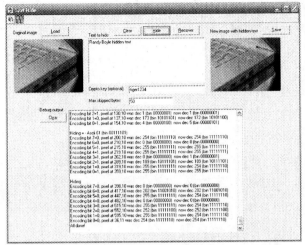

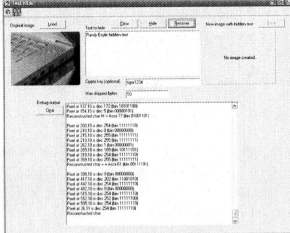

Figure 14-16: New image with text hidden inside.

Figure 14-17: Loaded image with hidden text (now recovered).

19. Close Text Hide.
20. Open Text Hide. (See Figure 14-16.)
21. Click Load.
22. Select the .bmp image you just saved as YourNameSTEG.bmp.
23. Enter "tiger1234" for the crypto key (without quotes).
24. Click Recover. (See Figure 14-17.)
25. Take a screenshot.

THOUGHT QUESTIONS

1. Does the Text Hide program change the size of the image?
2. How much text can you store in the image?
3. Does the image with the hidden text look different from the original image?
4. Does Text Hide only work on bitmap images?

INVISIBLE SECRETS 2.1

In the prior example you saw how to hide plain text in a simple bitmap image. What would you do if you wanted to hide more than just plain text in a variety of different image types (or even audio/video)? Could you encrypt and hide an image inside another image?

Invisible Secrets® provides you with the ability to hide a variety of file types inside more than just bitmap images. It also allows you to add your own encryption algorithm and add additional carrier types. It even has an integrated FTP server connection to make uploading the image easier after you have hidden your data.

For this example we will use Invisible Secrets 2.1 which has limited functionality but is free. Invisible Secrets 4 is an upgraded version with a lot more functionality. If you are working with a lot of sensitive data it might be worth buying the full version ($40) to get some excellent additional features. Let's look at a simple example.

1. Download Invisible Secrets 2.1 from http://www.invisiblesecrets.com/ver2/index.html.
2. Click Download.
3. Click Save.

4. Select the C:\security folder.
5. If the program doesn't automatically open, browse to C:\security.
6. Double-click invsec2.exe.
7. Click Run, Next.
8. Select "I have read the End User... ."
9. Click Install, Install, Finish.
10. In Invisible Secrets click Options (to see that you can add additional carrier types and encryption algorithms). (See Figure 14-18.)

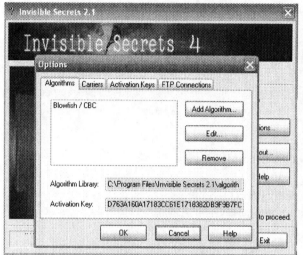

Figure 14-18: Select the algorithm you want to use.

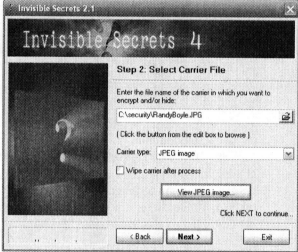

Figure 14-19: Select the original image.

11. Click Cancel to return to the main screen.
12. Click Next, Next.

Note: You are now going to copy any .jpg image on your computer and rename it YourName.JPG. This copy will be used as the carrier image. If you don't have any other .jpg images on your computer, you can use the Sample.jpg image that is in the Invisible Secrets 2.1 program folder. Once you have the image copy made you will hide a small program inside the image.

13. Open Windows Explorer.
14. Select any .jpg picture on your computer. (You can use any .jpg image you choose.)
15. Copy it and rename it YourName.jpg (in this case RandyBoyle.jpg).
16. Save the new YourName.jpg image in the C:\security folder.
17. In Invisible Secrets click on the folder next to the empty text box at the top of the screen.
18. Select the image labeled YourName.JPG in the C:\security folder (in this case RandyBoyle.jpg). (See Figure 14-19.)
19. Click Next.
20. In Invisible Secrets click Add Files.
21. Browse to the C:\security folder.
22. Select the Fport.exe program. (You can choose a different file, if you want.) (See Figure 14-20.)
23. Click Open, Next.
24. Enter "tiger" for the password. (The free version only allows five characters.) (See Figure 14-21.)
25. Click Next.

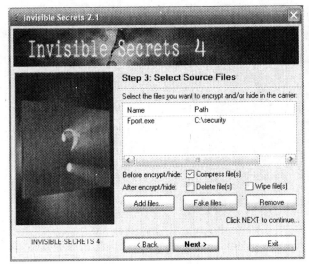

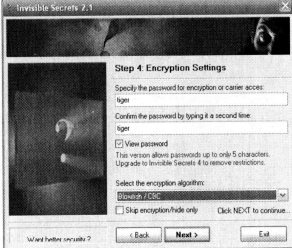

Figure 14-20: Select the file you want to hide.

Figure 14-21: Enter the recovery password.

26. In the target file text box enter YourNameHidden.jpg (in this case RandyBoyleHidden.jpg).
27. Take a screenshot. (See Figure 14-22.)
28. Click Next, Next.
29. Click Review Carrier File (to check and make sure the picture wasn't distorted). (See Figure 14-23.)
30. Take a screenshot.

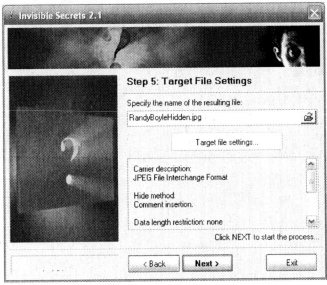

Figure 14-22: Name of the new image with hidden data.

Figure 14-23: New image with hidden data.

31. Click Finish.
32. Click Extract and/or Decrypt files from a carrier file.
33. Click Next.
34. Browse to C:\security.
35. Select the image labeled YourNameHidden.jpg. (See Figure 14-24.)
36. Click Next.

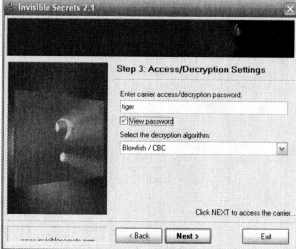

Figure 14-24: Select the image with the hidden data.

Figure 14-25: Enter the password to recover the data.

37. Enter "tiger" for the password. (See Figure 14-25.)
38. Click Next.
39. Take a screenshot showing the files that it can decrypt and unhide (in this case Fport.exe). (See Figure 14-26.)
40. Click Next.
41. Click Explore Extracted Data.
42. Take a screenshot of the window showing your recovered file. (See Figure 14-27.)

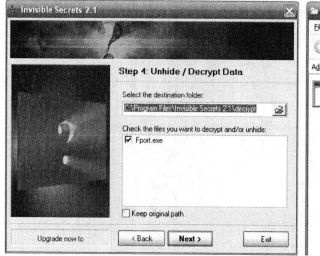

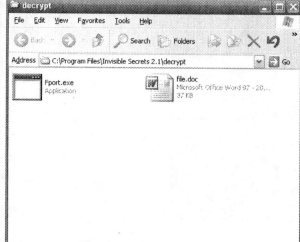

Figure 14-26: Recovered data.

Figure 14-27: Saved data that was once hidden.

THOUGHT QUESTIONS

1. Why would Invisible Secrets allow you to use your own custom encryption algorithms?
2. What different carrier types would be beneficial to use? Why?
3. Could this program be used to "watermark" an image (or other file type) to prove ownership?
4. Could this program be used to covertly sneak secret information through a secure corporate network?

STEGDETECT

Like most IT security tools, steganography can be used for both good and/or bad purposes. It's those bad purposes we are worried about. IT security professionals need to be able to detect images that may contain inappropriate content. Steganography detection tools are of interest to corporate security officers, law enforcement, and a variety of national security organizations (i.e., FBI, CIA, DEA, etc.).

In the previous example you learned how to hide a file inside an image. In this example you are going to learn how to scan your system and detect images that may have hidden payloads. Stegdetect[®] by Niels Provos is one of the few free tools available that can detect images with hidden content. There are other tools available to law enforcement but they are expensive.

Let's see if Stegdetect can scan your C:\security folder and find the YourNameHidden.jpg image that has a file hidden inside of it. The xsteg.exe program we will run is the front-end GUI to the Stegdetect program.

1. Download Stegdetect from http://www.outguess.org/detection.php.
2. Click Download.
3. Click on the link below the heading labeled Stegdetect 0.4—Windows Binary.
4. Click Save.
5. Select the C:\security folder.
6. If the program doesn't automatically open, browse to C:\security.
7. Right-click stegdetect-0.4.zip.
8. Select 7-Zip, Extract to "stegdetect-0.4\".
9. Browse to C:\security\stegdetect-0.4\stegdetect.
10. Double-click xsteg.exe. (See Figure 14-28.)

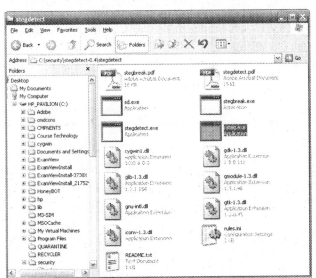

Figure 14-28: Xsteg.exe program.

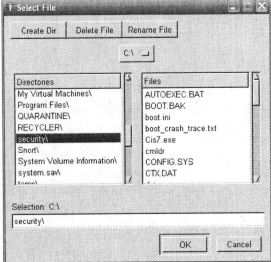

Figure 14-29: Select the directory or drive to scan.

11. In the xsteg window click File, Open.
12. Browse to C:\security. (See Figure 14-29.)
13. Click OK.

14. Take a screenshot showing the detection of the YourNameHidden.jpg file you created in the earlier project. (If you didn't do the earlier project, you won't see any results.) (See Figure 14-30.)

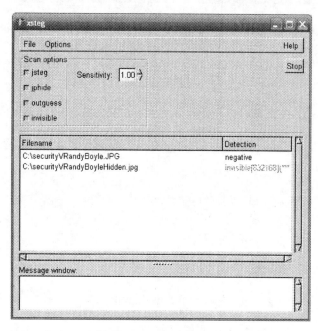

Figure 14-30: Image with hidden data is detected.

THOUGHT QUESTIONS

1. How would you open an image that contains hidden data?
2. Could you use the Stegbreak.exe tool to determine the password for a hidden file inside an image?
3. Could you write an automated program to scan a Web site, or the entire Internet, for images that may contain hidden data?
4. Could you scan all of your email attachments (images) for hidden data?

TRUECRYPT

TrueCrypt makes securing your private files quite easy. Using TrueCrypt you can create a mountable drive from part of your existing C: drive. The new drive is then fully encrypted. You can just drag-and-drop your files into this new drive. Once you are done accessing your files you just unmount the drive with TrueCrypt and it will look like a normal file (albeit a big one). All your data is safely encrypted. You can mount the drive again with TrueCrypt to access your files.

The ability to move files directly to another drive without having to enter a password for each individual file saves a lot of time and effort. TrueCrypt reduces the overall cognitive load on end users. If you are working with a large volume of files that must be encrypted, then TrueCrypt is a great solution. And it's Free! Let's go through a quick example.

1. Download TrueCrypt from http://www.truecrypt.org/downloads.
2. Click Download for the Windows version.
3. Click Save.
4. Select the C:\security folder.

5. If the program doesn't automatically open, browse to C:\security.
6. Double-click TrueCrypt Setup 6.1a.exe.
7. Click I Accept, Accept, Next, Install, OK, No, Finish.
8. Double-click the TrueCrypt icon on your desktop.
9. Click Tools, Volume Creation Wizard.
10. Click Next, Next, Select File.
11. Browse to C:\security.
12. Select any text file with your YourName showing (or create your own new text file) (in this case RandyBoyle.txt from C:\security). (See Figure 14-31.)
13. Click OK.
14. Take a screenshot.

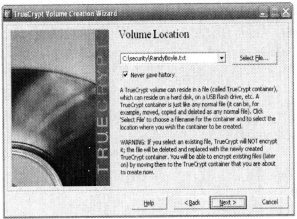

Figure 14-31: Select file to act as a hidden encrypted drive.

Figure 14-32: Select the size of the new hidden drive.

15. Click Next, Next.
16. Enter 20 MB for the size of the container. (See Figure 14-32.)
17. Click Next.
18. Enter a password that you can remember (in this case "tiger1234" without quotes).
19. Click Next, Format, Yes.
20. Click on the G: drive.
21. Click Select File.
22. Browse to C:\security.
23. Select the text file you chose earlier (in this case RandyBoyle.txt).
24. Click Open.
25. Click Mount. (See Figure 14-33.)
26. Enter the password you chose earlier.
27. Click OK.
28. Open Windows Explorer.
29. Drag-and-drop any file from C:\security to the newly created drive (in this case the G: drive).
30. Take a screenshot. (See Figure 14-34.)
31. Close Windows Explorer.

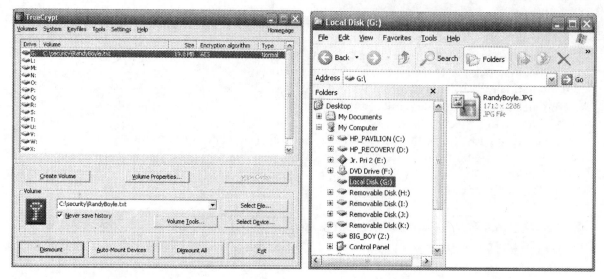

Figure 14-33: Mount the new volume.

Figure 14-34: Copy file to the new drive.

32. Back in TrueCrypt click on the G: drive.
33. Click Dismount.
34. Open Windows Explorer.
35. Browse to C:\security.
36. Note the size of the text file you selected earlier. (In this case RandyBoyle.txt is now 20MB.)
37. Take a screenshot showing your new text file.

THOUGHT QUESTIONS

1. What would you see if you opened the text file you used in this project?
2. What is the purpose of a "hidden" volume? (This was an option when you created the first volume.)
3. What are keyfiles and how do they work?
4. Can TrueCrypt encrypt an entire drive (e.g., an external hard drive)?

CHAPTER 15: SECURITY READINGS

The IT industry moves quickly. Five years in the IT world is the equivalent of 25 years in any other industry. Software, processes, functionality, connectivity, and capacity (CPU, memory, storage, etc.) are changing at a dizzying rate. IT security has been changing even more quickly.

Multiple new viruses are reported every day. Criminal hackers are coming up with creative (devious) forms of malware. The variety of criminal behaviors occurring on computers is expanding rapidly. Identity theft, credit card fraud, DOS attacks, phishing scams, corporate espionage, financial fraud, laptop theft, employee abuse, system penetration, and intellectual property theft are all serious concerns.

The same is true of exploits. Every time a new page of code is written there is the possibility of new vulnerabilities. There are billions of pages of code currently in use today. This creates a substantial number of potential vulnerabilities. Hackers are becoming more adept at automating tools to take advantage of these vulnerabilities.

It's impossible for you to know everything that is happening in the IT security field. However, it is beneficial to be aware of industry-wide trends and the latest developments in your specific area of IT security. It's a good idea to read current IT security news at least one hour every day. You also need to read books, whitepapers, and/or research articles about your area of interest. They make great reading during boring meetings.

Below are just a few Web sites that provide information about IT security developments. This is not a comprehensive list. Due to space limitations we are unable to include many good Web sites and blogs. It's worth the time to search out those Web sites and blogs that you are interested in.

SANS & SECURITY POLICIES

SANS® is a great source for information about current IT security trends. It also has an excellent collection of security-related whitepapers to help keep you current. If you are planning on working in the IT security field, it would be a good idea to look into their RSS feeds. SANS also has several ready-made templates to help you write a good security policy for your business or organization.

We will look at just a few of the resources on the SANS Web site. It's worth taking a few minutes to click through the entire site to see all of the resources available to you. As you learn more about IT security, you may find that SANS has some great resources that will help you as your career develops.

1. Open a Web browser and go to www.sans.org.
2. Click Resources, Top 10 security trends. (See Figure 15-1.)
3. Take a screenshot. (See Figure 15-2)
4. Click Back, Resources, 2008 Salary Survey.
5. Scroll down to page 5 showing the salary statistics for IT security professionals. (See Figure 15-3.)
6. Take a screenshot.
7. Click Back, Resources, Reading Room.
8. Click Top 25 Papers Based on Views.
9. Click on the first paper in the list. (See Figure 15-4.)
10. Take a screenshot.

Figure 15-1: SANS main page.

Figure 15-2: Top 10 security trends.

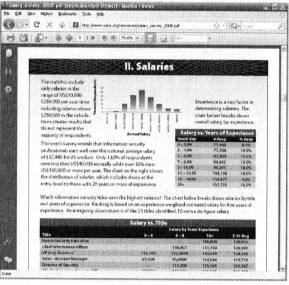

Figure 15-3: Salary statistics for IT security professionals.

Figure 15-4: SANS Reading Room.

11. Click Back.
12. Click Resources, Security Policy Project.
13. Click "Need an Example Policy or Template?"
14. Click Download Word Template under the heading labeled Acceptable Use Policy. In the MS Word window press Ctrl-F.
15. Click on the Replace tab. (See Figure 15-5.)
16. In the Find what text-box enter "<Company Name>."
17. In the Replace with text-box enter "YourName Company" (in this case RandyBoyle Company).
18. Click Replace All.
19. Take a screenshot of your new policy. (See Figure 15-6.)

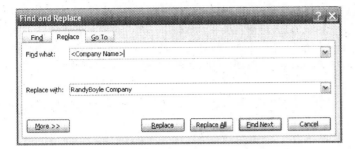

Figure 15-5: Dialog box for replace tab.

20. Return to SANS.org
21. Click Storm Center, Reports.
22. Click Top Sources.
23. Click the first IP address with the greatest number of attacks.
24. Scroll down until you can see which country the IP address originated from.
25. Take a screenshot. (See Figure 15-7.)

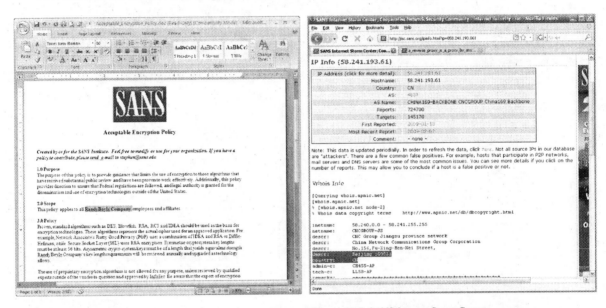

Figure 15-6: Security policy.

Figure 15-7: SANS Internet Storm Center.

THOUGHT QUESTIONS

1. Where does SANS get all of the information about attacks that are occurring?
2. Who contributes to the SANS Reading Room?
3. What type of training or certification does SANS provide?
4. What does the SANS Top-20 list tell you?

SECURITY FOCUS

SecurityFocus® is an excellent Web site that provides a comprehensive mailing list of current computer vulnerabilities (BugTraq) and a searchable database of known vulnerabilities. You can sign up for a variety of mailing lists depending on your area of interest. SecurityFocus is a great resource to help you get the latest IT security-related information.

SecurityFocus also has a Tools section that provides a pretty good index and summary of IT security software. You can see what tools are available for a specific platform and download them for testing. They have a Jobs section that lists open positions in various parts of the world. Looking through the job postings can give you an idea of what skill sets are currently being used in the IT security field.

1. Open a Web browser and go to www.securityfocus.com.
2. Click BugTraq.
3. Click on the first link in the list.
4. Take a screenshot. (See Figure 15-8.)
5. Click Vulnerabilities.
6. Select Microsoft from the Vendor drop-down menu.
7. Select Windows XP from the Title drop-down menu. (See Figure 15-9.)
8. Click on the first vulnerability in the list.
9. Click on the Discussion tab to see a short synopsis of the vulnerability. (See Figure 15-10.)
10. Take a screenshot.

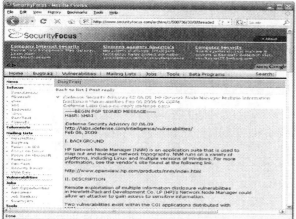

Figure 15-8: Click on the first link in the list for Bugtraq.

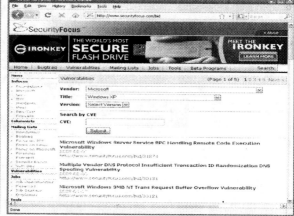

Figure 15-9: Request for information on vulnerabilities.

Figure 15-10: Details for a vulnerability.

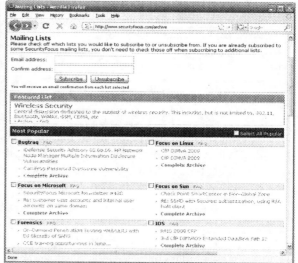

Figure 15-11: Subscription page for SecurityFocus email lists.

11. Click on Mailing Lists. (See Figure 15-11.)
12. Take a screenshot.
13. Click on Tools.

14. Scroll down to the Search Tools menu. (See Figure 15-12.)
15. Select Windows from the Platform drop-down menu.
16. Select Secure Deletion from the Category drop-down menu. (See Figure 15-13.)
17. Click Search.
18. Take a screenshot.
19. Click Jobs.
20. Under Job Seekers click Browse opportunities.
21. Scroll down and click on the first position.
22. Take a screenshot.

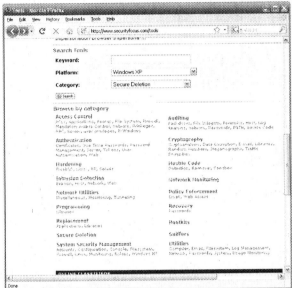

Figure 15-12: Search tools for known security tools.

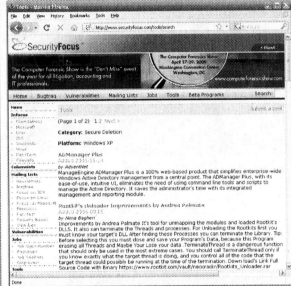

Figure 15-13: Software category listing for secure deletion tools.

THOUGHT QUESTIONS

1. How does SecurityFocus get security notices for BugTraq?
2. Why would an IT security software company want to submit a summary and link for their new software on SecurityFocus?
3. How does SecurityFocus provide these services for free and still operate?
4. In the job posting you looked at were there any specific skill sets or certifications required?

MILW0RM

Milw0rm® is a Web site that posts known vulnerabilities for a variety of software and operating systems. It has a large number of reported vulnerabilities going back several years. It gives the code for the vulnerability and helps you understand how it works.

It's a great resource for both software writers and administrators because it can alert them of potential weaknesses in their systems. Watching listings on Milw0rm (or getting the RSS feed) can help keep you current with potential software vulnerabilities. Let's browse a couple of the listings to give you an idea of the content available on Milw0rm.

1. Open a Web browser and go to http://www.milw0rm.com/.
2. Click on Platforms.

3. Click on Windows. (See Figure 15-14.)
4. Click on any one of the links that interest you. (See Figure 15-15.)
5. Take a screenshot.

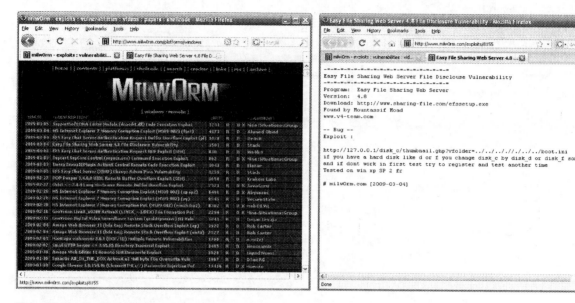

Figure 15-14: Milw0rm mainpage.

Figure 15-15: Details for a vulnerability.

6. Click Back, Back.
7. Click on the first link in the list under the "highlighted" section. (See Figure 15-16.)
8. Take a screenshot. (See Figure 15-17.)

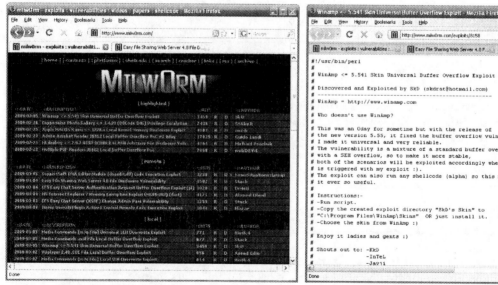

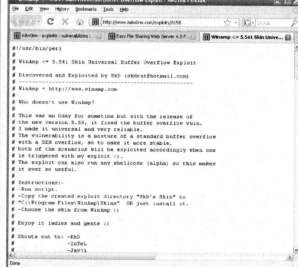

Figure 15-16: Highlighted vulnerabilities.

Figure 15-17: Details for a highlighted vulnerability.

THOUGHT QUESTIONS

1. Who reports these vulnerabilities?
2. If these are not executables, how would you use the information presented?
3. Would a software company want to know if their software has a weakness? Why?
4. Is posting information about these vulnerabilities illegal?

If you are new to the IT security field or just want a more accessible (i.e., less technical) news feed, you might want to read the Security section of eWeek.com® or The Register®. Sometimes you are just plain busy and only have time to look at a few articles. eWeek's Security section gives a good synopsis of some of the more important IT security developments in an easy-to-read format. The Register gives more articles separated by categories.

Because this is an introductory text on IT security we have included eWeek and The Register as options for readers that want to click through to a couple of Web sites and get a high-level overview of what is going on in the field. Let's look at some articles.

1. Open a Web browser and go to http://www.eweek.com/c/s/Security/. (See Figure 15-18.)
2. Click on an article that interests you. (See Figure 15-19.)
3. Take a screenshot.
4. Under the Security section click Security Reviews. (See Figure 15-20.)
5. Click on an article about an IT security product that interests you. (See Figure 15-21.)
6. Take a screenshot.

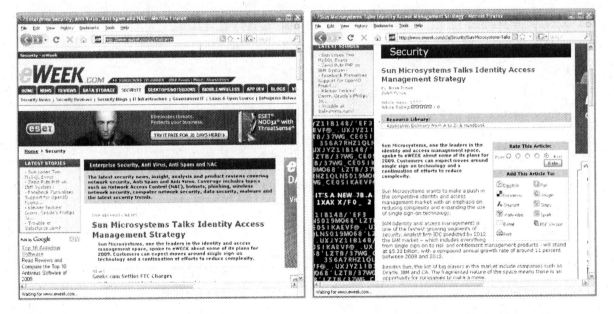

Figure 15-18: eWeek.com security section.   Figure 15-19: Security article from eWeek security section.

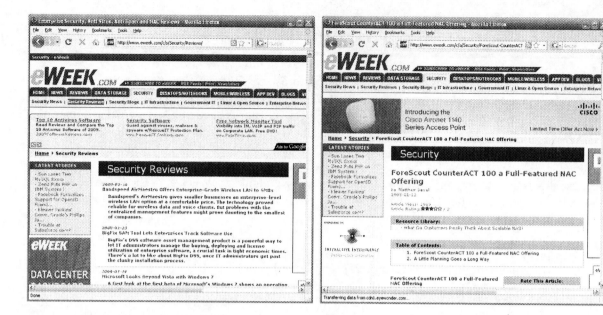

Figure 15-20: Security Reviews section of eWeek.

Figure 15-21: Details for a security review.

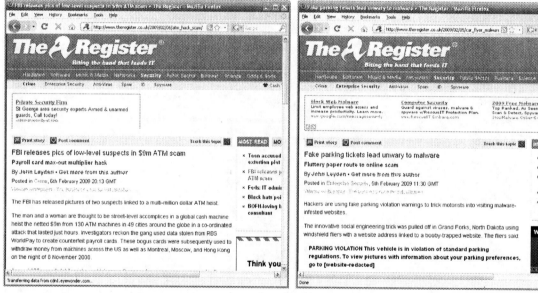

Figure 15-22: The Register security section.

Figure 15-23: An article on The Register.

7. Go to http://www.theregister.co.uk/security/.
8. Under the Security section click on Crime. (See Figure 15-22.)
9. Click on an article that interests you.
10. Take a screenshot.
11. Under the Security section click on Enterprise Security. (See Figure 15-23.)
12. Click on an article that interests you.
13. Take a screenshot.

1. How much time does your employer give you to read about current events related to your job?
2. How much free time do you think IT security professionals have?
3. Does reading current news articles really help IT security professionals in their daily jobs?
4. Is your company/organization more or less secure if you take the time to read about current events?

CSI COMPUTER CRIME SURVEY

The Computer Security Institute® (CSI) Computer Crime Survey® is an annual survey done of all reported computer crimes across a variety of industries. The CSI Survey is an invaluable tool because it tracks computer crime statistics over many years. It also reports figures for cost per incident type, amount of IT budget spent on security, percent of computer functions outsourced, and the types of technologies used to secure organizations.

IT security professionals are expected to perform miracles. They are supposed to secure vast computer systems from a bewildering number of attacks with almost no financial resources. When they suggest a solution to protect critical systems, they have to explain to the CEO that there typically is no ROI or breakeven. It's more like buying insurance. You hope you never have to collect.

The CSI Survey can help IT security professionals explain to non-technical managers how investments in IT security will protect them. It gives them an idea of how big the threat really is and how vulnerable their company may be. The hard facts provided in the CSI Survey help bolster the argument that additional resources need to be allocated to the IT security function.

1. Open a Web browser and go to http://www.gocsi.com/.
2. Click on CSI Survey.
3. Enter information in the fields that have an asterisk. (It's generally a bad idea to give out real information.)
4. Click Submit Form.
5. Click Download the 2008 Survey (or the latest one available).
6. Scroll down the CSI Survey until you get to the table showing a multi-year comparison of different types of incidents. (It was on page 16 in the 2008 version.)
7. Take a screenshot.
8. Scroll down until you see "Figure 21: Reasons for Not Reporting."
9. Take a screenshot.

1. Is the survey representative of all industry sizes and types?
2. How much does the average company spend on security?
3. Which type of incident is growing rapidly?
4. Which type of incident costs the most?

CHAPTER 16: WIRELESS

Most of the good wireless tools only work on the Linux platform. From a security point of view this may be a good thing because it may keep inexperienced users from doing bad things. Wireless is hard to secure and difficult to monitor. Wireless technology has had some well known problems that hackers are well aware of. Administrators have to fight to keep control of wireless networks that are ripe for the picking.

Wired networks are much easier to protect. You can secure the wires and keep people from attaching to the network. Wireless is more difficult because radio waves are hard to see. Do you know who is on your wireless network at all times? Could someone drive by and steal your data? Could a naïve VP plug in a wireless router and punch a gaping hole in your security perimeter? There are many ingenious ways to intentionally hack a wireless network or unintentionally open your network to unauthorized users.

The fact that you need to learn Linux may hinder script kiddies from using wireless tools inappropriately. As more wireless networks come online and software becomes written for the Windows platform you will see more problems arise. The 802.11 standard is hard enough to manage. Administrators are now starting to worry about potential security issues with cell phones. Cell phones are starting to include almost all the functionality you find in desktop computers.

Wireless at both the desktop and the cell phone levels will be a big challenge for IT security professionals for the next 10-15 years. In this chapter we will look at some of the basic tools that are available for Windows machines. Again, if you want to really learn more about wireless, you'll need to get a laptop and load a Linux distribution.

NETSTUMBLER

NetStumbler® gives information about how wireless networks are configured and the relative signal strength from your computer to nearby Access Points (AP). NetStumbler is a great tool for diagnosing wireless network problems like weak signal strength, dead zones, faulty APs, and causes of interference in the wireless signal on a network.

NetStumbler can also help find rogue access points. Often a new employee with limited knowledge about how wireless works will simply plug in an unsecured wireless router. This has the potential to open a serious security hole in your network. This happens more often than you would think. NetStumbler can help you identify those uninformed users and keep your internal network safe.

1. Download NetStumbler from http://www.netstumbler.com/.
2. Click Download NetStumbler 0.4.0.
3. Click Download.
4. Click Save.
5. Select the C:\security folder.
6. If the program doesn't automatically start, browse to the C:\security folder.
7. Double-click the netstumblerinstaller_0_4_0.exe program.
8. Click Run, I Agree, Next, Install, Close.
9. Click Start, All Programs, NetStumbler.

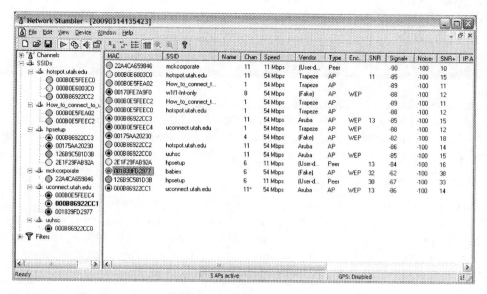

Figure 16–1: NetStumbler showing all available wireless networks.

10. Expand the SSIDs tree to show all lower levels. (See Figure 16-1.)
11. Take a screenshot.
12. Click on an AP that is showing green. (See Figure 16-2.)
13. Take a screenshot.
14. Click on an AP that is showing yellow. (See Figure 16-3.)
15. Take a screenshot.

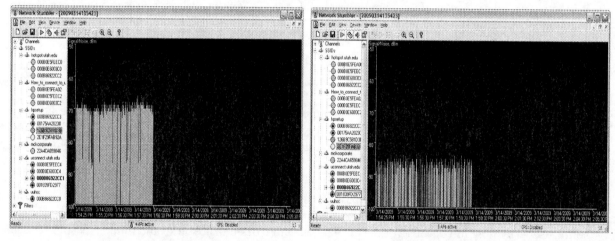

Figure 16-2: Signal strength for a close network.   Figure 16-3: Signal strength for a more distant network.

THOUGHT QUESTIONS

1. What is the signal-to-noise ratio and why is it important?
2. How does NetStumbler know the MAC address of those APs?
3. Why do some APs show their SSIDs and others don't?
4. Why do some networks appear to be encrypted but others don't? Are they really unencrypted?

Another useful wireless program is inSSIDer®. This has the same basic functionality as NetStumbler but is updated to work on newer Windows systems like Vista. It also has some integrated graphing functions that NetStumbler doesn't have. The relative signal strengths of various APs are easier to see using the inSSIDer graphical format.

Another benefit of inSSIDer is that it displays the encryption type used on a specific network. This is important information if you are doing a penetration test or a security audit. If your company is using wired equivalent privacy (WEP), it would be wise to switch to Wi-Fi protected access (WPA) or WPA2 (even better). There are several tools available that can crack WEP keys. Running a quick scan of your network using inSSIDer may help you determine if you need to make changes to your network. Let's look at a simple example.

1. Download inSSIDer from http://www.metageek.net/products/inssider.
2. Click Download inSSIDer.
3. Click Download.
4. Click Save.
5. Select the C:\security folder.
6. If the program doesn't automatically start, browse to the C:\security folder.
7. Double-click Inssider_Installer.msi.
8. Click Next, Next, Next, Close.

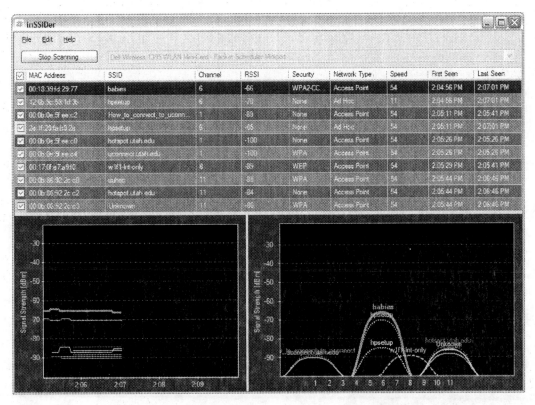

Figure 16–4: InSSIDer showing available wireless networks and their relative signal strengths.

9. Click Start, All Programs, MetaGeek, inSSIDer.
10. Select your wireless network card from the drop-down menu.
11. Click Start Scanning.

12. Wait a few minutes for surrounding networks to show up on the list. (See Figure 16-4.)
13. Take a screenshot.

THOUGHT QUESTIONS

1. What are channels? Would one be better than another?
2. Why is WEP considered cryptographically weak?
3. What is the difference between WPA and WPA2?
4. Why do some networks run at 11 Mbps and others at 54 Mbps?

WIFIDENUM

One of the ways hackers can access your wireless network is by exploiting vulnerabilities in your wireless network driver. Even if you are using WPA or WPA2, your network can still be compromised. You don't even have to be on a network to be attacked. Your firewall and Intrusion Prevention System may not be able to protect you from this type of attack.

WiFiDEnum® will scan your local wireless network card and retrieve its driver information. It will tell you the driver version, date, manufacturer, and if there are any known vulnerabilities. It's a good idea to keep your drivers updated if they are available. Unfortunately updating drivers is not a common occurrence and can cause substantial problems if done incorrectly. Let's see if you have any driver issues with your wireless network card.

1. Download WiFiDEnum from https://labs.arubanetworks.com/wifidenum.
2. Click on Security Tools.
3. Scroll down and click on the link labeled WiFiDEnum 1.2.0.
4. Click Save.
5. Select the C:\security folder.
6. If the program doesn't automatically start, browse to the C:\security folder.
7. Right-click wifidenum-1.2.zip.
8. Select 7-Zip, Extract to "wifidenum-1.2\".
9. Browse to C:\security\wifidenum-1.2\wifidenum-1.2.
10. Double-click WiFiDEnum.exe.

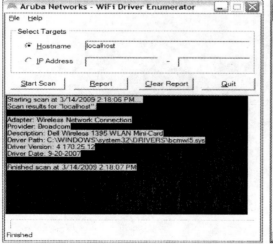

Figure 16-5: WiFiDEnum scanning the local computer.

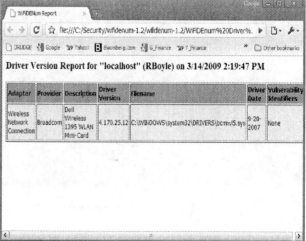

Figure 16-6: WiFiDEnum vulnerability report.

11. Click Start Scan. (See Figure 16-5.)
12. Click Report, Save, Yes (to view the report). (See Figure 16-6.)
13. Take a screenshot.

Note: Sometimes a computer may show the bottom panel in WiFiDEnum as all black. The results of the scan are being displayed. You just need to highlight them. WiFiDEnum works just fine on other computers. Both the lower pane and the HTML report show the same information.

THOUGHT QUESTIONS

1. What would you do if your driver listed a known vulnerability?
2. Have you ever updated your drivers?
3. What does a driver do exactly?
4. What tool would a hacker use to exploit a vulnerability associated with a wireless network card?

HOT SPOT DEFENSE KIT

One of the ways a hacker can cause problems is by creating an access point (AP) just like yours. He can then shut down your AP and provide service through his connection. All of your traffic is now passing through his network. You could lose a lot of confidential information to a hacker with a packet sniffer. The hacker would also be able to monitor all the internal activities within your organization.

You now have all your computers on a network controlled by a hacker. This is not good. If the hacker names the network with a similar name, you may not even know this has happened. The Hot Spot Defense Kit® allows you to monitor which network you are connected to. If you switch to a different network, it will notify you that something has changed. Let's see how this works.

1. Download Hot Spot Defense Kit from http://airsnarf.shmoo.com/.
2. Click HERE for the link labeled "Download the Hot Spot Defense Kit for Windows XP."
3. Click on Download.
4. Click Save.
5. Select the C:\security folder.
6. If the program doesn't automatically start, browse to the C:\security folder.
7. Right-click hotspotdk.zip.
8. Select 7-Zip, Extract to "hotspotdk\".
9. Browse to C:\security\hotspotdk\bin\release.
10. Double-click HotSpotDK.exe.
11. Right-click the HotSpotDK icon on the taskbar. (It looks like a bubble.)
12. Select properties.
13. Select Trusted for your network. (See Figure 16-7.)
14. Take a screenshot.

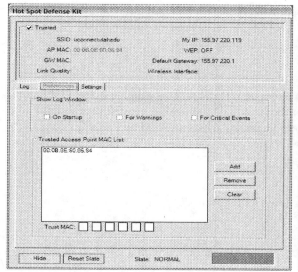

Figure 16-7: Showing a trusted AP.

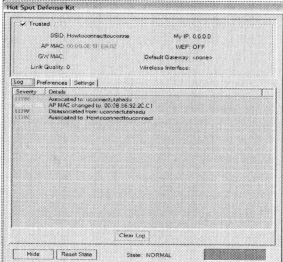

Figure 16-8: Showing which AP your computer is connected to.

15. Click the Log tab. (See Figure 16-8.)
16. Take a screenshot.
17. Click Hide to minimize HotSpotDK to the taskbar.

If you are on a large campus, you can walk around the campus and watch the status bar change. You'll likely switch APs several times.

THOUGHT QUESTIONS

1. Can a hacker use the exact same SSID as the one being used by your network?
2. Could law enforcement use the hackers same technique to re-route traffic in order to catch criminals? Would there be an easier way that is actually legal?
3. Can you keep your SSID from being broadcast?
4. Could you use another tool in this book to prove that you may be using a rogue AP?

WIGLE.NET

Wigle.net® is a Web site that gives you geographical maps with locations of wireless networks. It has recorded over 16 million networks from almost a billion observations since 2001. It has maps for almost every single street in the United States. It also has maps for Europe, Asia, and the Middle East.

Supporters of Wigle.net drive around and collect observations automatically. Then they upload these observations to Wigle.net to be included in the geographic map. They also collect general statistics about the network observations. This is a fun Web site to see the vast number of wireless networks that are in operation where you live. The fact that these observations were all voluntary contributions makes this an amazing Web site. Let's do a couple of quick searches.

1. Open a Web browser and go to http://www.wigle.net/.
2. Click on Web Maps at the top of the page.
3. Enter your zip code into the text box labeled Zip.
4. Click show address. (See Figure 16-9.)
5. Take a screenshot.

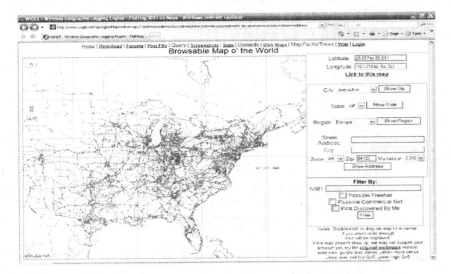

Figure 16-9: Wigle.net map of the United States.

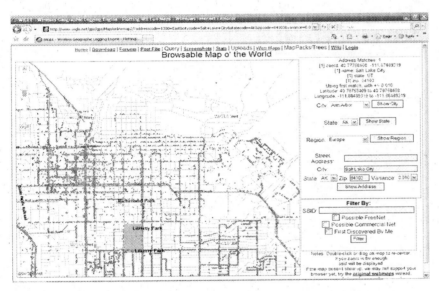

Figure 16-10: Showing wireless networks in Salt Lake City, Utah.

6. Drag the screen so it is approximately centered over your location.
7. Click the "In" button about 4 to 5 times (so you can zoom in and see the SSIDs). (See Figure 16-10.)
8. Take a screenshot.
9. Zoom back out to the zip code level.
10. Select the filter labeled "Possible FreeNet."
11. Click Filter. (See Figure 16-11.)
12. Take a screenshot.
13. Choose a large city from the City drop-down menu.
14. Click Show City. (See Figure 16-12.)
15. Take a screenshot.

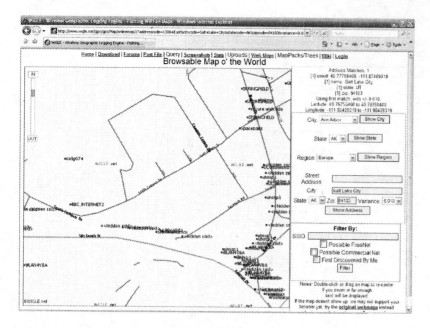

Figure 16-11: Street-view showing wireless networks.

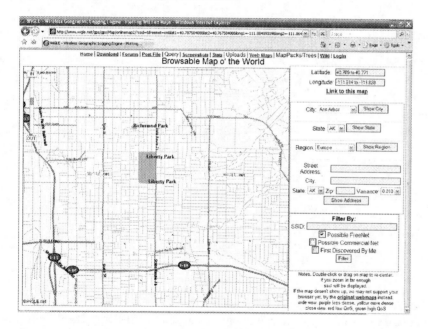

Figure 16-12: Possible free networks.

THOUGHT QUESTIONS

1. Who collects all these data points?
2. What equipment would you need to contribute to this Web site?
3. Does Wigle.net keep statistics on the number of networks with WEP, WPA, etc?
4. Which manufacturer is listed most frequently in all submissions?

CHAPTER 17: SQL INJECTION

SQL injection is when someone takes advantage of database vulnerabilities by submitting malicious parameters through a Web interface. SQL injection techniques can be thwarted by using parameterized statements or filtering the input before it is processed. Unfortunately, you are not going to learn how to protect against SQL injection attacks here.

Even mentioning SQL injection can be problematic. When is it appropriate to teach students about how SQL injection works? Most good IT security professionals know how SQL injection works and how to protect against it. Talking about SQL injection is the equivalent of having the birds-and-the-bees talk with your child. You know it has to be done sooner or later. You just don't want them to learn incorrect or inappropriate ideas from other children.

Do NOT use any of the information presented below on real Web sites. The projects below are intended to give the beginning IT security student an idea of how SQL injection works. They are NOT intended to be used inappropriately. Remember, everything you do on the Internet can be (and probably is) logged. You don't want to get into legal trouble for being curious.

There are several good books and a multitude of online Web sites that have more than enough information about SQL injection. Please feel free to learn more about it. If you learn how SQL works you'll become indispensible to companies that need to secure their databases from hackers. You will have a long and successful career.

HACME BOOKS 2.0

We will NOT be looking at automated software that analyzes all the potential SQL vulnerabilities. There are plenty of those types of software available. The aim of this book is to introduce students to the basics of IT security—not to teach them how to break things.

Foundstone has created some training simulators that you can practice on without harming a real Web site. As mentioned previously, Foundstone produces some great software. The Hacme® series consists of several inherently weak Web sites that you can test for vulnerabilities. Each Web site has many different weaknesses. If you are interested in learning more about how SQL injection really works, you should go through the entire series and buy some books.

We will only look at parts of two simulated Web sites. You can try several different techniques on any of the Web sites. Each Web site has its own unique functions that you can test. Each test Web site also comes with a manual (in PDF format) that has additional explanation and guided projects. It is well worth the time and effort to go through them all. If you are worried about SQL vulnerabilities in your own company, Foundstone does offer services to help you fix potential weaknesses (shameless plug for Foundstone since they give away such great software).

Let's get all of the components loaded and do a quick example.

1. Download Hacme Books 2.0® from http://www.foundstone.com.
2. Click Resources, Free Tools.
3. Scroll down and click on Hacme Books under Foundstone SASS Tools.
4. Click Download Installer.

5. Scroll to the bottom of the Terms of Use page and click Download Now.
6. Click Save.
7. Select the C:\security folder.
8. If the program doesn't automatically open, browse to C:\security.
9. Right-click hacmebooks2_installer.zip.
10. Select 7-Zip, Extract to "hacmebooks2_installer\".
11. Browse to C:\security\hacmebooks2_installer.
12. Double-click hacmebooks2_installer.exe.
13. Click I Agree, Next, Install.
14. Click "Yes" if prompted to install the Java Development Kit®. (You will have to restart after installation). If not, please skip down to step 31.

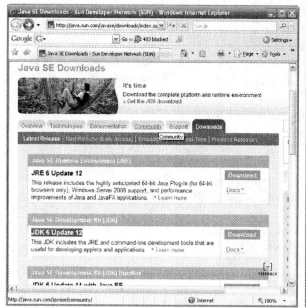

Figure 17-1: JDK 6 update options.

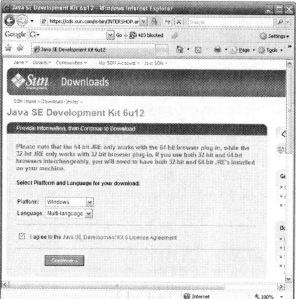

Figure 17-2: JDK 6 download options.

15. In the new browser window click download for the JDK 6 Update. (See Figure 17-1.)
16. Select Windows for the platform.
17. Select "I agree to the Java…"
18. Click Continue. (See Figure 17-2.)
19. Click on the file labeled jdk-6u12-windows-i586-p.exe.
20. Click Save (or Run if using Internet Explorer).
21. Select the C:\security folder.
22. If the program doesn't automatically open, browse to C:\security.
23. Double-click the program labeled jdk-6u12-windows-i586-p.exe.
24. Click Run, Run, Accept, Next. (Wait a couple of minutes.)
25. Click Next.
26. Close the download window if you still have it open and click Retry.
27. Click Finish.
28. Browse to C:\security\hacmebooks2_installer.
29. Double-click hacmebooks2_installer.exe.
30. Click I Agree, Next, Install.
31. Click Close. (Pick up here if you didn't have to install the JDK update.)
32. Save any files you have open.
33. Restart your computer. (Continue to the next step after your computer has restarted.)

34. Click Start, All Programs, Foundstone Free Tools, Hacme Books 2.0, Hacme Books Server START. (This starts a back-end Web site on your computer that you will access through your own Web browser. Do NOT close this DOS prompt or the Web site will crash.)

35. Click Start, All Programs, Foundstone Free Tools, Hacme Books 2.0, Hacme Books v2.0.

36. Click Start, All Programs, Foundstone Free Tools, Hacme Books 2.0, Hacme Books User and Solution Guide v2.0. (This manual, in pdf format, explains how this simulator works—just in case you get lost.)

37. In the Web browser showing Hacme Books 2.0 enter an apostrophe in the search text box. (See Figure 17-3.)

38. Click Search. (This will give us information about the back-end database.) (See Figure 17-4.)

39. Take a screenshot.

40. Click Main to return to the Hacme Books 2.0 mainpage.

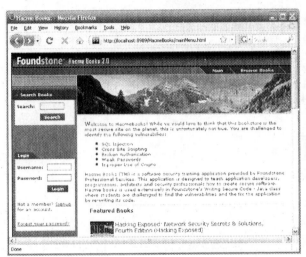

Figure 17-3: Hacme Books main page.

Figure 17-4: Information about the database backend.

41. Enter `';+SHUTDOWN;` into the Search text box.

42. Click Search. (This should effectively shut down the database, which would be extremely bad if it were a real company.)

43. Take a screenshot and notice the third line of the output shows the session "closed." (See Figure 17-5.)

44. Click Main to return to the main page.

45. Click on Details for the Hacking Exposed book. (You should get an error screen indicating that the entire database is shut down.)

46. Click Start, All Programs, Foundstone Free Tools, Hacme Books 2.0, Hacme Books Server STOP. (This will stop the server.)

47. Click Start, All Programs, Foundstone Free Tools, Hacme Books 2.0, Hacme Books Server START. (This will restart the server and get the database back up.)

48. Click Main to return to the main page.

49. Click on Details for the Hacking Exposed book. (You should get the correct page.)

50. Log onto the Web site by entering the following login information:

Username: testuser
Password: password

Figure 17-5: Shutdown database due to SQL injection.

Figure 17-6: Log in to Hacme Books Web site.

51. Click on Details for the Hacking Exposed book. (See Figure 17-6.)
52. Copy the following text (from the HacmeBooks UserGuide PDF).

```
my feedback', 735); insert into products (title, description,
popularity, price, vendor, category, publisher, isbn, author, imgurl,
quantity) values ('Eat my shorts you pointy haired boss','A great
book',4,29.95,'Amazon','Technical','Addison
Wesley','1234567890123','Disgruntled Employee','http://',1); --
```

53. Paste the above text into the Feedback text box. (See Figure 17-7.)
54. Click Submit Feedback.
55. Enter "eat my shorts" into the search text box.
56. Click Search.
57. Click on the link labeled "eat my shorts you pointy haired boss."
58. Take a screenshot. (You just added a book to their Web site through the feedback text box.) (See Figure 17-8.)

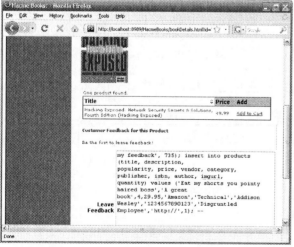

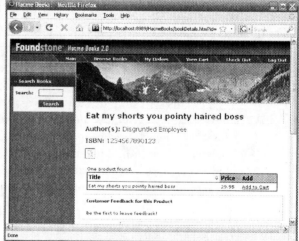

Figure 17-7: SQL injection through a comment box.

Figure 17-8: Results of the SQL injection.

59. Click Main.
60. Click Details for the Writing Secure Code book.
61. Copy and paste the following code into the feedback text box. (See Figure 17-9.)

```
You should buy our latest bestseller instead of this book.
<script>
location="http://localhost:8989/HacmeBooks/addShoppingCart.html?productId=1470"
</script>
```

62. Click Submit Feedback.
63. Click Main.
64. Click Details for the Writing Secure Code book.
65. Take a screenshot. (You just forced any user that clicks on the details for the Writing Secure Code book to add the book titled "Eat my shorts you pointy haired boss.") (See Figure 17-10.)

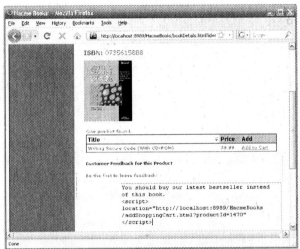

Figure 17-9: SQL injection.

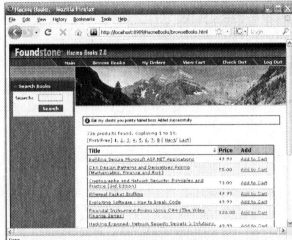

Figure 17-10: Successful SQL injection.

THOUGHT QUESTIONS

1. How long would it take you to learn SQL?
2. Have most real Web sites taken measures to secure their databases against SQL injection?
3. What is Cross-Site Scripting?
4. What are the advantages for IT security professionals having a training environment like the Hacme platform?

HACME CASINO

Hacme Casino® is a variation of the Hacme Books example above. In this example we will look at a basic SQL injection technique using the login box of a fictitious casino. We will also look at a weakness in the session handling that allows us to quit a card game before our losses are recorded. There are several other projects that are detailed in the Hacme Casino Manual that we will not cover. It's advisable that you go through them if you want to learn more about SQL injection.

Again, Do NOT use any of the information presented in this text on real Web sites. This book is not intended to be a hacker training manual. It is intended to give beginning IT security professionals an idea of what SQL injection is all about and how it works. Additional materials are available if you want to learn how to secure your databases and Web sites against attack. Let's look at one more example.

1. Close any windows that may be open from the prior Hacme project.
2. Download Hackme Casino from http://www.foundstone.com.
3. Click Resources, Free Tools.
4. Scroll down and click on Hackme Casino under Foundstone SASS Tools.
5. Click Download Installer.
6. Scroll to the bottom of the Terms of Use page and click Download Now.
7. Click Save.
8. Select the C:\security folder.
9. If the program doesn't automatically open, browse to C:\security.
10. Right-click hacmecasino_installer.zip.
11. Select 7-Zip, Extract to "hacmecasino_installer\".
12. Browse to C:\security\hacmecasino_installer.
13. Double-click HacmeCasinoSetup.exe.
14. Click I Agree, Next, Install, Close.
15. Click Start, All Programs, Foundstone Free Tools, Hacme Casino 1.0, Hacme Casino Server START.
16. Click Start, All Programs, Foundstone Free Tools, Hacme Casino 1.0, Hacme Casino v1.0.
17. Click Start, All Programs, Foundstone Free Tools, Hacme Casino 1.0, Hacme Casino User and Solution Guide 1.0.

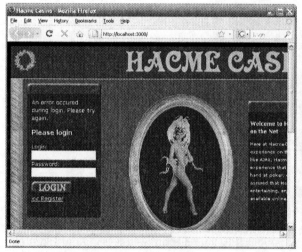

Figure 17-11: Hacme Casino main page login error.

Figure 17-12: Different login error.

18. Enter the following into the Login field: '
19. Click Login. (See Figure 17-11.)
20. Take a screenshot.
21. Enter the following into the Login field: ' OR 1=1--
22. Click Login.
23. Take a screenshot. (Notice that the error messages are different.) (See Figure 17-12.)
24. Enter the following into the Login field: ') OR 1=1--
25. Click Login. (See Figure 17-13.)
26. Take a screenshot. (You should be in the Web site now.) (See Figure 17-14.)

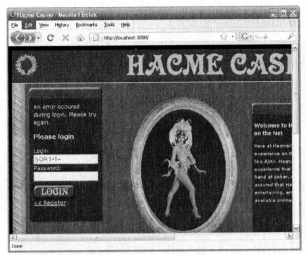

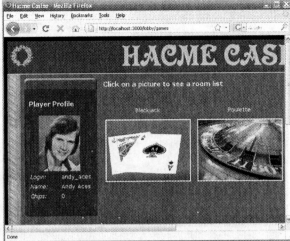

Figure 17-13: SQL injection to bypass login.   Figure 17-14: Successful SQL injection and entry to Web site.

Note: You can refer to the Foundstone manual for Hacme Casino about how to use a cross-site scripting trick to get money from other players. It has more detailed instructions on how this works. We are just going to log into another account and transfer the funds manually.

27. Click Logout.
28. Login using username: **bobby_blackjack** and the password: **twenty_one**
29. Click Options.
30. Enter 1000 into the Amount field under the "Transfer chips to another player" section.
31. Make sure Andy Aces is showing in the Recipient field.
32. Click Transfer chips. (See Figure 17-15.)

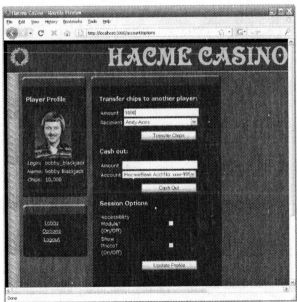

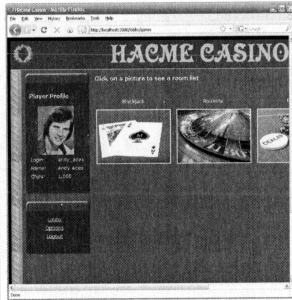

Figure 17-15: Transferring chips.   Figure 17-16: Chips added.

33. Click Logout.
34. Enter the following into the Login field: `') OR 1=1--`
35. Click Login.
36. Take a screenshot. (You should have $1000 in chips.) (See Figure 17-16.)
37. Click on Blackjack.

Figure 17-17: Betting five chips.

Figure 17-18: Play if you get a good hand, quit if you don't.

38. Enter 5 in the Bet text box. (See Figure 17-17.)
39. Click Bet.
40. If you get a good hand, click Stay.
41. If you get a bad hand, click Lobby on the left-hand side before you click Hit or Stay.
42. Keep betting until you win a couple of hands.
43. Take a screenshot showing you have more than 1,000 chips. (See Figure 17-18.)

THOUGHT QUESTIONS

1. What is "improper session handling" and why did the Hacme Casino application allow you to leave without deducting points after you had seen your cards?
2. Why does `') or 1=1--` allow you to get past the login screen?
3. Could you see behind the code to determine which cards were going to be dealt next? How?
4. The program Paros, mentioned in the Hacme Casino manual is a program that can "trap" packets sent to and from your Web browser. Why would that be helpful?

CHAPTER 18: LINUX PRIMER

Most of the best IT security software is written for the Linux/Unix/BSD platform. Many of the top Web sites run their Web servers on Linux/Unix/BSD machines. Given the popularity of Linux as an enterprise-level operating system it's surprising so few people have actually used Linux. With incrementally smaller functional innovations being incorporated into traditional operating systems like Windows it's probable that Linux adoptions could increase. Many online computer merchants are selling computers with Linux pre-loaded.

This section will give you a cursory overview of Linux. You will see what a Linux desktop looks like and run through some basic Linux commands. Most people are surprised at the functionality available in the various Linux distributions. You can get many of the same programs in Linux that you use in Windows and you don't have to pay a penny. It's also likely that Linux will be more stable, more secure, faster, easier to use, and less costly than Windows. Actually, it turns out that Linux is totally free!

Linux is like ice cream. There are lots of flavors but in the end it's all ice cream. You will see many different "flavors" of Linux that you can download and experiment with. Each flavor of Linux comes with its own benefits and features but shares the same basic functionality. If you are open to trying different flavors of Linux, you will be able to see exactly what those differences are.

Any IT security professional worth his/her salt will have at least a couple of Linux machines and be intimately familiar with the operating system. You need to take the time to become proficient with command-line Linux. It might be a little intimidating at first, but you will quickly get the hang of it.

VMWARE PLAYER

VMware® is the industry leader in virtualization software. VMware Player® is a piece of software that allows users to download pre-installed and configured "virtual computers" that can be used on a local machine. This means that you can use a Windows XP computer and a virtual Linux computer (running inside an XP window) at the same time. The Linux computer will share all the hardware that your Windows XP computer is using and still have all the functionality that you would see if you loaded it on a stand-alone machine. Not only could you run Windows and Linux at the same time, but you could run a variety of pre-loaded operating systems.

You can download a wide variety of pre-loaded VM machines (from www.vmware.com) for just about every operating system available. You can then choose which one to load and experiment with. VMware Player is great for users that are new to the Linux platform. It allows them to try Linux without getting rid of their native XP environment.

Another advantage of virtual machines is that if you don't like them you can easily delete them. You don't have to deal with the litany of installation issues that unavoidably arise when you set up a new system. Virtual machines are fast and easy. Once you see how easy VMware is to use you'll probably download several images.

In this example we are going to load a Linux distribution called openSUSE®. Feel free to try another Linux flavor (Ubuntu®, Mandriva®, Fedora®, Debian®, etc.). If your instructor has already downloaded the images it will save you a lot of time. Let's get a Linux machine up and running.

1. Download VMware Player from http://www.vmware.com/download/player/download.html.
2. Click Download for VMware Player for Windows.
3. Click Save.
4. Select the C:\security folder.
5. Click Run, Run, Next, Next, Next, Install, Next, Finish.

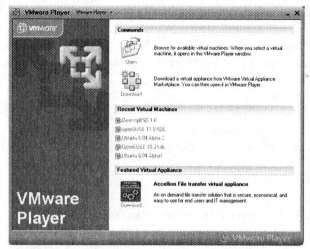

Figure 18-1: VMware Player.

Figure 18-2: VMware Virtual Appliance Marketplace.

6. Double-click the VMware icon on your desktop. (See Figure 18-1.)
7. Click download.
8. A Web browser window will open and you will enter "openSUSE 11.0" in the text box labeled Search Virtual Appliances. (See Figure 18-2.)
9. Press Enter.
10. Click on the link that lists "OpenSUSE 11.0." (See Figure 18-3.)

Figure 18-3: Search results for openSUSE.

Figure 18-4: Download for openSUSE.

11. You need to write down the primary account information (Username: vmplanet and Password: vmplanet.net) on a piece of paper. (See Figure 18-4.)

Note: If you download a different virtual image of OpenSUSE (or any other appliance) the primary username and password will be different. It will be difficult to log in if you don't have the correct username and password. Stop at this point and write down the username and password on a piece of paper. You can change it later.

12. Click Download this Appliance.
13. Click on the link that reads, "No thanks, take me directly to …" (See Figure 18-5.)
14. Click on the link that reads, "OpenSUSE VMware image" to download the image. (See Figure 18-6.)

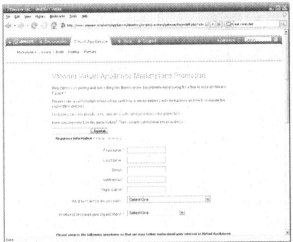

Figure 18-5: Download link for openSUSE.

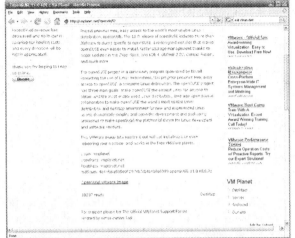

Figure 18-6: Username and password for openSUSE virtual machine.

15. Click Save.
16. Select the C:\security folder.

Note: These images are large and may take awhile to download. Now that you have the VMware player installed and the image downloaded you need to unzip the image and start the virtual machine. The VM images are zipped because they are large. Some of the Linux images are now coming in a .7z file format. This is a free file compression format that does a great job. Let's download the 7z program and unzip the VM image you just downloaded.

17. Download 7z from http://www.7-zip.org/download.html.
18. Click Download for 7-Zip 4.57 (Windows, 32-bit, .exe or .msi). (See Figure 18-7.)
19. Click Save.
20. Select the C:\security folder.
21. Double-click the executable file you just downloaded (7z457.msi or 7z457.exe) to install the 7z program.
22. Click Next, I Accept, Next, Next, Install, Finish.
23. Locate the VM image you downloaded from the Web (openSUSE-11.0-KDE.7z) and Double-click it to open.
24. Highlight the folder named openSUSE-11.0-KDE. (See Figure 18-8.)

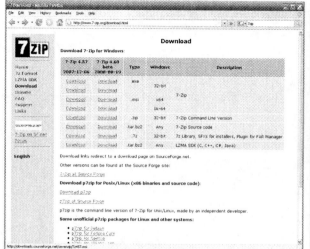

Figure 18-7: 7-Zip download page.

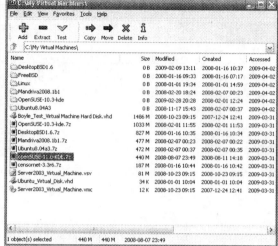

Figure 18-8: Uncompressing openSUSE download.

25. Click Extract To.
26. Click OK and it will unzip the compressed image to the current folder. (This may take a minute.)
27. Go back to the VMware Player screen and click Open.
28. Navigate until you find the folder you just unzipped and select the image named openSUSE 11.0 KDE.vmx.
29. Click Open.
30. If you see a window asking you if you moved/copied the virtual machine, just click "I moved it." (See Figure 18-9.)
31. Click OK and wait for the OS to load for the first time. (Subsequent boot sequences will be much faster.)

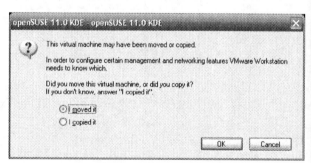

Figure 18-9: Opening the openSUSE virtual machine.

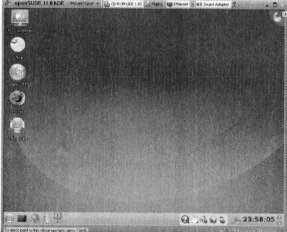

Figure 18-10: Desktop GUI for openSUSE.

Note: A few users may have an issue with their desktop not restarting after the images are loaded. This may be due to a screen resolution issue. Most users should not have this problem but if you see a black command-line enter the command **startx** and the desktop should start immediately.

32. Click on the virtual machine screen and your mouse/keyboard will be locked in the virtual machine. (To return to your host machine, press Ctrl-Alt.) (See Figure 18-10.)
33. Click on the SUSE icon on the bottom left-hand side of the screen to open the SUSE menu.

34. Click on Word Processor to open the OpenOffice Writer program (like Microsoft Word).
35. Type your name in the document.
36. Leave the virtual machine by pressing Ctrl-Alt.
37. Take a screenshot of the OpenSUSE virtual machine with your name showing. (See Figure 18-11.)

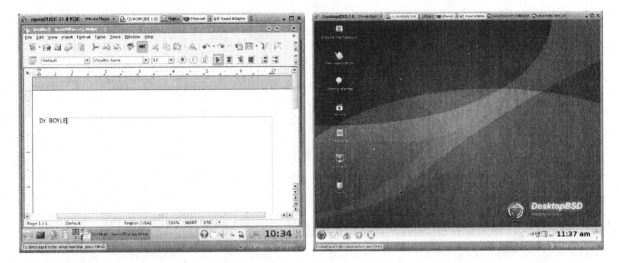

Figure 18-11: Screen display of the OPENSUSE virtual machine showing your name.

Figure 18-12: Example of a desktop version of Free BSD.

Now you know how to run VMware Player and load a virtual machine. You also have an idea of what it would take to run any version of Linux, FreeBSD, or UNIX as a virtual machine. The time and cost savings from using virtual machines, rather than loading them on dedicated boxes, can be substantial.

Take some time to explore this Linux virtual machine and see what you can do with Linux. People are surprised to learn that many of the mainstream versions of Linux have all the functionality of Windows and more. They are easy to use and come with a large amount of free software.

For many people this will be the first time they have seen Linux. The FreeBSD desktop is also worth trying out. The above screenshot is an example of a desktop version of FreeBSD. (See Figure 18-12.) After you're done you can just delete them without affecting your host machine. You can always keep them and show your friends.

THOUGHT QUESTIONS

1. Does Linux come with an Office suite similar to Microsoft Office?
2. Who makes Linux distributions and how do they make money?
3. Is Linux more secure than Windows or MAC? Why?
4. Why are the latest IT security tools written to run in a Linux/Unix environment before being ported to Windows?

LINUX COMMAND-LINE PRIMER

Now that you have a Linux machine up and running we will go through some of the basic commands you will need to know if you are going to use the command-line. Command-line is important to know because some critical systems use command-line exclusively. This is done to conserve system resources and improve stability.

You will need to practice these commands many times to become moderately proficient. Only after entering them hundreds of times will they become second nature to you. You can complete similar tasks using command-line in a fraction of the time it would take you to complete them in Windows. We will just go over the basic commands.

You might need a better tool to take screenshots of the virtual machine window to show your work. MWSnap® is a useful tool that allows you to take a screenshot of any size you want. You just start the program and press F6 when you are ready to take the screenshot. Let's load MWSnap and then start the command-line project.

1. Download MWSnap from http://www.mirekw.com/winfreeware/mwsnap.html.
2. Click on the download link for site 1 or site 2.
3. Click Save.
4. Select the C:\security folder.
5. If the program doesn't automatically start, browse to the C:\security folder.
6. Double-click the MWSnap300.exe program.
7. Click Run, Next, Next, Next, Finish.
8. Click Start, All Programs, MWSnap, MWSnap3.
9. Minimize the MWSnap window.

Note: Now that MWSnap is running in the background you can just press the F6 button anytime you want to take a screenshot. Then you click your starting and ending points for the screen capture area. The image will be transferred to the MWSnap program. In the MWSnap program you can click Edit and then Copy. Then you can paste the image into another document.

Let's get back to the Linux tutorial. Remember, you are going to press Enter after typing each command unless otherwise directed.

10. Double-click the VMware icon on your desktop.
11. Click the link for the OpenSUSE virtual machine you opened in the prior exercise.
12. Click the K-Menu icon (like the Start button in Windows) in the bottom left-hand side of your screen.
13. Click Applications, Terminal, Terminal Program. (See Figure 18-13.)
14. Click Close if a "tip of the day" opens.

Figure 18-13: Main menu for openSUSE.

Figure 18-14: Linux ls command.

15. Enter **ls** to see a listing of the files in the current directory.
16. Enter **ls -l** to see a listing of files in long format.
17. Enter **ls -al** to see a listing of files including hidden files.
18. Take a screenshot. (See Figure 18-14.)
19. Enter **man ls** to see the manual page for the ls command.
20. Press **q** to exit the man page.
21. Enter **man man** to see the manual page for the man command. (See Figure 18-15.)
22. Take a screenshot.
23. Enter **date** to see the current time and date.
24. Enter **cal** to see the current month's calendar.
25. Enter **uptime** to see how long the system has been up and running.
26. Enter **w** to see who is logged on to the system.
27. Enter **whoami** to see who you are logged on as.
28. Enter **finger opensuse** to see who "opensuse" is. (See Figure 18-16.)
29. Take a screenshot.
30. Enter **clear** to clear the screen.

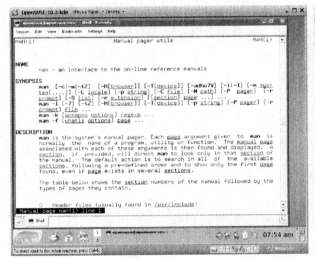

Figure 18-15: Linux MAN pages.

Figure 18-16: Linux date, cal, uptime, whoami, and finger commands.

31. Enter **df** to see how much of your hard disk you have used up.
32. Enter **touch YourName.txt** to create a simple text file. (In this case RandyBoyle.txt.)
33. Enter **ls** to verify that you did create the text file. (You should see the new text file with your name on it.)
34. Enter **vi YourName.txt** to enter the vi editor and enter text into the new file you created.
35. You are now in the vi editor. Press the **i** key to enter insert mode. (It will say insert at the bottom of the screen.)
36. Enter your name three times.
37. Press the ESC key.
38. Press **ZZ** to save and exit the vi editor. (Yes, it is cap sensitive.)
39. Enter **vi YourName.txt** to open the vi editor back up and verify that it did save the text you entered. (See Figure 18-17.)
40. Take a screenshot.
41. Press **ZZ** to save and exit the vi editor.

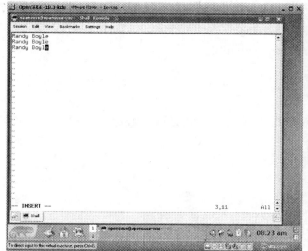

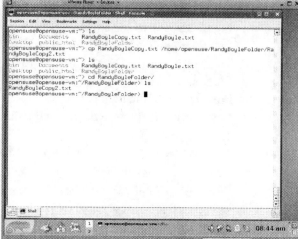

Figure 18-17: Editing with vi.   Figure 18-18: Linux cp command.

42. Enter **mkdir YourNameFolder** to create a folder in your home directory.
43. Enter **ls** to verify that you did create the new folder (directory).
44. Enter **cd YourN** but don't hit the enter key (in this case cd RandyB), instead press the **Tab** key to finish the name of the directory and then press enter.
45. Enter **pwd** to see the full path.
46. Enter **cd..** to move back one level in the directory structure to your home directory.
47. Enter **ls** to verify you are back in your home directory. (See Figure 18-18.)
48. Enter **cp YourName.txt YourNameCopy.txt** to create a copy of your text file. (In this case YourName will be RandyBoyle for the remainder of this project).
49. Enter the following command to make a copy of the copy. Move it into the directory you just created, and give it a new name. (It is cap sensitive.):

cp YourNameCopy.txt home/opensuse/YourNameFolder/YourNameCopy2.txt

50. Enter **cd YourNameFolder** to enter your subdirectory.
51. Enter **ls** to view the new file you just copied over.
52. Take a screenshot.
53. Enter **cd..** to move back to your home directory.
54. Enter **ls** to display the contents of your home directory.
55. Enter **rm YourNameCopy.txt** to delete the copied file in your home directory.
56. Enter **ls** to confirm the deletion of the YourNameCopy.txt file.
57. Enter **rm -r YourNameFolder** to remove the directory and its contents.
58. Enter **ls** to confirm the deletion of the directory. (See Figure 18-19.)
59. Enter **! !** to repeat the last command.

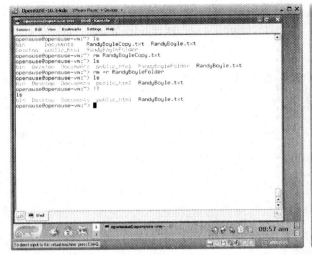

Figure 18-19: Linux rm and !! commands.

Figure 18-20: Linux find command.

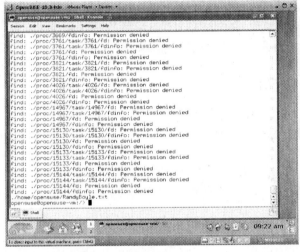

Figure 18-21: Linux command-line.

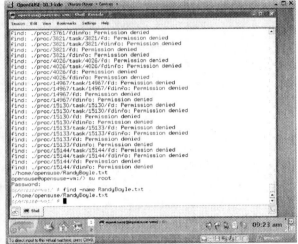

Figure 18-22: Running as root.

60. Take a screenshot.
61. Enter **cd..** to move to the home directory.
62. Enter **cd..** to move to the root directory.
63. Enter **ls** to see a listing of all the directories in root. (See Figure 18-20.)
64. Enter **find -name YourName.txt** to find your text file. (This will take about a minute.) (See Figure 18-21.)
65. Enter **su root** to switch into the administrator account.
66. Enter **opensuse** for the password. (Don't worry; it's taking your password even though it's not showing the characters.)
67. Enter **find -name YourName.txt** to find your text file. (See Figure 18-22.)
68. Take a screenshot.
69. Enter **exit** to exit root and lower your privileges back down.
70. Enter **cd home** to move into the home directory.
71. Enter **cd opensuse** to move into your home directory.
72. Enter **ls** to confirm you are back in your home directory.
73. Enter **grep name** where "name" is your last name all lowercase.

74. Enter **grep Name** where "Name" is your last name with the first letter capitalized to show all lines of the YourName.txt file where your last name appears. (See Figure 18-23.)

75. Take a screenshot.

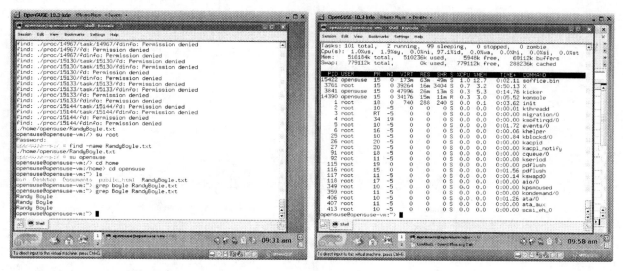

Figure 18-23: Linux grep command.   Figure 18-24: Linux top command.

76. Enter **tar cf RandyBoyleArchive.tar RandyBoyle.txt** to create a compressed file (like a zip file) of your text file.

77. Enter **ls** to confirm the creation of the tar file.

78. Enter **rm RandyBoyle.txt** to delete the text file.

79. Enter **ls** to confirm the deletion of the text file.

80. Enter **tar xf RandyBoyleArchive.tar** to extract the files from the archive.

81. Enter **ls** to confirm that the archive did extract your text file into your home directory.

82. Take a screenshot.

83. Enter **top** to see a listing of the processes currently running. (See Figure 18-24.)

84. Enter **q** to exit back to the command prompt.

85. Click on the K Menu button, Applications, Office, Spreadsheet. (Enter a couple of random values in the cells.)

86. Enter **top** again and see if you can locate the new process called soffice.bin and write down the process ID. (In this case 15344.)

87. Enter **q** to exit back to the command prompt.

88. Enter **kill 15344** (or whatever your process ID was).

89. Take a screenshot.

90. Enter **top** again to verify the process was killed. (You'll also notice that the spreadsheet program shut down.)

91. Enter **ping www.google.com** to ping one of Google's Web servers. (See Figure 18-25.)

92. Press Ctrl-C to cancel the ping command after about four responses.

93. Press the up arrow key to scroll through prior commands until you get to the ping www.google.com command and press enter.

94. Press Ctrl-C to cancel the ping command after about four responses.

95. Take a screenshot.

96. Enter **dig www.google.com** to see detailed information about some of Google's servers. (See Figure 18-26.)

97. Take a screenshot.

98. Enter **exit** to close the command shell.

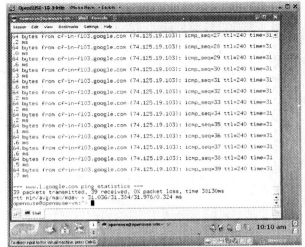

Figure 18-25: Ping command in Linux.

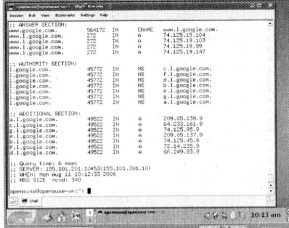

Figure 18-26: Dig command in Linux.

THOUGHT QUESTIONS

1. Do these commands work on a MAC? Why?
2. How many commands are there to learn? Are there cheat sheets available?
3. How can knowing command-line Linux save you time?
4. Do IT security professionals really use Linux command-line?

LINUX SOFTWARE INSTALLATION

When people first start learning Linux they are amazed at the amount of high-quality, free software that is available. They likely grew up on Windows or MAC and never knew there was an alternative. There are literally thousands of pieces of software available for Linux that provide the same functionality you will find on a Windows or MAC. In fact, there is more advanced IT security software available on the Linux platform.

In this project we will go through a simple example on how to install Linux-based software. OpenSUSE uses YaST® (Yet Another Setup Tool) to manage all the software you will install. It allows you to search for software and automatically install it on your machine. It works similar to the Add/Remove Programs function in Windows but has the ability to search many different software repositories for just about any software you would ever want.

Learning how to install Linux-based software is important because many of the best IT security tools are written exclusively for Linux/Unix. Let's look at a simple example.

1. Double-click the VMware icon on your desktop.
2. Click the link for the OpenSUSE virtual machine you opened in the prior exercise.
3. Click the K-Menu icon (like the Start button in Windows) in the bottom left-hand side of your screen.
4. Click Computer, Install Software.
5. Enter **opensuse** for the password.

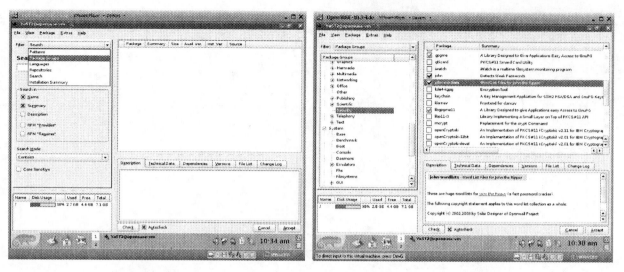

Figure 18-27: YaST software management.   Figure 18-28: Selecting a piece of security software to install.

6. Select Package Groups in the Filter drop-down menu. (See Figure 18-27.)
7. Scroll down the Package Groups list and click on Security.
8. Scroll down on the right-hand side until you see a package called John. (You used this program to audit your passwords in an earlier example.)
9. Check john and john-wordlists for installation. (You'll get 13.5 MB of wordlists!) (See Figure 18-28.)
10. Take a screenshot.
11. Click Accept. (Wait a minute or so depending on your Internet connection speed.)
12. Click "Yes" to install more packages.

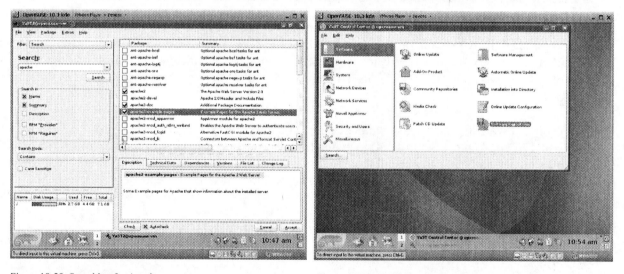

Figure 18-29: Searching for Apache.   Figure 18-30: YaST Control Center.

13. In the Search text box enter Apache.
14. Click Search.
15. In the results window select Apache2, Apache2-doc, and Apach2-example-pages.
16. Take a screenshot. (See Figure 18-29.)
17. Click Accept, Continue.
18. Click No to exit.
19. Click the K-Menu icon (like the Start button in Windows) in the bottom left-hand side of your screen.

20. Click Computer, Administrator Settings. (See Figure 18-30.)
21. Enter **opensuse** for the password.
22. Click Software Repositories. (See Figure 18-31.)

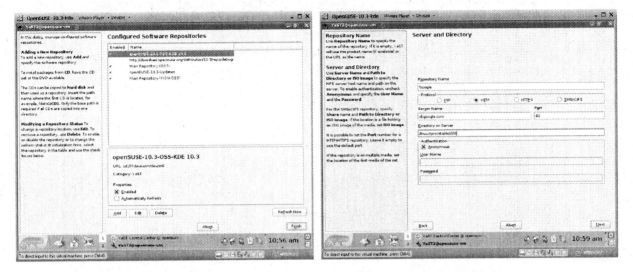

Figure 18-31: Configured software repositories.   Figure 18-32: Adding software repository.

23. Click Add.
24. Select HTTP, Next.
25. Enter **Google** for the Repository Name.
26. Enter **dl.google.com** for the Server Name.
27. Enter **/linux/rpm/stable/i386** for the directory name. (See Figure 18-32.)
28. Click Next, Finish.
29. Click Trust and Import the Key.
30. In the YaST Control Center click Software Management. (This will take a minute or two.)

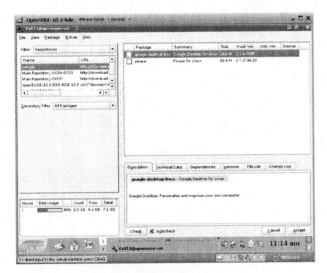

Figure 18-33: Repository successfully added.

31. In the Filter drop-down menu select Repositories.
32. Click on Google. (See Figure 18-33.)
33. Take a screenshot.
34. Close the YaST Manager.

1. Why doesn't Microsoft Windows have a similar software package manager that allows you to download free software?
2. Why are there different repositories and who manages them?
3. Does the software really install with one click?
4. Can you install software on Linux from the command-line?

CHAPTER 19: WEB SERVERS

Major Web sites in the United States are under attack every day of the week. Hackers set up fake Web sites to trick innocent users into giving away their private information. The number of defaced Web sites has grown too large to track. In general, Web sites are becoming bigger targets for potential criminals because businesses are putting more of their critical systems online. Web servers are potential security hazards that can critically injure your organization.

It's imperative that IT security professionals have a good understanding of Web servers to protect their organization. It's somewhat surprising how many people don't know how to make a basic Web site or set up a Web server. Web servers are really quite straightforward pieces of software. It's well worth your time to get to know Apache® and IIS®.

In this chapter we will install and configure both Apache and IIS. Both are important to know due to their dominance in the Web server market. We will also look at the basics of how a phishing scam works and how to protect you from phishing scams.

INSTALL APACHE, CREATE A WEB SITE, AND HOST PAGES

One of the more common questions asked by students and entrepreneurs is "How do I make a Web site?" They are actually asking about more than just making a Web site. They are actually asking about hosting, maintenance, administration, connecting the Web site to a backend database, etc.

You can set up a basic Web server, make a Web site, and start serving Web pages in about four minutes. This is a good project to show you what is involved in the creation, hosting, and eventual maintenance of a Web site. You probably won't be ready to start your own hosting company after doing this project as there is plenty more to learn, but it should be fun.

Apache is the leading Web server in the world and it's free! You can load Apache on your Windows box and serve pages directly from your computer. If you want to run your own Web site you will have to register your IP address through a company like Godaddy.com. Let's get started and see how it all works.

1. Download the Apache Web Server from http://httpd.apache.org/download.cgi.
2. Click Download for the file named apache_2.2.11-win32-x86-no_ssl-r2.msi. (Make sure it has the MSI extension.)
3. Click Save.
4. Select the C:\security folder.
5. Click Run, OK.
6. If your download doesn't automatically unzip and run, you should run the file apache_2.2.9-win32-x86-no_ssl-r2.msi. (Just double-click it.)
7. Click Run, Next, I accept, Next, Next.
8. Enter your first name and your last name followed by .com for the network domain; (e.g., YourName.com, RandyBoyle.com).
9. Enter www.YourName.com for the server name; (e.g., www.RandyBoyle.com).
10. Enter an email address. (I recommend entering a fake one.) (See Figure 19-1.)

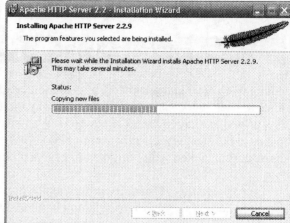

Figure 19-1: Apache configuration screen.　　　　　Figure 19-2: Installing Apache.

11. Take a screenshot.
12. Click Next, Next, Next, Install, Finish. (See Figure 19-2.)

Note: You have just installed the Apache Web server. We will now proceed to make a generic Web site using Microsoft Publisher® 2007. Microsoft Publisher 2003 will have a slightly different menu system but the same options are available. A standard Web site can be made in about 28 seconds. Customizing it may take longer.

If you don't have Publisher you can copy/paste the following code into a text file and save it as index.htm (not index.htm.txt). This is the code to create a basic first Web site. You can learn basic HTML in a weekend and easily make a better looking page. Replace YourName with your first and last name. If you make your own index.htm page from the code below you can skip down to step 27, otherwise continue to step 13.

```
<html>
<body>
This is YourName's first Web site!!
</body>
</html>
```

13. Open Microsoft Publisher.
14. In the middle pane select Web Sites. (See Figure 19-3.)
15. Select any template from the center pane. (I chose Summer.) (See Figure 19-4.)
16. Click Create.
17. Select all the options on Your Site Goals. (See Figure 19-5.)

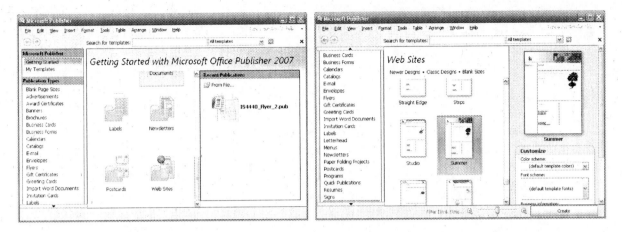

Figure 19-3: Creating a Web site from a template.　　　　Figure 19-4: Standard Web site templates.

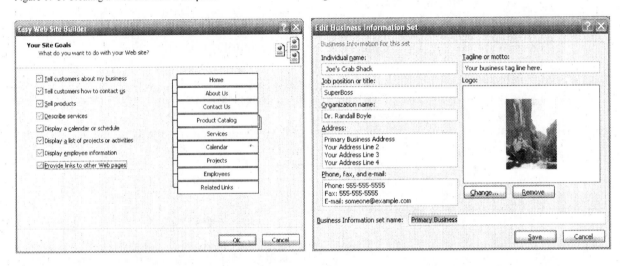

Figure 19-5: Standard pages to include in Web site.　　　Figure 19-6: Business information to include on Web site.

18. Click OK.
19. On the file menu click Insert, Business Information.
20. In the left-hand pane click Organization Name, Change Business Information.
21. Click Edit.
22. Change the Organization Name to your full name; (e.g., Randy Boyle). (See Figure 19-6.)
23. Click Save, Update Publication.
24. On the file menu click File, Publish to the Web, Save.
25. Select Other location. (By default it will save to your desktop.)
26. Click Next.

Note: You have just created a full Web site and saved it in your working directory. (Mine was My Documents.) Your main Web page will be called index.htm and all other pages will be in a folder called index_files located in your working directory. We are going to move your main page (index.htm) and all subsequent pages/graphics (located in the index_files folder) to your Apache folder named htdocs. Once we move these files and start your Apache Web server the world will be able to see your new Web site.

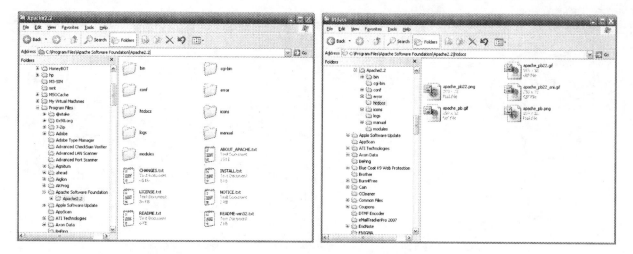

Figure 19-7: Place Web site in htdocs folder.

Figure 19-8: Delete default Web site.

27. Open Windows Explorer and navigate to C:\Program Files\Apache Software Foundation\Apache2.2. (See Figure 19-7.)
28. Open the htdocs folder.
29. Delete any file named index.htm or index.html. (These are the default pages that come included with the server.) (See Figure 19-8.)
30. Go back to your working directory where your new index.htm file and your index_files folder are located.
31. Copy both the index.htm file and the index_files folder from your working directory into the htdocs folder in C:\Program Files\Apache Software Foundation\Apache2.2. (See Figure 19-9.)

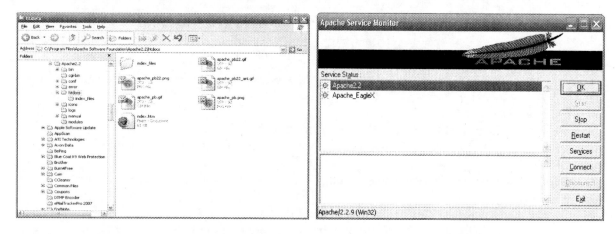

Figure 19-9: Copy your new Web site into the htdocs folder.

Figure 19-10: Start your Apache Web server.

32. Right-click the apache icon in the lower right-hand corner of your screen. (It looks like a little red feather.)
33. Open the Apache Monitor.
34. Select Apache 2.2.
35. Click Start. (It may already be started.) (See Figure 19-10.)
36. Open a Web browser and enter your IP address in the address bar. (If you don't know your IP address, you can enter the word *localhost*.) (See Figures 19-11 and 19-12.)

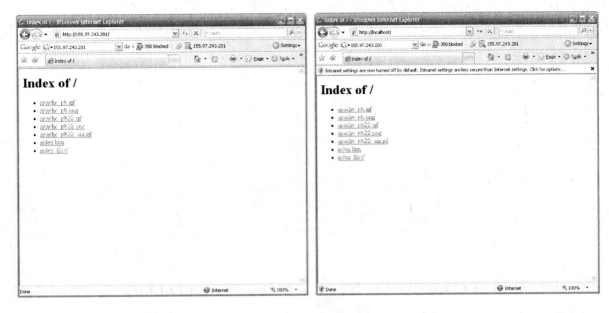

Figure 19-11: Enter your IP address into the address bar.   Figure 19-12: You can also enter "localhost" into the address bar.

Note: Your Web page did not come up. However you were able to get a listing of all the Web pages and files that your Web server does have. You can see that your index.htm is one of them. If you click on this link your full Web site will come up. However, we want it to open when people visit for the first time.

The reason it didn't open was because the default page for Apache is index.html not index.htm. (The difference is the "l" at the end.) We will now change the configuration file so that Apache will open index.htm by default.

37. Open Windows Explorer and navigate to C:\Program Files\Apache Software Foundation\Apache2.2\conf.
38. Open the text file named httpd.conf.
39. Scroll down until you see a heading that reads "# DirectoryIndex: sets the file that Apache will serve if a directory is requested." (See Figure 19-13.)
40. Change the text four lines below from "DirectoryIndex index.html" to "DirectoryIndex index.htm index.html." (There must be a space between index.htm and index.html.) (See Figure 19-14.)
41. On the file menu click File, Save.
42. Close the text file named httpd.conf.

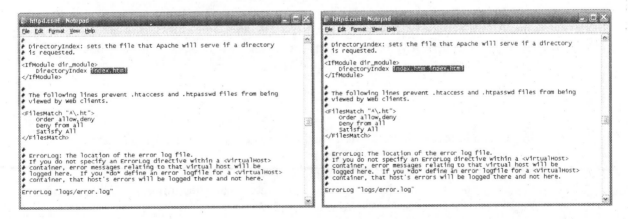

Figure 19-13: Apache httpd.conf file.   Figure 19-14: Adding "index.htm" so your Web site will load.

43. Right-click the apache icon in the lower right-hand corner of your screen.
44. Open the Apache Monitor.
45. Select Apache 2.2.
46. Click Restart.
47. Return to your Web browser and click refresh (or press F5).
48. Take a screenshot of the main page that shows your name. (See Figure 19-15.)

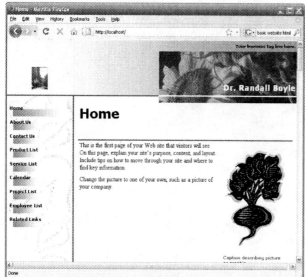

Figure 19-15: Your standard Web site.

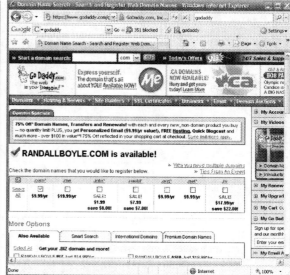

Figure 19-16: Register your Web site at GoDaddy.com.

You have successfully loaded a Web server, created a Web site, edited a configuration file, and served Web pages. Anyone that enters your IP address into their web browser will see your Web pages. If you register your Web address (e.g., www.YourName.com) with your IP address, then the world can just enter your Web address without having to know your IP address. You can register your domain name through any number of private companies. As of May 10, 2009 www.godaddy.com will register www.YourName.com for $9.99/year. (See Figure 19-16.)

Running a corporate Web site is a bit more complicated than what you just did (understatement), but this project does run you through the basics of how to get started. With practice you can do this entire project for friends/clients in less than 3.5 minutes. It's also worth buying a book and learning about Apache. There are plenty of free online references if you are price sensitive.

Make sure and stop your Apache Web server before you do the next project so port 80 will be available. You will get an error message if you don't stop it before you get IIS up and running. Right-click the Apache icon on the taskbar and select Open Apache Monitor. Select your Web site and click stop.

THOUGHT QUESTIONS

1. Why did you have to edit the configuration file rather than using a GUI interface?
2. Do large companies like CNN use Apache? Why?
3. Can you host multiple Web sites on a single computer?
4. If you can turn your computer into a Web server then what is the difference between your computer and the "servers" in the racks at Google?

INTERNET INFORMATION SERVER (IIS) INSTALLATION

In this project you will install and configure the second most popular Web server in use today (Apache is #1). Microsoft ships IIS with Windows XP. Most people don't even know that they have the ability to run a Web server on their personal computer.

The IIS interface is easier for beginners to learn than Apache. It comes with a nice GUI and is pretty intuitive. If you run it on Server 2003 you can run as many Web sites as you want! Running IIS on your Windows XP machine is a great way to start learning the basics of administering a Web site. Let's look at an example.

Make sure to stop your Apache Web server from the prior project so that port 80 is available for this project. Right-click the Apache icon on the taskbar and select Open Apache Monitor. Select your Web site and click stop.

1. Click Start, Control Panel.
2. Double-click Administrative Tools.
3. Double-click Add/Remove Programs.
4. On the left-hand side click Add/Remove Windows Components.
5. Check Internet Information Services. (Make sure all subcomponents are selected.)
6. Click Next, Finish.
7. In the Control Panel double-click Administrative Tools.
8. Double-click Internet Information Services.
9. Expand the file tree until you see the Default Web Site. (See Figure 19-17.)
10. Right-click on the folder labeled Web Sites.

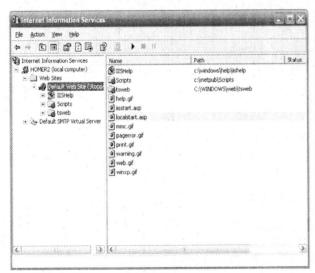

Figure 19-17: IIS default Web site.

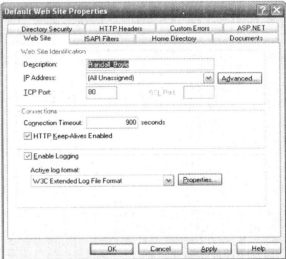

Figure 19-18: Web site configuration options.

11. Select Properties.
12. On the Web Site tab enter YourName in the Description. (See Figure 19-18.)
13. Take a screenshot.
14. Click on the Home Directory Tab and note that all the Web pages are located in the directory labeled c:\inetpub\wwwroot. (This is where you are going to put your Web site.) (See Figure 19-19.)
15. Click on the Documents tab.

16. Click Add.
17. Enter index.html. (See Figure 19-20.)
18. Click OK.
19. Select index.html and click the up arrow until it is at the top.

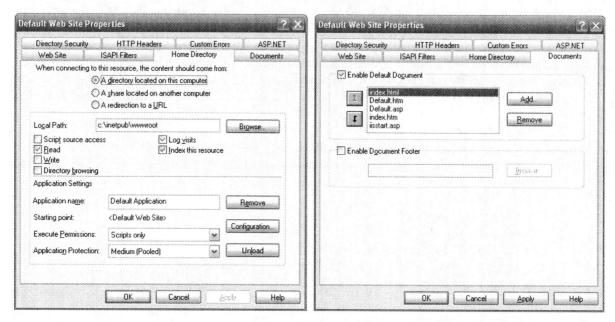

Figure 19-19: Designate a home directory for your Web site.   Figure 19-20: Designate a main page for your Web site.

20. Open Internet Explorer (IE) by clicking Start, All Programs, Internet Explorer.
21. In the address bar enter *localhost* or 127.0.0.1.
22. Take a screenshot of the default page. (See Figure 19-21.)

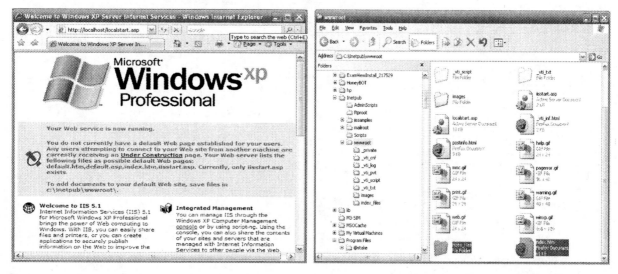

Figure 19-21: Default page.   Figure 19-22: Copy your Web site to the wwwroot folder.

Note: The default page is just a generic "Under Construction" page. The page is actually named localstart.asp. We will add a whole new Web site with real content. We will take the Web site you made in the previous example and put it in the directory labeled C:\Inetpub\wwwroot.

23. Select the folder where you saved your index.htm file and index_files folder. (Mine was in the My Documents folder.)
24. Copy both the file labeled index.htm and the folder labeled index_files.
25. Paste them in the directory labeled C:\Inetpub\wwwroot. (See Figure 19-22.)
26. Return to your Internet Explorer window and enter localhost or 127.0.0.1 into the address bar.
27. Take a screenshot of your Web site that shows your name. (See Figure 19-23.)

Figure 19-23: Your standard Web site.

Figure 19-24: Modified HTML code.

28. Enter http://www.pearsonhighered.com/boyle into your Web browser.
29. Click File, Save Page As. (This Web page may look different due to updates on the www.pearsonhighered.com Web site.)
30. Browse to C:\Inetpub\wwwroot.
31. Save the file as index.html. (The "l" at the end of index.html is important.)
32. Click OK.
33. In your browser enter localhost again. (Note that the saved version of http://www.pearsonhighered.com/boyle comes up.)
34. Browse to C:\Inetpub\wwwroot.
35. Right-click the file labeled index.html. (The "l" at the end of index.html is important.)
36. Select Open With, Notepad.
37. After the first two tags (<html><head>) press enter several times to create some blank space.
38. Enter the following text in the blank space: **<H3> YourName </H3>** (in this case <H3> Randall Boyle </H3>). (See Figure 19-24.)
39. Click File, Save.
40. Click refresh on your Web browser (or press F5).
41. Take a screenshot that shows your name on the saved http://www.pearsonhighered.com/boyle page. (See Figure 19-25.)

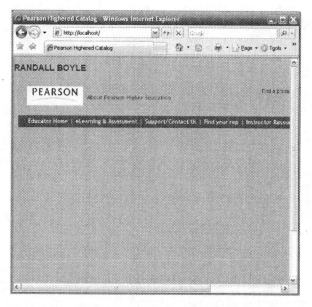

Figure 19-25: Modified Web site running locally on your computer.

You have successfully installed and configured ISS. If you have a valid IP address anyone that enters your IP address into their Web browser will be able to see your new Web site (as long as your network administrator isn't filtering out port 80 from internal machines to the outside world). As you can see there is a lot to learn about IIS. Most beginning users find it easier to learn on than Apache.

THOUGHT QUESTIONS

1. If you moved index.htm above index.html in the Documents tab in ISS, which Web site would show?
2. If you enter a search term into the saved Google page it doesn't return any results. Could you get it to work?
3. Can you password protect your Web site? How?
4. Can you require the use of SSL on your Web site?

PHISHING AND HOSTS FILE

Phishing scams are fairly easy to set up but somewhat difficult to execute. You need to copy a Web site (easy), host it on a machine you broke into (somewhat difficult), email out a believable link to hundreds of thousands of people (getting harder every day), get the stolen data off the machine before it is shut down (tricky), and get away without being tracked (difficult and dangerous).

In the prior example you saw how easy it was to save http://www.pearsonhighered.com/boyle and have it come up on your local machine. However, it still said localhost or 127.0.0.1 in the address bar. This isn't very believable. One of the easiest ways of identifying phishing scams is to look at the URL. If it looks funny, don't click on it. Legitimate Web sites don't have funky URLs. Unfortunately, there are people that don't even know what a URL is.

In the summer of 2008 there was a major DNS vulnerability in the news. This vulnerability could have allowed malicious individuals to re-route Internet traffic to any computer they designated. IT security experts were concerned but the general public appeared ambivalent. It might have been due to the fact that few people understood what DNS actually does. DNS is like a phone book. A phone book is used to resolve a person's name into the address where they live. Similarly, DNS changes domain names into IP addresses. It changes www.google.com into 74.125.19.103.

In the following example we will modify the local hosts file to redirect traffic. When you type in a domain name like http://www.pearsonhighered.com, it first checks your local hosts file for an entry. If it doesn't find an entry then it sends out a request to a DNS server. This example shows how dangerous a compromised DNS vulnerability might be.

1. Open the Control Panel by clicking Start, Control Panel.
2. In the Control Panel double-click Administrative Tools.
3. Double-click Internet Information Services.
4. Expand the file tree until you see the Default Web Site.
5. Make sure the Web site you modified in the prior project is running. (If not, start it.)
6. Open a Web browser.
7. Enter localhost or 127.0.0.1 into the address bar. (You should see the fake Web site.)
8. Open Windows Explorer by clicking Start, All Programs, Accessories, Windows Explorer.
9. Browse to C:\WINDOWS\system32\drivers\etc.
10. Right-click the file labeled "hosts."
11. Select Open.
12. Scroll down and select Notepad.
13. Click OK.

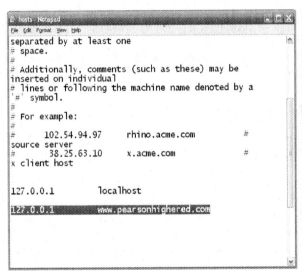

Figure 19-26: Modifying your "hosts" file.

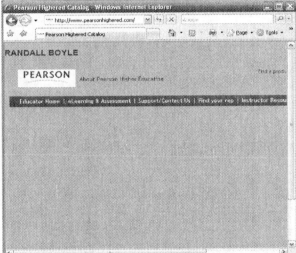

Figure 19-27: Modified Web is actually locally hosted.

14. Enter the following at the bottom of the page just below the entry labeled "127.0.0.1 localhost":

    127.0.0.1   www.pearsonhighered.com

15. Click File, Save. (See Figure 19-26.)
16. In your Web browser enter www.pearsonhighered.com.
17. Take a screenshot showing your fake Web site with www.pearsonhighered.com in the address bar. (See Figure 19-27.)
18. Open a command prompt by clicking Start, Run, CMD.
19. Type **ping www.google.com**
20. Write down the IP address (in this case 74.125.19.103).
21. Type **ping www.yahoo.com**

22. Write down the IP address (in this case 209.131.36.158).
23. Back in your hosts file add the following two entries. (Yes, they are intentionally reversed!)

74.125.19.103   www.yahoo.com
209.131.36.158   www.google.com

24. Click File, Save.
25. Close your Web browser.
26. Open your Web browser.
27. Enter www.google.com.
28. Take a screenshot showing Yahoo® with www.google.com in the address bar.
29. Enter www.yahoo.com.
30. Take a screenshot showing Google® with www.yahoo.com in the address bar.
31. Delete the following entries from your hosts file to return your hosts file back to normal. (You should only have "127.0.0.1 localhost" listed.)

74.125.19.103   www.yahoo.com
209.131.36.158   www.google.com

32. After deleting the new entries in your hosts file click File, Save.
33. Close your hosts file.

THOUGHT QUESTIONS

1. If a hacker or disgruntled worker was able to maliciously modify a large DNS server could they cause problems? How?
2. How many root DNS servers are there?
3. How could you tell if you were being redirected to an incorrect Web site?
4. Could a virus modify your hosts file and cause you problems?

CHAPTER 20: UTILITIES & OTHER

Below are a few miscellaneous tools that are important for IT security students to learn how to use. IT security professionals use them every day and you'll need to know them. This is just a small sampling of the vast number of additional IT security tools available. A large number of books could be written about the litany of useful IT security tools. We wish there were room for all of them.

Having an array of useful tools and knowing how to use them will increase your personal IT skill set and the value you add to an organization. Reading and actively searching for new IT security tools should be a daily event. You just need to get into the habit of reading about, testing, and implementing new tools. IT security professionals are lucky to be in such a dynamic field that is changing every day. You'll never be bored.

REMOTE DESKTOP

Remote Desktop® is an extremely useful tool for IT professionals. It allows you to login to a remote computer and use it as if it were a local machine. You have access to drives and printers on both machines. Remote Desktop comes pre-loaded on all Windows-based computers that have Windows XP (or a newer version of Windows). The ability to remotely administer a computer/system is nice because an administrator can remote into multiple machines in different locations at one time.

Many employees and employers are taking advantage of working remotely from home. The cost savings for all parties involved are tremendous (e.g., reduced commercial office space, no commute, flexible hours, environmentally friendly, etc.). Remote Desktop is also compatible with most Linux distributions. In order for Remote Desktop to work correctly make sure you check the following:

(1) Have the remote computer turned on
(2) Have it configured with a password-protected user account
(3) Enable Remote Desktop connections
(4) Allow Remote Desktop connections through the firewall (port 3389)
(5) Do NOT have WinXP Home Edition

For some reason Microsoft does not allow Remote Desktop connections INTO WinXP Home Edition but you can remote OUT OF a computer with WinXP Home Edition. You can remote into any computer as long as you know the IP address. You can work on computers that are literally hundreds and thousands of miles away as if you were sitting right in front of them.

For this project you will need two computers. You can work with a classmate or a friend to complete the project. Your instructor might give you the IP address of a test machine that you can use to complete this project. First, you will need to determine the IP address of both your computer and the "remote" machine. It's a good idea to write down the IP addresses of the computers you want to remote into until you memorize them. Let's see what IP address is assigned to your computer.

1. Click Start, Control Panel.
2. Double-click System.
3. Click on the Remote tab.
4. Select "Allow users to connect remotely to this computer." (See Figure 20-1.)

5. Click OK.
6. In the Control Panel double-click Windows Firewall.
7. Click the Exceptions tab.
8. Make sure Remote Desktop is selected. (See Figure 20-2.)
9. Click OK.
10. Open a command prompt by clicking Start, All Programs, Accessories, Command Prompt.
11. Type `ipconfig /all`
12. Write down your IP address. (In this example it was 155.97.60.71.)
13. Go to another computer. (This could be a friend's computer or another computer in your house.)

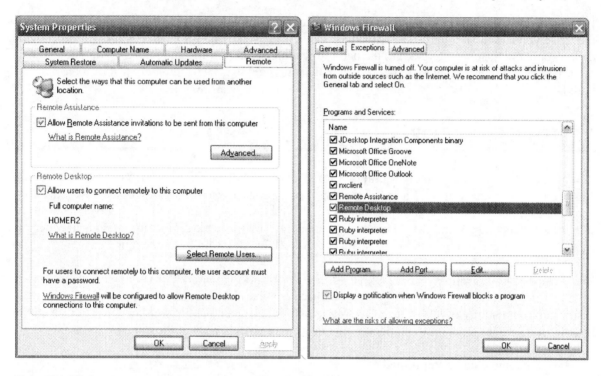

Figure 20-1: Windows remote settings.   Figure 20-2: Allow Remote Desktop through your firewall.

Figure 20-3: Remote Desktop connection.

14. Click Start, All Programs, Accessories, Communications, Remote Desktop Connection. (See Figure 20-3.)
15. Click Options.
16. Click Local Resources. (See Figure 20-4.)
17. Select Printers and Clipboard.
18. Click More.
19. Select all options for Local Devices and Resources. (See Figure 20-5.)
20. Click OK.

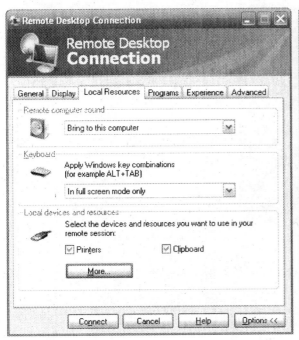

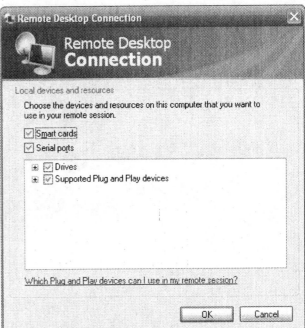

Figure 20-4: Local resource options for remote connections.

Figure 20-5: Allow drives to be shared during remote sessions.

21. On the Remote Desktop Window enter your IP address.
22. Click Connect. (See Figure 20-6.)
23. Enter your username and password just as if you were logging into your home computer. (See Figure 20-7.)
24. Click the Restore Down button in the top right-hand corner of the window so the remote desktop will be a smaller window (so you can take a screenshot of the whole window).
25. Take a screenshot of your whole local desktop with the Remote Desktop window in the middle. (See Figure 20-8.)

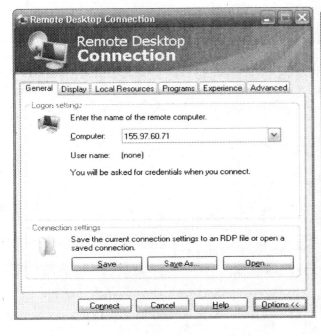

Figure 20-6: Remote Desktop connection.

Figure 20-7: Login for remote connection.

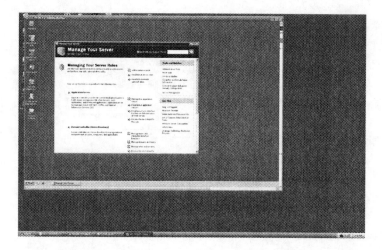

Figure 20-8: Working remotely.

THOUGHT QUESTIONS

1. Can you remote into more than one computer at a time?
2. Can you remote through a chain of multiple computers?
3. Can you copy files from a remote desktop and paste them to the local desktop?
4. What keeps the bad guys from using remote desktop to access your computer?

PROCESS EXPLORER

Even though you may only be running two programs (i.e., MS Word, Firefox, etc.) you will likely have a couple dozen processes running behind the scenes. Viruses, worms, and malware can run as processes without the user even knowing they are loaded into memory. Faulty programs can also take up large amounts of physical memory or CPU speed. It's critical to have the ability to identify the offending program and/or process and kill it.

IT security professionals use Process Explorer® (or a program similar to it) all the time. They need to know exactly which programs and processes are running. They also need to know which DLLs are being used, the location of the process, what the process does, who made it, if it's sending or receiving information, etc. Process Explorer turns out to be an invaluable diagnostic tool. Let's go through a simple example looking at just a few of the more basic functionalities.

1. Download Process Explorer from http://technet.microsoft.com/en-us/sysinternals/bb896653.aspx.
2. Click Download Process Explorer.
3. Click Save.
4. Select the C:\security folder.
5. If the program doesn't automatically open, browse to C:\security.
6. Right-click ProcessExplorer.zip.
7. Select 7-Zip, Extract to "ProcessExplorer\".
8. Browse to C:\security\ProcessExplorer\.
9. Double-click procexp.exe. (If you find this to be a useful tool, you might want to make it a shortcut on your desktop.)
10. Open a Web browser (in this case Firefox).
11. Scroll down the list of processes open until you find your Web browser.
12. Select your Web browser. (See Figure 20-9.)

13. Take a screenshot.
14. Double-click the line with your Web browser highlighted. (See Figure 20-10.)
15. Take a screenshot.
16. Click Kill Process to close your browser.
17. Click OK to close the properties window for that process.

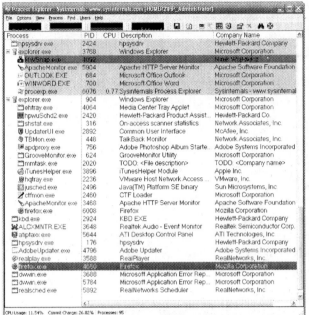

Figure 20-9: Processes shown with firefox.exe highlighted.

Figure 20-10: Details for firefox.exe.

18. In Process Explorer click View, System Information. (See Figure 20-11.)
19. Take a screenshot.
20. Click View, Lower Pane View, DLLs. (See Figure 20-12.)
21. Take a screenshot.

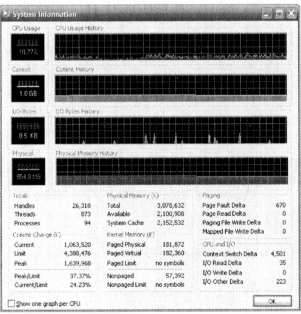

Figure 20-11: System information.

Figure 20-12: Detailed DLL information.

1. Why are all these processes started?
2. Can you keep these processes from starting? How?
3. Are there any processes you recognize or don't recognize?
4. What do DLLs do and why are they associated with a specific process?

CHANGE MAC ADDRESS

A security concern with wireless networks is that packets are tagged with each sender's MAC address. Bad guys can use a packet sniffer and learn the MAC addresses of all wireless clients on a network. This information could pose a potential security risk. A malicious person could redirect traffic from any host.

There are also privacy concerns. User activity can be monitored and tracked by any number of organizations based on MAC addresses. Privacy advocates worry that tracking information based on MAC addresses could be used inappropriately and violate basic civil rights.

Being able to change MAC addresses can facilitate an exact copy of an existing system for a hot-site backup. If a company is using an application that requires specific registered MAC addresses then an exact duplicate would be necessary. Being able to change MAC addresses is also a great tool to help troubleshoot network problems. Let's look at a tool that can change your MAC address.

1. Download MAC Address Changer v5® from http://tmac.technitium.com/tmac/index.html.
2. Click Download Now, Download Now.
3. Click Save.
4. Select the C:\security folder.
5. If the program doesn't automatically open, browse to C:\security.
6. Right-click TMACv5_Setup.zip.
7. Select 7-Zip, Extract to "TMACv5_Setup\".
8. Browse to C:\security\TMACv5_Setup\.

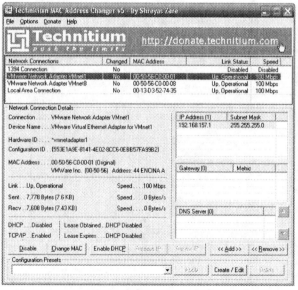

Figure 20-13: List of your network adapters.

Figure 20-14: Changing your MAC address.

9. Double-click TMACv5_Setup.exe.
10. Click Next, I Agree, Next, Next, Next, Finish.
11. Double-click the TMACv5 icon on your desktop.
12. Click on one of the VMware virtual network adapters. (You should have at least one of them visible from the prior VMware project. If not, you can use any existing NIC.) (See Figure 20-13.)
13. Click Change MAC.
14. Click Random MAC Address. (See Figure 20-14.)
15. Click Change Now!
16. Click "Yes."
17. Take a screenshot.

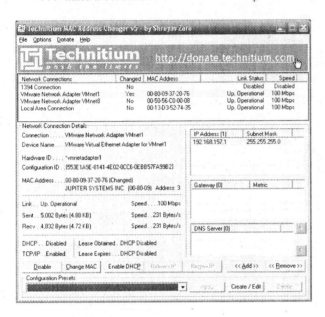

Figure 20-15: Change your MAC address back.

18. Select the same network adapter you just changed.
19. Click Change MAC.
20. Click Original MAC. (See Figure 20-15.)
21. Click "Yes."
22. Take a screenshot.

THOUGHT QUESTIONS

1. How could a large organization benefit from changing their MAC addresses?
2. Do certain Web-based applications filter requests based on MAC address?
3. Why do we need MAC addresses anyway? Aren't IP addresses sufficient?
4. What would happen if there were two computers with the same MAC address on the same network?

HOTFUSION (BINDERS)

A binder is a tool that can combine multiple separate programs into a single executable. Hotfusion® is a tool that can bind any file type or program, encrypt/decrypt files, move each file to a designated directory on extraction, run each program on extraction, add bound programs to startup, and self-destroy itself on extraction. Binders can save a system administrator time if he/she has to configure a lot of different hosts. A single executable can install and run several disparate programs with a single click.

Binders are also important to study in a security setting because they are one of the tools that can be used to create malicious software. Showing you that binders do exist, and can potentially be used to bind malicious software with legitimate software, helps you learn not to click on every executable program you get as an attachment in an email. Binders, like any tool, can be used for good and/or bad purposes.

1. Download Hotfusion from http://hotfusion.xtreemhost.com/dld.php.
2. Click on the download v0.9.2 (or the latest version).
3. Click Save.
4. Select the C:\security folder.
5. If the program doesn't automatically open, browse to C:\security.
6. Right-click hotfusion-0.9.2-installer.zip.
7. Select 7-Zip, Extract to "hotfusion-0.9.2-installer\".
8. Browse to C:\security\hotfusion-0.9.2-installer\.
9. Double-click Setup.exe.
10. Click Next, Next, Next, Install, Finish.
11. Browse to C:\WINDOWS\system32.
12. Copy freecell.exe.
13. Paste freecell.exe into the C:\security\ folder.
14. Browse to C:\WINDOWS\system32.
15. Copy sol.exe.
16. Paste sol.exe into the C:\security folder. (See Figure 20-16.)
17. Click Start, All Programs, Xeus Technologies, Hotfusion, Hotfusion (or double-click the icon on your desktop). (See Figure 20-17.)
18. Click Add File.
19. Click the button labeled "…"
20. Browse to the C:\security folder.

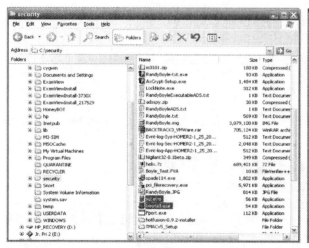

Figure 20-16: Copy two programs to bind.

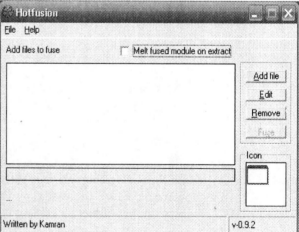

Figure 20-17: Hotfusion main screen.

21. Select freecell.exe.
22. Click Open.
23. Click the button labeled "{v}."
24. Scroll down and select the destination labeled {DESKTOPDIRECTORY}. (See Figure 20-18.)
25. Click OK.
26. Select Run on extract.

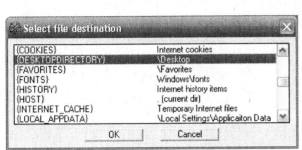

Figure 20-18: Select a destination directory.

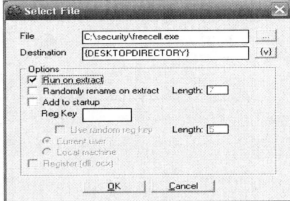

Figure 20-19: Select what to do with the program on extraction.

27. Click OK.
28. Click Add File.
29. Click the button labeled "…"
30. Browse to the C:\security folder.
31. Select sol.exe.
32. Click Open.
33. Click the button labeled "{v}."
34. Scroll down and select the destination labeled {DESKTOPDIRECTORY}.
35. Click OK.
36. Select Run on extract. (See Figure 20-19.)
37. Click OK.

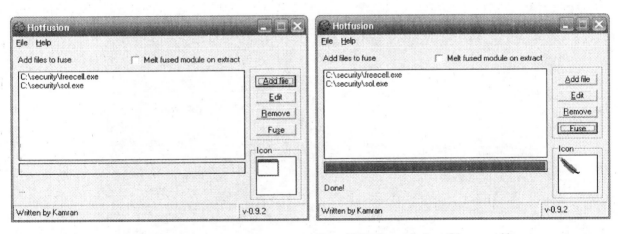

Figure 20-20: Listing of files to bind.

Figure 20-21: Change the icon of the executable.

38. Click on the graphic below the word Icon. (See Figure 20-20.)
39. Browse to the C:\Program Files\Apache Software Foundation\Apache2.2\manual\images.
40. Select the icon labeled favicon.ico. (See Figure 20-21.)
41. Click Open.
42. Take a screenshot.
43. Click Fuse.
44. Browse to the C:\security folder.
45. In the File name text box enter YourName.exe (in this case RandyBoyle.exe). (See Figure 20-22.)
46. Click Save.
47. Click OK.

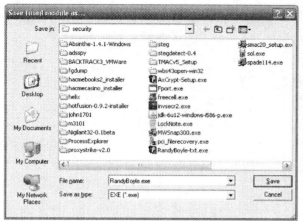

Figure 20-22: Save the executable.

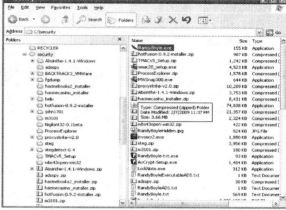

Figure 20-23: Two programs successfully bound.

48. Browse to the C:\security folder.
49. Double-click the program labeled YourName.exe. (See Figure 20-23.)
50. Right-click your taskbar.
51. Select Task Manager.
52. Take a screenshot showing freecell.exe running. (See Figure 20-24.)
53. Take a screenshot showing freecell.exe and sol.exe on your desktop. (See Figure 20-25.)

Figure 20-24: Programs running after being extracted.

Figure 20-25: Programs automatically copied on extraction.

THOUGHT QUESTIONS

1. What does the "Melt fused module on extract" option do?
2. How could Hotfusion help an administrator?
3. How do you know the sol.exe and freecell.exe programs were started after they were extracted?
4. Could this program be used for malicious purposes?

BUFFER OVERFLOW

Buffer overflows are a fairly common vulnerability. They can crash an application, allow unauthorized people access, process unintended payloads, etc. Most students just learning about the field of IT security hear about buffer overflows but don't really understand how they work.

The following online example is a great demonstration of how buffer overflows actually work. It really helps students understand how buffer overflows work if they can see a graphical representation. They can visualize the memory space and how the overflow may affect the underlying code. Let's look at just one example of a buffer overflow written by Dr. Susan Gerhart.

1. Open a Web browser and go to http://nsfsecurity.pr.erau.edu/bom/. (Additional buffer overflow examples are available for download at http://www.pearsonhighered.com/boyle.)
2. Scroll down and click on the link labeled "Spock."
3. Click Play.
4. After it stops enter the first eight characters (ONLY 8 characters) of your last name as the password. (If your last name has less than 8 characters, you can fill in the last characters with "X"; in this case BOYLEXXX.) (See Figure 20-26.)
5. Click Play.
6. Take a screenshot. (See Figure 20-27.)

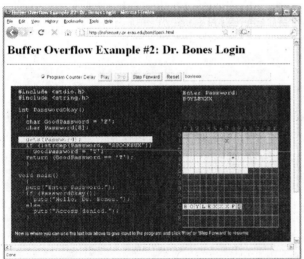
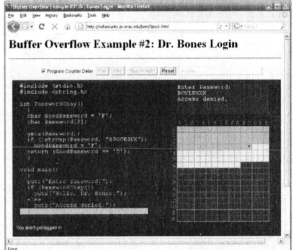

Figure 20-26: Entering an incorrect password.   Figure 20-27: Denied access.

7. Click Reset.
8. Click Play.
9. After it stops enter the first eight characters (ONLY 8 characters) of your last name as the password AND the letter "**T**" at the end. (If your last name has less than 8 characters, you can fill in the last characters with "X;" in this case BOYLEXXXT.) (See Figure 20-28.)
10. Click Play.
11. Take a screenshot. (See Figure 20-29.)

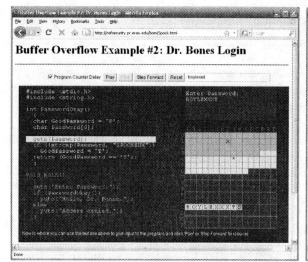

Figure 20-28: Incorrect password with "T" at the end.

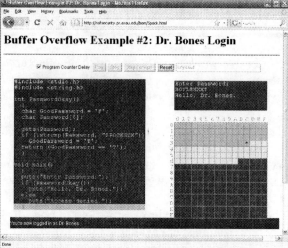

Figure 20-29: Access granted.

THOUGHT QUESTIONS

1. Why did the addition of the letter "T" allow you to bypass the login with a fake password?
2. What would happen if you entered a 15 character password consisting of all X's?
3. Could the code behind this login be fixed to stop this buffer overflow? How?
4. Are there different overflow attacks? (Hint: Look at the other examples shown.)

CHAPTER 21: INTERMEDIATE & ADVANCED

If you've made it this far in the book you've seen a variety of IT security tools. Below are a few examples of larger packages/distributions that contain many different tools. These are great resources because you have all the tools you need on one disk and one interface. You can do the same work but in a fraction of the time.

These "suites" are also nice because they are updated fairly often. Updated versions of each tool are included and new tools are also bundled with existing software. Some distributions come as live disks, virtual machines, and/or can be loaded directly from a USB drive. These are powerful tools that are worth burning to a disk and learning how to use. If you are going to be involved in penetration testing for your job these are the tools to get.

BACKTRACK

One of the best Linux distributions that focuses on IT security tools is BackTrack®. BackTrack comes with over 300 different tools focused specifically on IT security and penetration testing. You can download a copy as a virtual machine or burn it on a CD/DVD. There is also a bootable USB version. If you had to learn one suite of tools, this would probably be it. As of this writing the latest version is BackTrack 3 and BackTrack 4 is in beta testing. By the time you read this there might be a more current version.

You will need VMware Player to load the BackTrack virtual machine. You should have it loaded from a previous project. If you don't have it loaded, you will have to go back and install it before continuing with the rest of this project.

1. Download BackTrack from http://remote-exploit.org/backtrack.html.
2. Click on the download.
3. Scroll down and click on "Click here" to download the VMware version of BackTrack 3 (or the latest VMware version). (See Figure 21-1.)
4. Click Save.
5. Select the C:\security folder.
6. Right-click BACKTRACK3_VMWare.rar.
7. Select 7-Zip, Extract to "BACKTRACK3_VMWare\".
8. Browse to C:\security\ BACKTRACK3_VMWare\.
9. Double-click the VMware Player icon on your desktop.
10. Click Open.
11. Browse to C:\security\ BACKTRACK3_VMWare\BACKTRACK3\.
12. Select the image named Other Linux 2.6.x kernel.vmx.
13. Click Open.

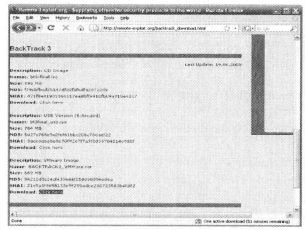

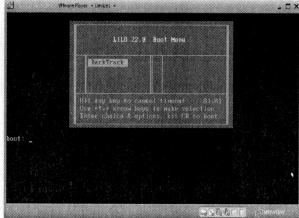

Figure 21-1: BackTrack download page.   Figure 21-2: BackTrack boot menu.

14. If you see a window asking you if you moved/copied the virtual machine, just click "I moved it."
15. Click OK. (Subsequent boot sequences will be much faster.)
16. Press the Enter key on the boot menu. (See Figure 21-2.)
17. Type **root** as the username.
18. Type **toor** as the password.
19. Type **startx** to start the graphical interface.
20. Click the K-Menu icon (like the Start button in Windows) in the bottom left-hand side of your screen. (See Figure 21-3.)
21. Click BackTrack, Penetration, Framework Version 3, Framework3-Msf-GUI.

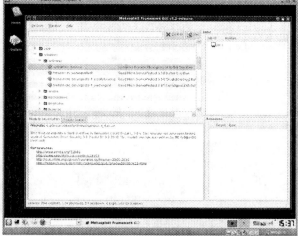

Figure 21-3: BackTrack desktop.   Figure 21-4: Metasploit GUI.

22. Click Exploits, Windows, Antivirus. (See Figure 21-4.)
23. Take a screenshot.
24. Double-click the first link. (See Figure 21-5.)
25. Take a screenshot.

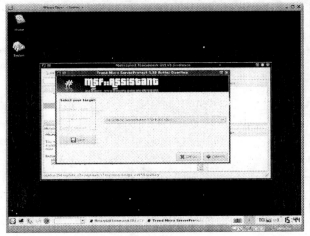

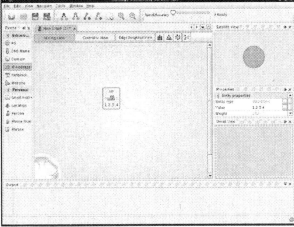

Figure 21-5: Metasploit vulnerability.

Figure 21-6: Maltego start screen.

26. Click the K-Menu icon (like the Start button in Windows) in the bottom left-hand side of your screen.
27. Click BackTrack, Information Gathering, Maltego®.
28. Wait for the nag screen to stop counting and click "Start using Maltego."
29. Drag-and-drop the icon labeled IP Address from the left-hand pane to the center of the screen.
30. Click on the icon you just moved over. (See Figure 21-6.)
31. Change the IP address from 1.2.3.4 to your IP Address (in this case 155.97.243.201). (But don't use this IP address for your project, use your own.) (See Figure 21-7.)

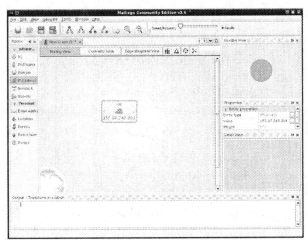

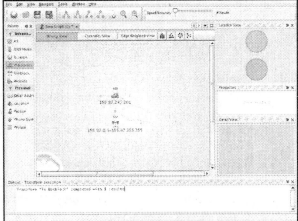

Figure 21-7: Enter your IP address.

Figure 21-8: Your block of IP addresses.

32. Right-click the icon with your IP address showing.
33. Select Netblocks, To Netblock. (See Figure 21-8.)
34. Right-click the icon with your IP address showing.
35. Select DNSNamesForThisIP, To DNS Name [DNS]. (See Figure 21-9.)
36. Right-click the DNS icon that appeared.
37. Select All, To Domains [DNS]. (See Figure 21-10.)
38. Take a screenshot.

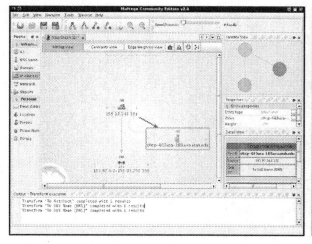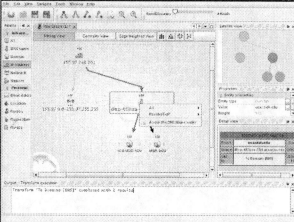

Figure 21-9: Resolved DNS names for the IP.　　　　Figure 21-10: Resolved to domains.

THOUGHT QUESTIONS

1. Are most of the tools included in BackTrack GUI or command-line? Why?
2. What does Metasploit® do?
3. What would someone use Maltego for?
4. Where would you go to learn about all the tools in BackTrack?

OWASP

Another security distribution that comes with some excellent tools is Open Web Application Security Project® (OWASP). This set of tools focuses specifically on application security. It has some robust tools for testing the security of your existing Web applications. It also has some impressive training tools.

Organizations can either know how vulnerable their applications are or they can stick their heads in the sand and hope that nothing too embarrassing happens. Embarrassing and/or criminal incidents will undoubtedly occur. OWASP has a great training tool (WebGoat®) that will walk you through several of the main types of weaknesses. Anyone interested in application testing should be familiar with WebGoat and WebScarab® (a custom testing proxy).

We will just look at a small part of the OWASP distribution. Take some time and become familiar with the entire distribution. We will also install Sun's Virtual Box® to run OWASP as a virtual machine within your Windows box.

1. Download OWASP from http://mtesauro.com/livecd/index.php?title=Main_Page.
2. Scroll down to the section labeled VMware and Virtual Box Installs.
3. Click on the link labeled owasp-livecd-AustinTerrier-Feb2009.vdi.rar.
4. Click Save.
5. Select the C:\security\ folder.
6. Browse to the C:\security folder.
7. Right-click owasp-livecd-AustinTerrier-Feb2009.vdi.rar.
8. Select 7-Zip, Extract to "owasp-livecd-AustinTerrier-Feb2009.vdi\".

You will need Sun's Virtual Box to load the OWASP virtual machine. We will install it first and then open the OWASP virtual machine.

9. Download Virtual Box from http://www.virtualbox.org/wiki/Downloads.
10. Click on the "x86" link next to VirtualBox 2.1.4 for Windows hosts.
11. Click Save.
12. Select the C:\security folder.
13. Browse to the C:\security folder.
14. Double-click VirtualBox-2.1.4-42893-Win_x86.msi.
15. Click Next, I Accept, Next, Next, Next, Yes, Install, Finish.
16. Click Cancel on the registration window.

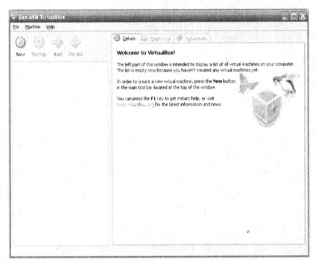

Figure 21-11: Creating a new virtual machine.

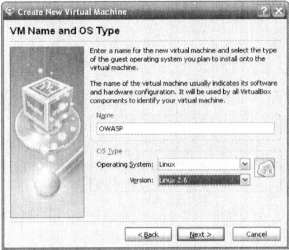

Figure 21-12: Creating a OWASP Linux virtual machine.

17. Click New, Next. (See Figure 21-11.)
18. Enter OWASP for the Name.
19. Enter Linux for the Operating System.
20. Enter Linux 2.6 for the Version. (See Figure 21-12.)
21. Click Next, Next, Existing.
22. Click Add.
23. Browse to the C:\security\owasp-livecd-AustinTerrier-Feb2009.vdi folder.
24. Select owasp-livecd-AustinTerrier-Feb2009.vdi. (See Figure 21-13.)
25. Click Open.
26. Click Select, Next, Finish.
27. Click Start. (See Figure 21-14.)

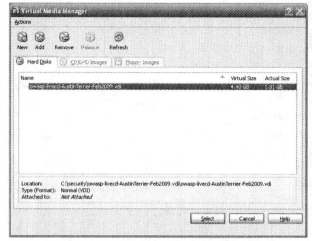

Figure 21-13: A new virtual hard disk.

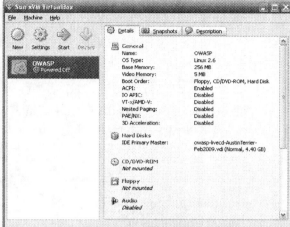

Figure 21-14: Virtual machine successfully created.

28. Select "Do not show again."
29. Click OK.
30. Click the K-Menu icon (like the Start button in Windows) in the bottom left-hand side of your screen. (See Figure 21-15.)
31. Click OWSP Live CD, WebGoat Manager.
32. Click Start, Go to WebGoat. (See Figure 21-16.)
33. Type "guest" for both the username and password.
34. Click OK.

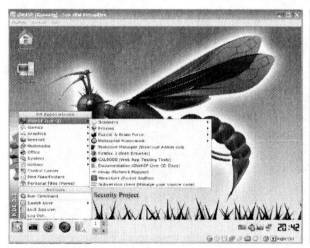

Figure 21-15: OWASP desktop.

Figure 21-16: WebGoat main page.

35. Scroll down and click Start WebGoat.
36. Click on Injection Flaws.
37. Click on String SQL Injection. (See Figure 21-17.)
38. Click on the link labeled Solution in the upper right-hand of the screen. (It will explain the SQL injection technique you are going to do.)
39. Close the solution window.
40. Type the following in the field asking for your last name: **Erwin' OR '1' = '1**
41. Click Go!
42. Take a screenshot showing "Congratulations." (See Figure 21-18.)

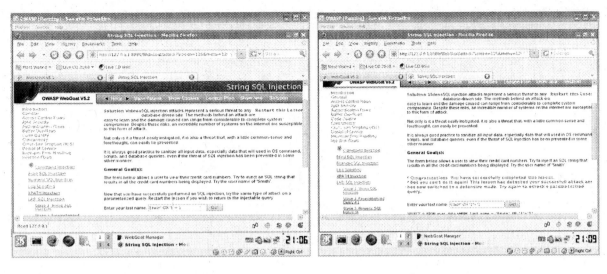

Figure 21-17: Practicing SQL injection in WebGoat.　　　Figure 21-18: SQL injection success.

THOUGHT QUESTIONS

1. What does the Web Scarab do?
2. What does CAL9000 do?
3. What does W3af do?
4. What is a Fuzzer?

CAIN & ABLE (PART 2)

Cain & Able integrates many of the tools you have seen in prior chapters into a single application. It's fairly easy to use once you become familiar with all of the components. If you were able to do the previous projects, you will find many of the components familiar. Some of the tools are interdependent. For example, Cain & Able can sniff certain packets and then send the results directly to a password auditor. Integrating tools can add additional value that neither tool may have had as a stand-alone tool.

WARNING Cain & Able does have certain functionality that could cause network problems if you randomly start pushing buttons. Do NOT push buttons if you're not sure what they do. It is worth the time and effort to learn more about the tool before you use it. Many of the most useful tools in the world (e.g.. knife, hammer, etc.) can be used improperly. Do not use Cain & Able improperly. If you follow the instructions you will be fine. Let's look at some of the functionality included in Cain & Able.

1. Download Cain & Able from http://www.oxid.it/cain.html.
2. Click "Download Cain & Abel v4.9.29 for Windows NT/2000/XP."
3. Click Save.
4. Select the C:\security folder.
5. If the program doesn't automatically open, browse to C:\security.
6. Double-click ca_setup.exe.
7. Click Next, Next, Next, Next, Finish, Install, Next, Next, I Agree.
8. If you see a window indicating that you have a prior version installed, just click "Yes."
9. Click OK, Finish.
10. Click Start, All Programs, Cain, Cain.

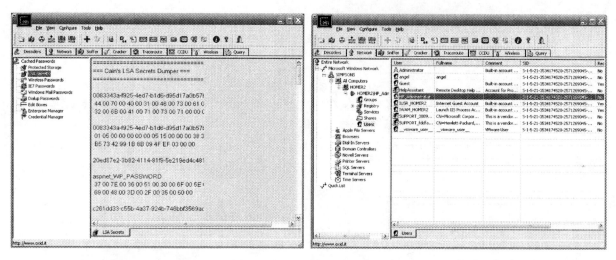

Figure 21-19: Cain's LSA Secrets Dumper.

Figure 21-20: Viewing users on your computer.

11. Click on the Decoders tab.
12. Select the first item in the list labeled Protected Storage.
13. Click the "+" button. (If you see a result, take a screenshot.)
14. Click on LSA Secrets. (See Figure 21-19.)
15. Click the "+" button.
16. Take a screenshot of the results.
17. Click on the Network Tab.
18. Expand the Microsoft Windows Network until you get to your computer.
19. Click on Users.
20. Click "Yes" to enumerate users.
21. Select your username. (See Figure 21-20.)
22. Take a screenshot.

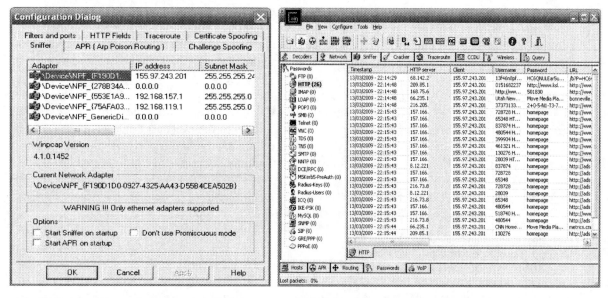

Figure 21-21: Cain sniffer configuration.

Figure 21-22: Sniffing passwords automatically.

23. Click on Configure.
24. Select your network card with your IP address. (In this case it was 155.97.243.201.)
25. Click OK. (See Figure 21-21.)
26. Click on the Start/Stop Sniffer icon. (It looks like a little green NIC.)

27. Click on the Sniffer tab.
28. Click on the Passwords lower tab at the bottom of the screen. (See Figure 21-22.)
29. Open a Web browser.
30. Go to several Web sites that you know have logon capabilities (not encrypted).
31. Take a screenshot of the results.

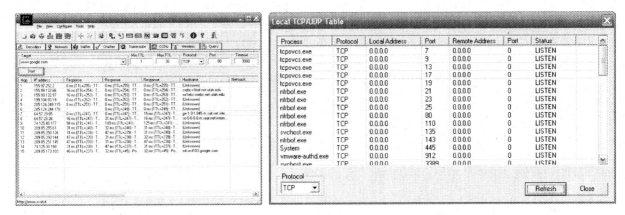

Figure 21-23: Cain's traceroute function.   Figure 21-24: Programs and their associated local ports.

32. Click on the Traceroute tab. (See Figure 21-23.)
33. Enter www.google.com.
34. Click Start.
35. Take a screenshot.
36. Click on Tools, Tcp/Udp Tables. (See Figure 21-24.)
37. Take a screenshot.
38. Click Close.
39. Click Tools, Hash Calculator.
40. Enter YourName in the text box that will be hashed.
41. Click Calculate. (See Figure 21-25.)
42. Take a screenshot.
43. Click Cancel.

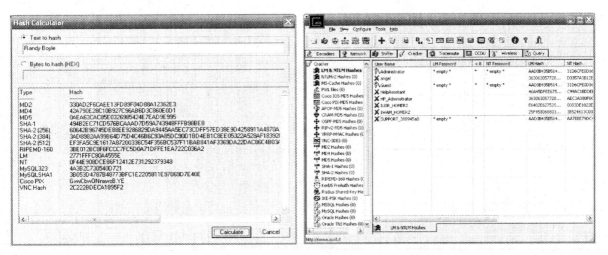

Figure 21-25: Built-in hash calculator.   Figure 21-26: Cain's password cracker.

44. Click on the Cracker tab.
45. Click on the LM & NTLM Hashes icon on the left-hand menu. (See Figure 21-26.)

46. Click the "+" button.
47. Click Next.
48. Take a screenshot.

THOUGHT QUESTIONS

1. What is ARP poisoning?
2. Does Cain & Able come with wireless tools?
3. What does the Query tab do?
4. What is spoofing and why would someone want to do it?

APPENDIX A

CREATING A VIRUS SCAN EXCEPTION FOLDER (MCAFEE)

Some of the programs shown in the projects may show up as viruses by well-known virus scanners. They aren't viruses. They just have functionality that the anti-virus company decided most users don't need and could be used to harm them. There are legal battles currently under way to get certain pieces of software off their virus lists.

The instructions below show you how to create a folder that will not be scanned by your anti-virus software. Basically you create an exception folder that you can place all your security software in and then tell the anti-virus scanner to ignore this folder when it scans for viruses.

1. Make a folder called "security" in C:\.
2. Open the McAfee VirusScan Console. (See Figure A-1.)
3. Open the On-Access Scanner. (See Figure A-2.)
4. Click on All Processes. (See Figure A-3.)

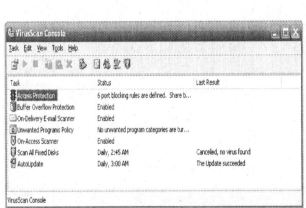

Figure A-1: VirusScan Console.

Figure A-2: General Settings.

Figure A-3: All Processes menu.

Figure A-4: Detection settings.

5.   Click on the Detection tab. (See Figure A-4.)
6.   Click on Exclusions. (See Figure A-5.)

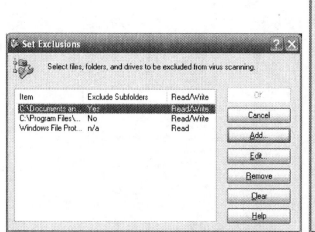

Figure A-5: Listing of exclusions.

Figure A-6: Folder to exclude.

7.   Click Add.
8.   Click Browse. (See Figure A-6.)
9.   Select the "security" folder on your C: drive. If you don't see a "security" folder, you'll need to create one first. (See Figure A-7.)
10. Keep clicking OK until you are done.
11. McAfee anti-virus will not scan that folder.

Figure A-7: Select the folder you want excluded.

CREATING A VIRUS SCAN EXCEPTION FOLDER (NORTON)

Some of the programs shown in the projects may show up as viruses by well-known virus scanners. They aren't viruses. They just have functionality that the anti-virus company decided most users don't need and could be used to harm them. There are legal battles currently under way to get certain pieces of software off their virus lists.

The instructions below show you how to create a folder that will not be scanned by your anti-virus software. Basically you create an exception folder that you can place all your security software in and then tell the anti-virus scanner to ignore this folder when it scans for viruses.

1. Make a folder called "security" in C:\.
2. Open your Norton Anti-virus software.
3. Click on Norton Security Options.
4. Click Exclusions on the left side.
5. Add the C:\security folder to the exclusions list.
6. Keep clicking OK until you close Norton.

GETTING FREE ANTI-VIRUS SOFTWARE

You should always have at least one anti-virus scanner on your computer. If you don't want to spend money on an anti-virus scanner, AVG has a free option. Below are instructions on how to install it. Compared to most free anti-virus scanners it does a fairly effective job of cleaning up viruses.

1. Download AVG from http://free.avg.com/.
2. Click "Get it now!" to get the free version.
3. Click Download for the free version.

4. Click Download now for the free version.
5. Click Download Now.
6. Click Save.
7. Select the C:\security folder.
8. If the program doesn't automatically open, browse to C:\security.
9. Double-click avg_free_stf_en_85_278a1439.exe.
10. Click Next, I Accept, I Accept, Next, Next.
11. Unselect the AVG toolbar.
12. Click Next, Finish, Finish.

GETTING FREE SPYWARE SOFTWARE

In addition to anti-virus protection you'll also likely need several good spyware scanners. Between a few good anti-virus scanners and three or four spyware scanners you should be sufficiently protected. Over time you'll likely notice that one scanner will catch malware that others won't. Then a new piece of malware will come out and one of the other scanners will catch it.

If you run into a problem (i.e., you get a virus) it's a good idea to start all your anti-virus and spyware scanners at once and leave them running for several hours. It may be a good idea to initiate the scans before you go to bed and view the results in the morning. In general you should set your anti-virus scanner to update every day and run a full scan sometime while you are asleep (e.g., 3:00 A.M.). Below are just a few suggestions for good spyware scanners.

Malware Bytes®: http://www.malwarebytes.org/

Spybot®: http://www.safer-networking.org/index2.html

Ad-Aware®: http://www.lavasoft.com/

Windows Defender®: http://www.microsoft.com/windows/products/winfamily/defender/default.mspx

APPENDIX B

SOFTWARE LINKS

Below is a listing of the software, and accompanying URLs, used in this book. Web links don't last forever and it's likely by the time you pick up this book at least one of the links listed below is out of date. If a link below is broken, chances are you will be able to find the software listed somewhere on the main page of the listed domain. You can also search for the name of the software through www.Google.com or www.Yahoo.com.

An updated list for all of the software listed below will be maintained on the Web site for this book. Please go to http://www.pearsonhighered.com/boyle for an updated listing.

Name	Company	Size	Link
ADS Spy	Merijn	30 KB	http://www.bleepingcomputer.com/files/adsspy.php
Advanced LAN Scanner	Famatech	0.5 MB	http://www.radmin.com/products/utilities/lanscanner.php
Apache	Apache Software Foundation	4.28 MB	http://httpd.apache.org/download.cgi
AppScan	IBM	116 MB	http://www.ibm.com/developerworks/downloads/r/appscan/?S_TACT=105AGX15&S_CMP=LP
AVG	AVG Technologies	60.8 MB	http://free.avg.com/
AxCrypt	Axantum Software AB	1.5 MB	http://www.axantum.com/AxCrypt/
BackTrack	Remote-Exploit.org	971 MB	http://remote-exploit.org/backtrack.html
BgInfo	Microsoft	387 KB	http://technet.microsoft.com/en-us/sysinternals/bb897557.aspx
Buffer Overflow	Dr. Susan Gerhart	--	http://nsfsecurity.pr.erau.edu/bom/
Cain & Able	Massimiliano Montoro	0.6 MB	http://www.oxid.it/cain.html
CAINE	Giancarlo Giustini	659 MB	http://www.caine-live.net/page5/page5.html
CCleaner	Piriform Ltd	2.6 MB	http://www.filehippo.com/download_ccleaner/
CSI Survey	TechWeb Networks	--	http://www.gocsi.com/
Default Passwords	phenoelit	--	http://www.phenoelit-us.org/dpl/dpl.html
DIR & CD	Microsoft	--	www.microsoft.com
Enigma	Geoff Sullivan	3.1 MB	http://cryptocellar.org/simula/m3/
Eraser	Heidi Computers Ltd.	8.74 MB	http://www.heidi.ie/node/6
Event Viewer	Microsoft	--	www.microsoft.com

e-Week Security	Ziff Davis Enterprise Holdings Inc.	--	http://www.eweek.com/c/s/Security/
F-Port	Foundstone (McAfee)	0.05 MB	http://www.foundstone.com/us/resources-free-tools.asp
FGDump	fizzgig	0.2 MB	http://swamp.foofus.net/fizzgig/fgdump/downloads.htm
File Verifier++	Tom Bramer	2.54 MB	http://www.programmingunlimited.net/siteexec/content.cgi?page=fv
Firefox	Mozilla	7.1 MB	http://www.mozilla.com/en-US/firefox/
Free Word and Excel Password Recovery Wizard	Mastermen Pty Ltd.	0.2 MB	http://www.freewordexcelpassword.com/index.php?id=download
GoDaddy.com	GoDaddy.com	4.28 MB	www.GoDaddy.com
Google	Google.com	--	www.google.com
Hacme Books	Foundstone (McAfee)	21.4 MB	http://www.foundstone.com/us/resources-free-tools.asp
Hacme Casino	Foundstone (McAfee)	8.43 MB	http://www.foundstone.com/us/resources-free-tools.asp
HashCalc	SlavaSoft Inc.	465 KB	http://www.slavasoft.com/hashcalc/index.htm
HoneyBOT	Atomic Software Solutions	1.04 MB	http://www.atomicsoftwaresolutions.com/download.php
Hot Fusion	Xeus Technologies	894 KB	http://hotfusion.xtreemhost.com/dld.php
Hotmail	Microsoft	--	www.hotmail.com
Hot Spot Defense Kit	The Shmoo Group	207 KB	http://airsnarf.shmoo.com/
IIS	Microsoft	--	http://www.iis.net/
inSSIDer	MetaGeek, LLC	1.03 MB	http://www.metageek.net/products/inssider
Internet Explorer	Microsoft	91 KB	www.microsoft.com
Invisible Secrets	NeoByte Solutions	1.9 MB	http://www.invisiblesecrets.com/ver2/index.html
IPAdress.com	IPAdress.com	--	http://www.ip-adress.com/trace_email/
Ipconfig	Microsoft	55 KB	www.microsoft.com
John the Ripper	Openwall Project	1.3 MB	http://www.openwall.com/john/
K9	Blue Coat Systems	235 KB	http://www1.k9webprotection.com/getk9/index.php
LCP	LCP Soft	2.3 MB	http://www.lcpsoft.com/english/download.htm
LockNote	Steganos GmbH	312 KB	https://www.steganos.com/us/products/for-free/locknote/overview/
MAC Address Changer v5	Technitium	1.24 MB	http://tmac.technitium.com/tmac/index.html
McAfee Anti-virus	McAfee Inc.	--	http://www.mcafee.com/us/
Milw0rm	milw0rm	--	http://www.milw0rm.com/
Microsoft Publisher	Microsoft	--	http://office.microsoft.com/en-us/publisher/default.aspx

MW Snap	Mirek Wojtowicz	644 KB	http://www.mirekw.com/winfreeware/mwsnap.html
Nessus	Tenable Network Security	20.5 MB	http://www.nessus.org/download/
Netstat	Microsoft	36 KB	www.microsoft.com
NetStumbler	Marius Milner	1.3 MB	http://www.netstumbler.com/
Nigilant 32	Agile Risk Management	349 KB	http://www.agilerm.net/publications_4.html
Nmap	Gordon Lyon	12.7 MB	http://nmap.org/download.html
Norton Anti-virus	Symantec Corp.	--	http://www.symantec.com/index.jsp
NotePad	Microsoft	--	www.microsoft.com
Nslookup	Microsoft	75 KB	www.microsoft.com
NST, Snort, BASE	networksecuritytoolkit.org	452 MB	http://networksecuritytoolkit.org/nst/index.html www.snort.org
OpenSUSE	Novell®	1.06 GB	http://www.opensuse.org/en/
Ophcrack	Objectif Sécurité	3.8 MB	http://sourceforge.net/project/showfiles.php?group_id=133599&package_id=148704
Outlook	Microsoft	--	http://office.microsoft.com/en-us/outlook/default.aspx
OWASP	Matt Tesauro	471 MB	http://mtesauro.com/livecd/index.php?title=Main_Page
Password Evaluator	George Shaffer	--	http://geodsoft.com/cgi-bin/pwcheck.pl
Password Generator	George Shaffer	--	http://geodsoft.com/cgi-bin/password.pl
PING	Microsoft	18 KB	www.microsoft.com
Process Explorer	Microsoft	1.58 MB	http://technet.microsoft.com/en-us/sysinternals/bb896653.aspx
Process Monitor	Microsoft	1.25 MB	http://technet.microsoft.com/en-us/sysinternals/bb896645.aspx
Recuva	Piriform Ltd	2.3 MB	http://www.recuva.com/download
Refog Keylogger	Refog	1.35 MB	http://www.refog.com/trial2.html
Remote Desktop	Microsoft	--	www.microsoft.com
7-Zip	Igor Pavlov	694 KB	http://www.7-zip.org/download.html
Sam Spade	Steve Atkins	1.80 MB	http://www.softpedia.com/get/Network-Tools/Network-Tools-Suites/Sam-Spade.shtml
SANS	The SANS™ Institute	--	www.sans.org
SecurityFocus	SecurityFocus	--	www.securityfocus.com
Sentinel	runtimeware.com	1.66 MB	http://www.runtimeware.com/sentinel.html
Shields Up	Gibson Research Corporation	--	https://www.grc.com/x/ne.dll?bh0bkyd2
Snadboy's Revelation	Snadboy	213 KB	http://www.snadboy.com/
SNARE for Windows	InterSect Alliance	758 KB	http://www.intersectalliance.com/

Snitch	Arne Vidstrom	0.02 MB	http://www.ntsecurity.nu/toolbox/snitch/
Spector 360	SpectorSoft Corporation	116 MB	http://www.spector360.com/OnlineDemos/index.htm#
Steg Detect	Niels Provos	2.3 MB	http://www.outguess.org/detection.php
SuperScan	Foundstone (McAfee)	0.2 MB	http://www.foundstone.com/us/resources/proddesc/superscan4.htm
Text Hide	Wuul	278 KB	http://members.lycos.co.uk/wuul/texthide/readme.html
The Register	The Register	--	http://www.theregister.co.uk/security/
TRACERT	Microsoft	12 KB	www.microsoft.com
TrueCrypt	TrueCrypt	3.01 MB	http://www.truecrypt.org/
Virtual Box	Sun Microsystems	37 MB	http://www.virtualbox.org/wiki/Downloads
VMware Player	VMware	177 MB	http://www.vmware.com/download/player/download.html
WhatIsMyIPAddress	WhatIsMyIPAddress.com	--	http://whatismyipaddress.com/
Whitepages.com	Whitepages.com	--	http://www.whitepages.com/reverse-lookup
WiFiDEnum	Aruba Networks, Inc.	308 KB	https://labs.arubanetworks.com/wifidenum
Wigle.net	arkasha & bobzilla	--	http://www.wigle.net/
Wireshark®	Wireshark Foundation	21.2 MB	http://www.wireshark.org/download.html
You Get Signal	Kirk Ouimet Design	--	http://www.yougetsignal.com/tools/visual-tracert/